Ethical Borders

Bill Ong Hing

Ethical Borders

NAFTA, Globalization, and
Mexican Migration

TEMPLE UNIVERSITY PRESS
Philadelphia

TEMPLE UNIVERSITY PRESS
Philadelphia, Pennsylvania 19122
www.temple.edu/tempress

Cover photo: An onion field near Lamont, California. The indigenous workers Fernando Gonzalez and Maria Antonia Mong top and bag onions at sunset. Onion harvesters work in the morning and evening; they do not work during the early afternoon, when the heat is unbearable. (Photo by David Bacon, from the series *Immigrants*, June 2006.)

Library of Congress Cataloging-in-Publication Data

Hing, Bill Ong.
  Ethical borders : NAFTA, globalization, and Mexican migration / Bill Ong Hing.
    p. cm.
  Includes bibliographical references and index.
  ISBN 978-1-59213-924-8 (cloth : alk. paper)
  ISBN 978-1-59213-925-5 (pbk. : alk. paper)
1. United States—Emigration and immigration. 2. Mexico—Emigration and immigration. 3. Foreign workers, Mexican—United States. 4. Mexicans—Employment—United States. I. Title.
  JV6465.H56 2010
  325.73—dc22
                                                                    2009032109

Printed in the United States of America

2 4 6 8 9 7 5 3

*For the countless Mexican workers
who have been displaced by NAFTA and globalization.
Perhaps someday we'll make up for
the wrong you have suffered.*

Contents

Acknowledgments

For some time now, I have been troubled by the venom directed at undocumented workers who have crossed borders in search of a better life. Since the 1970s, I have had the privilege and opportunity to meet and represent countless individuals whom the anti-immigrant lobby and the mass media have dubbed "illegal" immigrants. These are decent folks who deserve respect and much better treatment. I am thankful for having met these people and their families. They continue to inspire me to search for the truth on their behalf and to share what I learn with others.

Since the 1990s, I have wanted to investigate the causes of the mounting desperation that the border crossers from Mexico I encounter have demonstrated. Why have their pesos been devalued time and again? Why are manufacturing jobs on the decline? Why is U.S. corn cheaper for Mexicans than their own corn? Why do many risk life and limb to cross the border? Why must they look to *El Norte*—the North—for a better life.

As I sought answers to these questions, my findings were troubling. As I delved deeper into this project and realized how the phenomenon of globalization controls the lives of average workers from Mexico, Sir Thomas More's criticism of the English justice system of the 1500s kept coming to mind: "For if you suffer your people to be ill-educated, and their manners to be corrupted from their infancy, and then punish them for those crimes to which their first education disposed them, what else is to be concluded from this, but that you first make thieves and then punish them?"[1]

U.S. economic policies, trade strategies, and the multinational corporations that promote trade agreements have created the environment and institutions that induce the movement of workers across borders. The workers are pushed and pulled into the U.S. workforce. We then demonize and, in some situations, criminalize these migrants. To characterize them as culprits is simply dishonest.

I could not have undertaken a project of this size and nature without substantial assistance and support. Most of the research funds and resources for this project were provided by Rex Perschbacher and Kevin Johnson of the University of California (UC), Davis, School of Law. Over the years, Rex and Kevin have been wonderful colleagues and have become dear friends. This project is as much theirs as it is mine. Jeff Brand of the University of San Francisco (USF) School of Law also gave me partial research support for the project. The USF law faculty offered very useful feedback on the project at a lunch presentation. Laura Carlsen of the Americas Policy Program and Ted Lewis of Global Exchange offered me early guidance. Jennifer Allen and Fernando Garcia of the Border Action Network and Oscar Chacón of the National Alliance of Latin American and Caribbean Communities, provided great insight. I particularly thank Janet Francendese, the superb editor-in-chief at Temple University Press, for her faith in my efforts and the rigor with which she challenged me to be accurate, complete, and fair. She deserves great credit for the quality of the final product.

Several UC Davis law students provided excellent research assistance: Vandana Balakrishnan, Samantha Grant, Victoria Hassid, Natalie Johnston, Tally Kingsnorth, Julia Mendoza, Ramaah Sadasivam, and Caroline Swindells. Without them, the project could not have progressed. My friends at the Immigrant Legal Resource Center remain my greatest source of inspiration: Kathy Brady, Eric Cohen, Chris Godwin, Jonathan Huang, Angie Junck, Sally Kinoshita, Shari Kurita, Deirdre O'Shea, Nora Privitera, Tim Sheehan, Mark Silverman, Byron Spicer, Shellie Stortz, Sai Suzuki, and Daniel Torres. Their hard work and dedication on behalf of all immigrants is extraordinary. I also appreciate the assistance of the library staff of the UC Davis School of Law and the San Mateo Public Library.

I am blessed with a family that is completely supportive of the work I do. My wife, Lenora, and our children, Eric, Sharon, and Julianne, continue to demonstrate tireless dedication to community service. They set the bar high with their efforts, and every day I learn something from them about low-income groups, the disadvantaged, and immigrant communities. They encourage me to do good work and expect me to get it right.

Introduction

A Time to Think Broadly

The vitriol and hate rhetoric directed at undocumented immigrants in the United States is as palpable as ever: "They are lawbreakers!" "They take our jobs!" "They don't learn English!" "They commit crimes!" "They run up costs of schools, medical care, and public services!" "We should place the military at the border!" "They should all be deported!" With this level of rancor, is it any wonder that the estimated 12 million undocumented immigrants in the country have become the victims of increased enforcement efforts?[1]

However, the stepped-up efforts by U.S. Immigration and Customs Enforcement (ICE) agents to round up undocumented immigrants in factories and neighborhoods has led to outcries by citizens and co-workers who have witnessed the operations. Allegations that ICE is using "Gestapo tactics" have become common. Residents decry the inhumane treatment to which their friends and neighbors have been subjected. Local business owners wonder why things have to be done this way.

Consider the raid in Stillmore, Georgia, on the Friday before Labor Day weekend in 2006. Local residents were outraged over the action. Nestled amid pine trees and cotton fields, undocumented Mexican immigrants supplied a stable workforce for a thriving poultry industry and for the onion fields in Vidalia only a few miles away. Descending shortly before midnight, ICE agents arrested and deported 125 undocumented workers over a three-day period.[2] Most of those captured by ICE were men, while their wives and children fled to the woods to hide.[3] In the weeks after the raid, at least 200 more immigrants left town. Many of the women whose husbands were deported used their spouses' final paychecks to purchase bus tickets to Mexico.[4]

The impact was evident, underscoring just how vital the undocumented immigrants were to the local economy. Trailer parks were abandoned. The poultry plant scrambled to replace more than half of its workforce. Business dried up at stores where Mexican laborers had once lined up to buy groceries, household goods, and other living essentials. The former community of about a thousand people became a ghost town.

Neighbors and friends witnessed the events, as ICE officials raided local homes and trailer parks. At one trailer park, operated by David Robinson, immigrants were taken away in handcuffs. Robinson, who bought an American flag and flew it upside down in protest, commented: "These people might not have American rights, but they've damn sure got human rights. There ain't no reason to treat them like animals."[5] Officials were seen stopping motorists and breaking into homes, and there were even reports of officials threatening people with tear gas.[6] Witnesses reported seeing ICE officials breaking windows and entering homes through floorboards.[7] Mayor Marilyn Slater commented, "This reminds me of what I read about Nazi Germany, the Gestapo coming in and yanking people up."[8]

When ICE agents raided several of Swift and Company's meatpacking sites a few weeks after the Stillmore raid, about thirteen hundred undocu-mented workers—mostly from Mexico—were arrested. Swift and other large companies across the country have come to rely on migrant workers for their hard-to-fill jobs. Nationwide production was severely affected, prompting the following call for immigration reform from company officials: "The impact of this is so widespread. We're being indirectly impacted—Main Street businesses and social services are all impacted. There has to be a better method."[9]

In places like Santa Fe, New Mexico, and Richmond, California, ICE agents have arrested parents walking their children to school or waiting at public-school bus stops. These invasive neighborhood tactics have left communities in fear: Children are afraid to go to school, worried that their parents may be arrested. These enforcement strategies have left a trail of bewilderment and anger in the residents left behind, who wonder how this took place in a society that prides itself on its fairness and support of family values.

Although the vast majority of Americans favor amnesty for undocument-ed immigrants,[10] Congress has been mired in debate on the topic. In 2007, comprehensive efforts to reform immigration laws in the U.S. Senate were derailed by the perception that any path to legalization for undocumented immigrants would amount to "amnesty" for lawbreakers. More precisely, enough senators—mostly right-wing Republicans—did not want to be perceived as supporting "amnesty for illegal immigrants" that a cloture motion requiring sixty senators was impossible. Despite the strenuous lobbying of the Bush administration to move the legislation forward, the proposed reforms ultimately failed to garner enough support to pass into law.

The "can't-support-amnesty-for-lawbreakers" camp claims the moral high ground. It argues that the United States should not forgive undocumented aliens for breaking our laws, because this would simply "reward lawlessness, which naturally encourages more lawlessness."[11] As the congressman and presidential candidate Tom Tancredo (R-Colo.) wrote, "We must keep maximum pressure on the U.S. Senate to stop this amnesty bill. If we fail, and this bill becomes law, we will have taken the first irrevocable step on the road to national suicide."[12] Senator Bob Corker (R-Tenn.) declared: "I think Americans feel they are losing their country."[13] Speaking at an anti-immigrant rally in Washington, D.C., in 2007 that began with the Pledge of Allegiance, T. J. Bonner, a U.S. Border Patrol agent, told the assembly: "What is happening on the border is anarchy. Millions are crossing over, reaping our benefits, taking our jobs, and the government is not doing a damn thing about it."[14]

Advocates for legalization respond to anti-immigrant sentiment by focusing on the contributions that undocumented immigrants have made to the economy. A journalist for *Time* magazine concluded: "[Amnesty is] a good thing for America. The estimated 12 million illegals are by their sheer numbers undeportable. More important, they are too enmeshed in a healthy U.S. economy to be extracted."[15] Barbara Ehrenreich, the author of *Nickel and Dimed*, agrees: "In case you don't know what immigrants do in this country, the Latinos have a word for it—*trabajo*. They've been mowing the lawns, cleaning the offices, hammering the nails and picking the tomatoes, not to mention all that dish-washing, diaper-changing, meat-packing and poultry-plucking. . . . There is still the issue of the original 'crime.' If someone breaks into my property for the purpose of trashing and looting, I would be hell-bent on restitution. But if they break in for the purpose of cleaning it—scrubbing the bathroom, mowing the lawn—then, in my way of thinking anyway, the debt goes in the other direction."[16]

I have argued elsewhere that undocumented immigrants' economic and social contributions should be recognized.[17] Immigrants are seeking the "right to live 'legally' and be recognized as . . . productive, valued member[s] of society."[18] I believe that, for a variety of reasons, the border should not be seen as a barrier to keep out the unwanted. Economic and practical reasons support a more open-minded approach to the border. And, as I hope to show in this volume, ethical reasons and conditions compel us to explore a more open-hearted solution to the challenge of undocumented immigration.

In contrast to the close-the-border perspective taken by some, others, such as former President George W. Bush, believe that U.S. businesses need a pool of low-wage workers and a large guest-worker program to thrive.[19] I sympathize with the latter perspective, but to me U.S. immigration policy should not revolve around businesses' need for workers; it should address the modern-day social, cultural, political, and economic relations between nations—particularly those in our hemisphere. We need to look at these relations in a way that would endorse the free flow of residents of these nations between borders. The flow of immigrants must, however, be addressed in a manner that ensures that a primary sending nation such as Mexico is not disadvantaged by a devastatingly large loss of able workers.

The need to develop an approach to address the challenge of undocumented migration is great—some might even say urgent. Low-wage workers continue to be needed and recruited, yet they are demonized by some political leaders and segments of society. The workers themselves are attracted to the work, yet they are susceptible to exploitation. And since the initiation of Operation Gatekeeper in the early 1990s, restrictive immigration laws enacted in 1996, and increased border militarization after September 11, 2001, the pattern of circular migration of workers to the United States and back to their homes in Mexico has been interrupted.

In spite of increased enforcement and growing resentment directed at them, undocumented migrants continue to flow across the U.S.–Mexican border in record numbers. Billions of dollars have been invested in the U.S. Border Patrol, new fencing, and high-tech surveillance systems at the border. ICE has stepped up raids of factories and neighborhoods where undocumented workers and their families work and live. State and local officials have entered the fray by enacting laws and ordinances aimed at making life difficult for undocumented families living within their jurisdictions. Yet the number of undocumented immigrants—especially from Mexico—has increased across the country. Demographers estimate that approximately half a million new undocumented immigrants enter the United States annually.

The phenomenon of continued undocumented Mexican migration raises two vital questions that I address in this volume: (1) Why do undocumented immigrants from Mexico continue to enter the United States? and (2) What can be done to reduce the undocumented flow? That they come here for a better life is only a partial answer to the first question. We also need to determine why that better life cannot be found in Mexico. Following that line of inquiry also helps us develop an analysis to answer the second question. When we understand the social and economic challenges within Mexico, we begin to understand what needs to be addressed to reduce emigration. We also begin to understand why popular answers to the second question, such as more border enforcement, employer sanctions, or ICE raids, have been ineffective in curbing undocumented migration.

On closer examination, we find that many of the economic challenges Mexico faces are directly linked to policies that have been supported by the United States, U.S. corporations, or institutions supported by the United States. For example, we were told that the North American Free Trade Agreement (NAFTA), involving the United States, Canada, and Mexico, would remedy the problem of undocumented Mexican migration. NAFTA would promote economic development in Mexico, creating jobs that would keep Mexicans home. The theory was that in a non-protectionist, free-trade environment, each country would specialize in areas and products in which it had a comparative advantage; middle-class jobs would flourish in every region; and Mexico—a poor country—would thrive.

Somehow, things did not turn out that way. Despite warnings from U.S. opponents of NAFTA that U.S. jobs would be lost to Mexico because the low-wage workforce would undercut higher-paid U.S. workers, Mexico has lost far more jobs than it has gained under NAFTA. Incredibly, because of the lifting of tariffs under NAFTA and continued U.S. farm subsidies, for example, Mexico is now importing most of its corn from the United States. Mexican corn farmers have gone out of business, undercut by U.S. prices. So farm workers who once harvested corn in Mexico lost their jobs, and where did they look for work? Across the border.

This project is not simply about pointing fingers. Yes, the United States shares culpability when it comes to Mexico's misfortunes. But corruption and the Mexican government's judgment on how to address economic challenges also are to blame. Yet the power and influence that the United States holds over Mexico positions the United States to play a positive role in Mexico's future. I believe that bold measures can be taken by the United States that would make a world of difference in the lives of Mexicans while bolstering the economy of the United States and affecting emigration.

In my view, the United States, Canada, and Mexico should pursue a true North American integration plan fashioned after the European Union (EU) model. NAFTA was a half-baked idea that left out the ingredients needed to bolster the Mexican economy. A true partnership that included serious support for infrastructure, development, and labor-migration avenues was absent. NAFTA has left the United States and Canada with a neighbor to the south that has a broken economy that loses more and more ground each day; we should not be surprised that Mexican workers look for jobs across borders. But when the wealthy nations of the European Union faced similar prospects, with poor states such as Ireland, Spain, and Portugal seeking membership, the wealthy nations invested heavily in the poorer countries. This helped to turn around their economies and avoided a flood of workers crossing borders, even though membership entitled EU nationals to free border passage.

The debate over whether millions of undocumented workers in the United States should be granted legalization distracts us from the more important questions about how we can structure the relationship among Mexico, the United States, and Canada in a manner that is good for all three countries. One day, the Minutemen, Lou Dobbs, or the former presidential candidate Tom Tancredo criticize legalization as a reward for lawbreakers and call for the absolute closing of the border. The next day, lawmakers are greeted with passionate calls by immigrant-rights advocates to recognize the contributions of undocumented workers who deserve our respect and lawful status. When President Bush called for a large, temporary guest-worker program in recognition of the needs of his business constituents, he faced resistance from both immigrant-rights advocates who want a path to legalization for workers and the Tancredo restrictionists who labeled the Bush plan an amnesty. While these debates rage on, no one talks about why the workers are here, beyond the standard understandings that they are here for a better life or that U.S. businesses need workers. No one pays attention to why the workers left Mexico in the first place or the effect that emigration of its workers has on Mexico.

Defining the debate in terms of what undocumented immigrants do or do not deserve, or even framing the answer around U.S. businesses' needs for workers, does not enable us to think broadly enough. Understanding the flow of workers between Mexico and the United States provides more than a glimpse of the effects of NAFTA, globalization, and social phenomena. Understanding modern-day social, cultural, and political, as well as economic, relations between nations—particularly those in our hemisphere—helps us begin to formulate a framework for our region that addresses concerns we may have about migration and immigrant rights. The EU model of heavy investment in poor nations, given with serious conditions and later coupled with open labor migration, is worth emulating. I believe that if we take the time to understand the reason for the phenomenon of migration, and if we plan and implement correctly, future undocumented migration among the United States, Mexico, and Canada will become passé.

To understand the flow of low-wage Mexican workers into the United States and why an EU model for North America provides valuable instruction, I explore several topics. I believe that these areas and concepts will help us develop the information that we need for a sensible, comprehensive approach to solving the challenge of undocumented Mexican migration. In Chapter 1, I take a close look at NAFTA and its effect on the economies and job forces of the United States, Canada, and Mexico. We begin to see in

Chapter 1 how Mexico was disadvantaged by the terms of NAFTA and why increased undocumented Mexican migration followed, especially given U.S. farm subsidies and manufacturing competition from China. Chapter 2 provides a historical overview of the economic and political history of Mexico, including the election of a new pro-NAFTA president in 2006 and the effect of the U.S. recession; an understanding of that history is necessary if we are to invest effectively in Mexico and rely on its leaders to follow through on those investments. Chapter 3 explores the Canadian experience to get a sense of what a country that engages in free trade with the United States must do to succeed. Lessons from Canada help us understand what needs to be done to develop a successful economy in Mexico but also allow us to understand that Canada has a responsibility to help resolve the migration issue, as well. Chapter 4 introduces the lessons from the European Union. While its process has not been perfect, the EU has developed a powerful structure and economy. The EU model is not simply important to use as a guide for how we might structure North American integration; as a force that must be reckoned with, the EU provides added incentive to re-create a North America that can compete with Europe. Chapter 5 on Ireland provides a closer look at the benefits of the EU approach to a formerly poor, emigrant-exporting country that has developed into an economically successful, immigrant-receiving country. While the analogy between Mexico and Ireland is imperfect, and Ireland recently has experienced new economic challenges, important lessons can still be retrieved from the EU–Irish experience for Mexico. Chapter 6 reviews current U.S. border and enforcement approaches to undocumented immigration and serves as a reminder of how those approaches have been shortsighted, unsuccessful, and wasteful. The stark failures and inhumane border strategy challenge us to think strategically and look for innovative approaches to the migration phenomenon. In Chapter 7, I outline what North American integration using an EU model would entail, including great investment in Mexico's infrastructure, as well as a more generous visa system. I also explain why, in the face of manufacturing competition from China, the United States as well as Mexico would benefit from bolstering Mexico's strategic position. In the Epilogue, I argue that we owe it to ourselves and to Mexico to look for innovation and to take a smarter approach to migration. Conceiving of the U.S.–Mexican border simply as a barrier for keeping out the unwanted has led us down a problematic, self-defeating path. There are economic, practical reasons for a more open-minded, regional approach. But ethical reasons and conditions compel us to explore a broader solution, as well.

Some may wonder why—in a discussion of undocumented immigration to the United States—I focus this volume solely on Mexican migration.

Mexicans may make up most—perhaps 60 percent—of the undocumented immigrants in the country, but there are others. I do so because, after thirty-five years of advocacy, representation, teaching, and research in the field, the big complaint that anti-immigrant groups and advocates have is about undocumented Mexican migration. I have seen and heard this in my work before the old Immigration and Naturalization Service and the current Department of Homeland Security. I have seen it in my work in opposition to California's Proposition 187 in the 1990s. I have seen it in my appearances before the courts and in my reading of court decisions. I have seen it in the raids at factories and homes. I have seen it in the expenditures at the U.S.–Mexican border. I have heard it in the audiences before whom I have appeared. And I have read it in the hate mail I receive. If we can resolve the challenge of undocumented Mexican migration, I think we can quiet most of the critics.

If we really want to solve the problem of undocumented Mexican migration, we should look honestly at the situation that we have helped to create with regimes such as NAFTA. Mexico is a friend and ally, and Mexican workers are coming to feed their families while contributing to the U.S. economy. We should take seriously the need to understand why they come here and the economic policies that must be implemented to keep them home if that is our goal. If we want to facilitate the entry of workers, as well, then we must do that above board. We should take to heart what we learn about the forces that affect the flow of labor migration. By doing so, we will begin to see that the answer does not lie in stepped-up militarization of the border that results in avoidable deaths, the harassment of families walking their children to school, or raids on factories and plants that inevitably end up hurting businesses, workers, and local communities. The answer lies in a broader vision of North America.

The NAFTA Effect

The North American Free Trade Agreement (NAFTA) of 1994, vigorously endorsed by the political leaders of the United States, Mexico, and Canada, was supposed to fix the problem of undocumented Mexican migration into the United States.[1] NAFTA would be the permanent solution. The idea was that economic development in Mexico would be enhanced under NAFTA and that development would create jobs in Mexico, encouraging Mexicans to stay home.[2]

In fact, NAFTA as a method of reducing undocumented migration failed miserably. Even though the agreement coincided with a new border-enforcement regime, illicit border crossings from Mexico continued to rise. The militarization of the border and Operation Gatekeeper, which closed off the easiest places to cross the border, simply shifted the entry points to more treacherous, and in many cases lethal, terrain.[3] Most demographers estimate that half a million undocumented immigrants enter the United States annually.[4]

NAFTA has not resulted in increased employment opportunities in Mexico for Mexican workers, and U.S. employers continue to recruit and rely on low-wage Mexican workers. Is it surprising that workers continue to enter without inspection, given no changes to immigration quotas since the passage of NAFTA? Some observers, like Douglas Massey, have criticized the situation as a shortsighted understanding of how NAFTA would work, arguing that the movement of people in addition to goods should have been anticipated.[5] While NAFTA's provisions facilitated the movement of goods and services as trade integration was unfolding, no provisions were incorporated to further the movement of labor beyond existing immigration-law categories.

North American economic integration under NAFTA and related developments in Mexico actually have promoted more, not less, labor migration.[6] Perhaps failing to provide for labor migration in NAFTA was an oversight or even a mistake. Whatever the reason, determining why heavy labor migration has persisted helps us understand how NAFTA failed to address the challenge of undocumented immigration.

A free-trade agreement is a pact between two countries or areas that agree to lift most or all tariffs, quotas, special fees and taxes, and other barriers to trade.[7] The purpose of free-trade agreements is to allow faster and more business between the two countries or areas, which should benefit both.[8] The economic theory underlying free-trade agreements is the concept of "comparative advantage," which asserts that in a free marketplace, each country will specialize in the activity in which it has a comparative advantage (that is, natural resources, skilled artisans, agriculture-friendly weather, etc.).[9] Since each country is specializing in a particular area or product, each country should mutually benefit from the agreement and generate more overall income.[10]

Free-trade agreements are controversial in the United States. Proponents support U.S. free-trade agreements because they believe that free trade (1) increases sales and profits for U.S. businesses, thus strengthening the economy; (2) creates jobs for the U.S. middle class over the long term; and (3) is an opportunity for the United States to provide financial help to some of the world's poorest countries. However, critics argue that free-trade agreements tend to increase globalization and the outsourcing of U.S. jobs to other countries.[11] Specifically, opponents of U.S. free-trade agreements believe that in the United States free trade has caused more job losses than gains, especially for high-wage jobs, and that many free-trade agreements are simply bad deals for the United States.[12] In terms of how NAFTA operated, we will see that free trade has created another problem: With an ailing economy, NAFTA was in fact a bad deal for Mexico because it could not compete with U.S. subsidies to its own businesses, thus producing job loss and migration pressures in Mexico.

The standard description of how NAFTA came about (as opposed to a more critical description set forth below) goes like this. Since the 1980s, Mexico has engaged in economic reforms that have relied on international trade. Mexico adopted major measures in 1986, when President Carlos Salinas de Gortari and a new ruling elite successfully pushed the country's entry into the General Agreement on Tariffs and Trade (GATT).[13] Soon after that,

Salinas approached the United States about establishing a continent-wide free-trade zone.[14] By 1990, President Salinas and President George H. W. Bush had announced the initiation of negotiations of a free-trade agreement between Mexico and the United States. Canadian Prime Minister Brian Mulroney soon joined in, setting the stage for the creation of a free-trade area covering all of North America. Within two years, the three leaders had signed NAFTA, beginning the implementation process. Although President Bush failed to be reelected, his successor, President Bill Clinton, followed through, insisting on side agreements pertaining to U.S. labor protection, environmental control, and certain limitations on imports. Tariffs and other barriers would be phased out over a fifteen-year period, and intellectual property rights would be protected.[15] By reducing restraints on trade, the idea was, commerce between the three nations would increase.[16]

The controversy over NAFTA was deep. Free-trade advocates, enamored by the accord, were pitted against liberal interest groups. In territory, population, and product, NAFTA would be larger than the first fifteen members of the European Union combined (almost 400 million people live in the three countries of North America).[17] Economists and chambers of commerce argued that the agreement would benefit all three nations. But organized labor worried that jobs would be lost, because employers would move their operations to Mexico.[18] The independent presidential candidate Ross Perot sarcastically asserted that the "giant sucking sound" was that of jobs that would be lost to Mexico under NAFTA.[19] Environmentalist claimed that Mexico's environmental protections were lacking and that the accord would harm the environment.[20]

NAFTA's failure to include a component for low-skilled laborers apparently was intentional. Kevin Johnson has explained that the debate over NAFTA "did not view the trade agreement and immigration as related. In part, this was a result of the fact that, in negotiating the trade agreement, the United States excluded the subject of labor migration from the bargaining table."[21] The only real discussion about migration was in negative rather than positive terms. Some critics urged opposition to NAFTA late in the process if Mexico did not agree to take steps to limit immigration and stem the flow of undocumented migrants.[22] The Mexican government objected to such a suggestion as a violation of the right to travel, and U.S. officials objected by saying that it was too late to add provisions on immigration controls.[23] Incredibly, when asked about immigration issues, the deputy U.S. trade representative involved in the NAFTA negotiations responded: "The issues of immigration . . . [are] not considered to be a subject of the free trade negotiations. . . . When we get into broad scale immigration, you're not dealing with trade. . . . [Y]ou're dealing with social issues . . . and we've agreed that will not be part of this negotiation."[24] As a result, NAFTA essentially did not deal with migration among the three countries.[25]

The Results of NAFTA in Mexico

NAFTA clearly has helped to increase trade between Mexico and the United States. Over the past twenty years, trade between the two nations has increased more than eight times.[26] Just since NAFTA was signed in 1994, trade and investment among Mexico, the United States, and Canada has tripled,[27] and by 2001 Mexico has become one of the largest suppliers of goods and services to the United States.[28] After Canada, Mexico was the second-biggest U.S. trading partner until 2004, when China moved into second place. Still, these are impressive figures for Mexico.

However, the increase in trade has not translated into more jobs for Mexicans at home. In fact, NAFTA has resulted in structural changes that encourage more labor migration from Mexico. Consider agriculture. In theory, agricultural free trade should reduce migration pressures from poorer countries, because agriculture is a huge source of low-wage employment in such countries; those countries should have a competitive advantage when it comes to agriculture. However, agricultural subsidies and mechanization in the wealthier countries can distort the outcome.[29] Those factors actually give the United States the comparative advantage when it comes to agriculture:

> American agriculture is the most mechanized and productive in the world, and government subsidies for farmers create market distortions, which in turn create a higher demand for cheap labor and for guest worker programs. If the goal of U.S. government policy is to reduce immigration from Mexico, it would make sense to address this distorting effect at the source. U.S. agricultural subsidies often support large-scale agricultural operations that create demand for immigrant labor. At the same time, these subsidies negatively affect agricultural production in developing countries that cannot afford to subsidize farms to the same degree and indirectly promote rural emigration. The result is both greater demand for and greater supply of guest workers.[30]

In contrast, the agricultural industry in Mexico is not powerful and vast. Certainly, some large farms located in northern Mexico grow fruit and vegetables aimed at U.S. markets. However, most Mexican farms are small and do not have credit. The sale of land in the form of cooperatives (*ejidos*) is permitted, but the government has few credit funds and little aid for small farmers.[31] Net exports from the northern part of Mexico grew after NAFTA, but that expansion paled in comparison with new imports of grain, oilseeds, and meat from the United States. After ten years under NAFTA, Mexico was dependent on the United States for much of its food.[32]

The effect of government subsidies to U.S. companies on undocumented migration is clear. Subsidies for U.S. agricultural entities actually promote the migration of unskilled workers because this "non-market stimulation" of the industry increases demand for employees and is accompanied by "negative effects . . . on developing countries which send migrant workers."[33] This was foreseeable when NAFTA began. For years, Mexico had provided support to rural areas through systems of price supports for producers and reduced prices of agricultural products to consumers, but Mexico withdrew this support after NAFTA.[34] However, the United States continued to produce subsidized corn in huge quantities at low prices, undercutting Mexico's corn prices. A major source of rural income for Mexicans was lost as Mexican corn farmers ceased operations, leaving their workers without jobs.[35] At best, the effects of NAFTA in Mexico have been uneven, especially in rural areas and among low-skilled groups; when those workers need work, they tend to migrate to the United States. Moreover, the wages for low-wage manufacturing workers have suffered as the rural poverty rate has increased. The creation of jobs by NAFTA that would reduce pressure to migrate simply has not occurred.[36]

Government intervention in and subsidies to the agricultural industry have always been a huge challenge for all three countries . A farm bill enacted by the U.S. Congress in 1996 actually eliminated subsidies to farmers while the United States was pressuring Europe to eliminate its farm subsidies. But U.S. crops began to get crowded out of the market as the global market was glutted and the U.S. dollar increased in value. As a result, the United States jumped in again, and by 2000 farm subsidies totaled $28 billion in the United States.[37] The 2008 farm bill included at least $25 billion in farm subsidies. In Michael Pollan's view, the U.S.-subsidized cheap corn is a "plague . . . impoverishing farmers (both here and in the countries to which we export it), degrading the land, polluting the water, and bleeding the federal treasury, which now spends up to $5 billion a year subsidizing cheap corn."[38] For example, federal subsidies account for nearly "half the income of the average Iowa corn farmer and represent roughly a quarter of the $19 billion U.S. taxpayers spend each year on payments to farmers."[39]

Thus, while agricultural liberalization may theoretically be good for a developing country in a trade relationship with a developed economy, that was not true for Mexico. Mexico started with an agricultural trade deficit with the United States before NAFTA, and the problem just got worse under the trade accord. Matters are still in flux because not all tariffs on certain crops in both the United States and Mexico have been eliminated. However, U.S. farm subsidies and the efficiency of U.S. farmers continue to make a difference. In the case of corn, U.S. corn is sold in Mexico at prices that are estimated to be at least 30 percent below the cost of production.[40]

Resulting agricultural job loss in Mexico has been severe. Prior to NAFTA, Mexico had 8.1 million agricultural jobs. That figure actually increased slightly after the peso crisis of the early 1990s, when unemployment led some workers back to the farm. Then a decline followed, and by 2006 only 6 million Mexican agricultural workers were employed—down 2 million from pre-NAFTA levels. While NAFTA cannot be blamed for all of these losses, Mexico has reduced its agricultural tariffs much more for the United States than for other trading partners. Clearly, agricultural trade liberalization is the "single most significant factor" in Mexico's agricultural jobs loss.[41]

The 2 million farmers forced to abandon their land ended up in Mexican cities, as migrant workers within Mexico, or in the United States.[42] Perhaps two hundred thousand have settled in wretched conditions in an agricultural area of the Mexican state of Sinaloa, where twenty families control the industry. Sinaloa is one of Mexico's prime, modern industrial-agricultural regions, as well as the core of country's drug trade. With pitiful wages, many survive on corn and beans they manage to grow, with poor housing, and no schools or health care available.[43]

NAFTA's failure to provide a long phase-out period for tariffs on basic crops led to the problems Mexican farmers have suffered. Nothing was done to help rural farmers face the adjustments that had to be made—no meaningful transition period, no assistance in shifting to competitive crops, no development of alternative job opportunities.[44] The effect of U.S. subsidies on Mexican products such as corn should have been anticipated when NAFTA was enacted. Anticipating the disadvantage to rural Mexican farmers was even more obvious in 2002 when U.S. farm-bill subsidies were increased.[45] As small, purportedly "inefficient" Mexican farmers were put at risk, no foreign investment into the rural sector for industrial development or value-added activities arrived to assist.[46]

Laura Carlsen, a program director of the Americas Program at the Center for International Policy in Mexico City, argues that the decline of Mexico's agricultural sector was actually a planned result of NAFTA. The 11.6 million acres farmed by small corn growers who would not be able to compete with U.S. imports were to be converted to other crops and uses, even though they constituted half of national production, and half of that land produced for family consumption. The claim was that the rural sector would receive investment for industrial development and value-added activities, and "inefficient" small farmers would be relocated to jobs in other sectors. But foreign investment did not pour into the rural sector. At the beginning of NAFTA, the sector was absorbing only .1 percent of total investment; by 2004, it was absorbing even less, at .09 percent. Much of the investment that arrived went to buying up existing productive capacity, including livestock operations and storage facilities. The absorption of Mexico's chicken production by Tyson and Pilgrim's Pride is a good example. Today the Ministry of Agriculture reports that only 6 percent of farms export.[47]

Agricultural job loss is emblematic of overall employment problems in Mexico exacerbated by NAFTA. Jobs in non-maquiladora manufacturing are fewer today than in 1994, except in informal-sector microenterprises. By June 2006, there were 130,000 fewer jobs (1.26 million) in non-maquiladora manufacturing than there had been prior to NAFTA. The U.S. recession and global changes such as competitive exports from China also have contributed to Mexican job loss in the past few years.[48]

Export-manufacturing jobs have increased modestly in Mexico during NAFTA. However, the loss of 2 million agricultural jobs greatly offsets the seven hundred thousand jobs gained in export manufacturing.[49] So although the number of foreign-owned factories increased, total manufacturing employment in Mexico declined to 3.5 million by 2004, from a high of 4.1 million in 2000.[50] Furthermore, a hundred thousand jobs in Mexico's domestic manufacturing sector were lost from 1993 to 2003.[51] Simply put, "The trade pact has not produced a strong gain in overall employment and, indeed, might have produced a net loss of jobs for Mexico."[52] As jobs that pay relatively well disappeared, Mexico's average wage for production workers, already low, fell further behind the average hourly pay of production workers in the United States, and Mexican manufacturing workers responded by migrating.[53]

The effect of NAFTA on Mexican wages as a factor in undocumented migration from Mexico is relevant, as well. Recent migration is a manifestation of historic restructuring of the Mexican economy.[54] After ten years of NAFTA, real wages in Mexico were lower, and income inequality grew, even though productivity was up.[55] Many Mexicans who have come to the United States looking for work were not unemployed in Mexico. That means that efforts to improve economic conditions in Mexico have to look beyond employment to wages, job quality, and perceptions of opportunity.[56] So the migration for these individuals is not so much about escaping abject poverty as it is about improving their economic situation in the new NAFTA economy.[57] In essence, given the growth in low-wage maquiladora jobs and decline in domestic manufacturing jobs, the gap between U.S. and Mexican wages actually widened under NAFTA. In 1975, Mexican wages were about

23 percent of U.S. wages; just before NAFTA was implemented in 1994, they declined to 15 percent; by 2003, they had dropped further, to 12 percent of U.S. wages.[58] Wages for manufacturing workers (both maquiladora and non-maquiladora) fell below pre-NAFTA levels. Even highly educated workers in manufacturing (e.g., professional, technical, and administrative staff) had lower wages in the late 1990s than in 1993.[59] So the average Mexican worker's wages and standard of living has not improved, despite increased exports and the attraction of some direct foreign investment to Mexico under NAFTA.

The gap between the rich and the poor in Mexico has widened during NAFTA, as well. In the early 1990s, income discrepancies between Mexico's rich and poor were already bad. Since that time, the wealthiest 10 percent of the population has claimed more of the share of national income, while the remaining 90 percent have lost or experienced no change in their income share. Regional inequalities also have worsened.[60]

U.S. imports from Mexico have increased under NAFTA. Prior to the agreement, imports were increasing at a rate of about 6.4 percent, compared with a 20 percent rate after. Interestingly, commodities liberalized by NAFTA did not grow as much as those that were not affected by liberalization. Apparently, export expansion in exports was primarily in manufacturing and "due primarily to industrial integration by North American firms."[61]

NAFTA definitely has affected Mexico more than the United States and Canada. The Mexican recession in 1995 principally resulted from government mismanagement and political crises, but growing dependence on foreign capital was also a challenge. In spite of these problems, through the end of the 1990s Mexico experienced annual growth rates of about 5 percent.[62] Mexico is the world's sixth-largest oil producer, its eighth-largest oil exporter, and the third-largest supplier of oil to the United States; its oil and gas revenues provide more than one-third of all Mexican government revenues.[63] NAFTA has transformed Mexico from an oil-dependent economy to one based on manufactured exports. Labor has moved out of the rural areas, and although about a fifth of the population live on farms, they produced only 5 percent of the country's output. This movement of workers to the cities affects Mexico's ability to compete in the industrial market.[64]

The costs can be severe under trade pacts. The losers are often those segments of society least able to cope with adjustment, due to "low skills, low savings, and low mobility," and the effect may be permanent due to limitations in education and skills, geographic isolation, and other factors.[65] Completely untangling the causes of the current situation in Mexico is impossible. But the main point to bear in mind is that NAFTA was not just a trade policy for Mexico. NAFTA was the cornerstone of Mexico's economic restructuring designed to lock in an export-oriented, market economy. After

NAFTA, Mexico went on to sign forty-two trade agreements modeled on the agreement, making it the free-trade champion of the world. However, these are "largely irrelevant" given that 90 percent of the nation's trade is with just one country: the United States.[66]

The Limitations of Maquiladoras

After the Bracero Program expired in 1964, unemployment in Mexican border towns reached critical levels, and the foreign exchange that had been generated for Mexico under the program was lost.[67] For more than twenty years, hundreds of thousands of Mexicans entered each year as temporary agricultural workers under the Bracero Program. After its expiration, Mexico looked for ways to replace the program with something that would create jobs, bring in foreign investment, increase industrial competitiveness, and enhance technology.[68] Attempting to attract capital and technology from abroad, Mexico eased legal restrictions that required foreign investments to be structured as joint ventures with majority Mexican control and protectionist tariffs that excluded foreign goods. At the same time, Mexico looked to the United States for help; under trade laws, the United States charged tariffs on products produced abroad even if the components were from the United States.[69]

The platform for maquiladoras was launched. First, Congress added the "807 Assembly Provision" in the tariff law. It provided that U.S. components could be exported "ready for assembly" and that the finished product imported back to the United States would not be assessed duties on the value of any U.S. components. In other words, U.S. firms could reduce manufacturing costs by using cheaper labor in Mexico.[70] Then through presidential decree (the "Maquiladora Decree") in 1965, Mexico permitted active foreign ownership of manufacturing and assembly facilities located near the U.S.–Mexican border. The decree also provided duty-free importation of raw materials and auxiliary materials (such as packaging and containers) irrespective of origin (including countries other than the United States), as long as the assembled or manufactured product was exported from Mexico within ninety days.[71] Non-maquiladora manufacturers in Mexico paid a price for these arrangements; without the advantage of duty-free components, they were disadvantaged for twenty-five years, until 1990, when the government lifted important duties on imported machinery, raw materials, and packaging.[72]

The maquiladora program's effect on the Mexican and U.S. economies was substantial. At the beginning of the 1990s, maquiladoras generated the second-largest source of foreign income and 45 percent of Mexico's exports to the United States.[73] New technology was also introduced to undeveloped towns and cities.[74] Yet during the 1980s, average Mexican wages fell to

30,000 pesos ($9.50) a day, a sign that low Mexican wages were subsidizing U.S. industrial restructuring, especially in the automotive and electronics industries. Thus, U.S. companies could save $25,000 per worker by using Mexican labor, amounting to $10 billion in 1990.[75]

By the end of the 1990s, the maquiladora program was being hailed as a success by many observers. Almost a million workers were employed in nearly three thousand factories, more than six hundred of whom were involved in manufacturing electronics.[76] Most of the electronics components come into Mexico duty-free from Asia, and with sufficient value added as a finished product, the product could qualify under NAFTA "rules of origin" to be exported duty-free to the United States or Canada as a NAFTA product.[77] In contrast, Asian components that came into the United States or Canada that were made into finished products were dutiable.

This advantage to Mexico did not go unnoticed in the negotiations over NAFTA. The United States and Canada had forced Mexico to give up the maquiladora advantage on the importing of duty-free components by January 2001, when duty deferrals or refunds ceased.[78] This placed Mexico in a difficult situation, and choices had to be made with respect to what to do to maintain revenue—for example, by attempting to export finished products to non-NAFTA countries or reducing external tariffs.[79]

Today, maquiladoras are concentrated in auto parts, electronics, and apparel. While maquiladora job growth cannot be primarily attributable to NAFTA, since the program predates it, the trade agreement stimulated apparel manufacturing due to tariff cuts. Maquiladora assembly plants added about 800,000 jobs between NAFTA's enactment in 1994 and peak maquiladora employment in 2001. But about 125,000 jobs had been eliminated by January 2006, so employment in this sector is up about 700,000 jobs since NAFTA began.[80] In the textile and apparel sectors, the number of jobs dropped by an average rate of 4.3 percent per year between 2001 and 2005.[81]

The great increase in apparel and other manufacturing in China since January 2005, when international limits on clothing exports expired, cannot be good news for maquiladora and other employment figures. The end of quotas on Chinese imports was a major reason that one Mexican stuffed-animal plant closed. "I couldn't compete with the Chinese anymore," the plant's owner complained.[82] While job loss in textiles and apparel is easily attributable to competition from factories paying even lower wages in China, that is not the sole problem. Mexico needs to do more to support export industries, from financing to technological backing.[83]

Mexico's maquiladora-dominated job growth reveals a real problem with a strategy that relies on the use of cheap labor for exports. For economic development to be sustained over time, the best paradigm would involve linking manufacturing companies with local businesses that supply materials, parts, or services. But maquiladoras are simply about low-wage workers, and the companies bring in components from outside Mexico, with little connection to local businesses and the rest of the economy.[84] Little transfer in technology occurs. This phenomenon occurs elsewhere around the globe, and the problem is that multinationals that set up shop this way can abandon a particular country when cheaper labor is found in a different country.[85]

Thus, China has become a real headache for Mexico. Low-wage competition on a world stage is a trap. Although maquiladora wages in 2001 were less than 10 percent of the manufacturing wage in the United States, two hundred thousand jobs were relocated to China between 2002 and 2003, where the wages were 3 percent of U.S. manufacturing wages. By 2003, China had replaced Mexico as the second-largest exporter to the United States.[86]

The Effect of NAFTA on the United States

During the 2008 presidential primaries, we often heard criticism of NAFTA from the Democratic hopefuls complaining that U.S. jobs were lost under the agreement. But depending on the calculus, measuring the effect of NAFTA in the United States can be tricky. One approach is to estimate the number of manufacturing jobs supported by a certain level of exports and to multiply the increase in exports to Canada and Mexico by that figure to calculate job growth. Others apply a multiplier formula to the trade deficit (which presumably reflects the greater increase of imports over exports). NAFTA's supporters do not use a multiplier formula to identify jobs lost due to imports, noting the lack of certainty that all imported goods substitute for U.S. goods that would have been produced in the absence of trade. Most agree, however, that all trade agreements produce both winners and losers, so one must look at both jobs created and jobs lost. Also, one has to keep in mind that factors beyond NAFTA are at play, such as other trade agreements and the creation of the World Trade Organization (WTO). Simple multiplier formulas may not truly capture all that is transpiring.[87]

The U.S. International Trade Commission (USITC) uses its own approach to measure the effect of trade agreements on the U.S. economy. Its model concluded that NAFTA and the Canada–United States Free Trade Agreement (CUFTA) had a combined positive effect on total compensation to U.S. workers by about $10 billion in 2001. The model is based on the trade-theory assumption that in full-employment economies, there is no change in total employment.[88] To the USITC, the effect of NAFTA on U.S. employment falls between a gain of 270,000 jobs and zero net change.[89] The problem with the USITC model (as well as others) is the failure to account for investment decisions to move production facilities from the United States to Mexico or Canada. Investment decisions based on market access may be captured, but other considerations, such as NAFTA's protections for U.S. investors, may be missed.[90]

Most researchers conclude that about half a million U.S. workers lost jobs as a result of NAFTA. However, the losses were likely offset by job increases. About half of the losses were due to production shifts to Mexico, apparel manufacturing producing the greatest number, about 28 percent, followed by electronics (13 percent), automobiles and parts (7 percent), and fabricated metals (6 percent).[91] But while more than ninety thousand jobs may have been lost in the United States each year, about two hundred thousand jobs were created each year in the 1990s, for example, making the losses "trivial in comparison."[92]

Overall, NAFTA has resulted in strong growth in manufactured exports but disappointing increases in manufacturing employment.[93] Mexican employment loss in domestic manufacturing and agriculture overwhelmed jobs created in export manufacturing. In the United States, the effect has been neutral or slightly positive, at best, in terms of employment, but certainly not negative.[94]

Canada and NAFTA

Prior to NAFTA, Canada was doing well economically, and that success has continued under the agreement. The Canadian economy ranked eighth in the world in 2006, and Canadian citizens enjoy a high standard of living that is comparable to that in the United States. Although the relative sizes of these national economies are clearly imbalanced, like that of the United States the Canadian economy is market-based and in recent decades has become service-sector-oriented. The United States is Canada's primary trading partner. In 2002, total trade between the two countries was $411 billion. But Canada also has strong trading relations with the EU.

Agricultural trade with Canada has flourished under NAFTA. Canada is the number-one market for U.S. agricultural exports, purchasing $8.7 billion worth in 2002. Since 1994, U.S. agricultural products to Canada have accounted for almost half of total growth in U.S. agricultural exports worldwide. The average annual growth rate of U.S. agricultural-product exports to Canada since the implementation of NAFTA was 5.1 percent, while that for the rest of the world was only 1 percent.

Canada has taken advantage of free-trade opportunities under NAFTA. Because of the agreement, 29 percent more merchandise flowed from Canada to the United States, and 14 percent more goods flowed from the United States to Canada. About one-half of the increase in Canadian exports to the United States between 1993 and 1997 was attributed to NAFTA. The flow of merchandise from Canada to Mexico increased by 12 percent, and the flow from Mexico to Canada increased by 48 percent. In this case, NAFTA was responsible for about one-quarter of the increase in Canadian exports to Mexico during the period and roughly 60 percent of the increase in Canadian imports from Mexico.

As the closer look at Canada in Chapter 3 shows, unlike Mexico, Canada entered into NAFTA with a strong economy and has been able to do fine under the agreement.

Multinational Interests and NAFTA

A more critical exploration of NAFTA's background, what it represents, and how it came about reveals a disturbing history with multinational corporate links that certainly did not coincide with working-class interests. That history provides a better understanding of why undocumented Mexican migration has increased since the enactment of NAFTA and related events, such as the peso crisis of the 1990s. The history also raises concerns about the ethics of the approach the United States takes toward its southern border and toward low-wage workers from Mexico.

NAFTA represented a sea change in the manner that international trade was addressed by the United States. Until then, different sectors of the economy competed against each other for advantages, uniting various sectors' workers, managers, and investors on the issues of tariffs and trade policies. Manufacturers, food producers, shipping companies, and other sectors sought advantages so that each could do well. But with NAFTA, class divisions emerged between workers on one side and managers and investors on the other, the latter side realizing that it could make money by investing elsewhere, regardless of where the workers were located.[95]

The long negotiation period leading up to NAFTA made clear that the agreement was not about workers' rights. Just about all of the members of the U.S. Advisory Committee for Trade and Policy and Negotiations (ACTPIN) were representatives of multinational corporations. Likewise, trade unions, environmental groups, and other civil-society organizations were not invited to the negotiation table by Mexico or Canada. The message was clear: Trade agreements were business matters.[96] And more than anything, NAFTA represented an opportunity to dismantle public regulation of business, and the business class was able to write its own ticket.[97]

Up against a novice and compliant Mexican negotiating team—and behind the backs of both publics—U.S. negotiators achieved terms favorable to large corporations such as an investment-promotion provision, intellectual-property protection, new markets, and access to resources that included cheap labor. The result was a trade agreement that was unprecedented in the world. Even strategic products and services were slated for tariff and barrier eliminations under NAFTA, and the Mexican state relinquished basic development policy tools, such as government-procurement preferences to support local industry, management of the basic food chain, and performance requirements for foreign companies regarding technology transfer, backward linkages, or adoption of state-of-the-art environmental practices.[98] Although the U.S. economy was more than fifteen times larger than Mexico's and the Mexican economy suffered from major disadvantages, no weight was given to the need to compensate for the disparities between the two, as was done in the EU when poor countries were integrated. NAFTA sought to "lock in" a broad range of economic reforms, including tariff elimination but also investment guarantees.[99]

Supporters of NAFTA (including President Clinton) and the media advanced three common justifications for the new global-economy agreement. One was economic: Jobs would be created, and the U.S. standard of living would increase. A second was related to immigration: Free trade would bolster Mexico's economy, thereby stemming the flow of undocumented migration. The third was political: The forces of democracy epitomized by President Carlos Salinas had to be supported.[100] The immigration rationale appealed to many who were concerned about the flow of undocumented immigrants in the early 1990s.[101]

As we have seen, the job-creation theme was misleading. The real benefits of free trade come in the form of lower prices rather than more jobs. Free trade means larger markets that increase economies of scale; businesses can specialize more and sell products at lower prices. Although being able to buy more is a form of wealth creation, being able to buy cheaper products was not something typical taxpayers had in mind when their congressional representatives voted for NAFTA.[102] But even Jimmy Carter got into the act. Perhaps concerned with EU consolidation and the early signs of a Chinese economic movement, he endorsed NAFTA, fearful that "the Japanese and others will move in and take over markets that are rightfully ours."[103]

Multinational interests were solidifying as the agreement neared completion. Corporate enterprises would be freed of national trade restrictions. Already connected to others in their worldwide business networks, the enterprises would not longer be constrained by national boundaries . Profitmaking across boundaries for multinationals from all three countries would be enhanced.[104]

Workers could have benefited under NAFTA if a single internal market had been created—a customs union (think EU). In that vision, a protected, internal market would emerge. Businesses from all three countries could benefit from economies of scale, access to raw materials and technology, and shared research and development, training, and business subsidies.[105] But what emerged was far different. Instead, NAFTA was crafted to enhance profitmaking for big business, not for everyday workers. Each country maintained its own markets, but multinationals could trade freely across borders, taking advantage of whatever each country had to offer.

A union of the three countries from which workers and businesses would all benefit from a protected market would have amounted to a social contract that big business did not support. To big business, NAFTA was not about making North America or each country more competitive; it was about making corporate investors more competitive by giving them access to cheap labor and even government assets in Mexico. NAFTA was not a commitment to North America; it was about cheap labor, no matter where the labor was located.[106] Big business made substantial contributions to the Clinton campaign in 1992 after he advocated more open markets and less protectionism.[107]

Since NAFTA promoters today do not have the evidence to claim that major job growth and higher wages have resulted, they emphasize how the agreement brought about lower prices for consumers. A few years ago, the Office of the U.S. Trade Representative asserted that a family of four benefited by $1,300 to $2,000 per year as a result of NAFTA and the WTO. However, the estimate was based on a simulated model that did not consider unemployment or dislocation costs.[108]

One would surmise that cheaper prices are meaningful for Mexicans. Surely some Mexicans benefit from cheaper U.S. and Canadian products. But the Mexican poverty rate is above 50 percent, and the cost of living in Mexico has risen. The minimum wage in 1994 (about $4.20 per day) bought 44.9 pounds of tortillas compared with only 18.6 pounds in 2003. In 2003, the minimum wage bought seven liters of gas, down from 24.5 liters in 1994.[109] While being the most vulnerable to job loss, poor families have experienced the highest proportional increase in the cost of living. The tortilla crisis of January 2006 and the government's decision to place an additional tax on gas and gasoline set off a chain of price hikes that affected basic goods. In the first nine months of 2007, the cost of the "basic basket"—forty-three products defined as fundamental to Mexican subsistence—rose 34 percent.

During the same period, the legal minimum wage and the average contractual wage rose only 4 percent.[110] Consider the economic challenges faced by one maid in Mexico City. She "collects $8 a day, or about 80 pesos—almost double the minimum daily wage. But her earnings are spent as soon as she makes them. Six pesos a day for bus fare for each of the three days she works. Twenty-four pesos a day for her youngest child's bus fare to school. Thirty pesos a day for the oldest child's bus fare to high school. That leaves 20 pesos a day to buy food and clothing and pay for any doctor's bills or medicine, since her family is among the 63 percent of the population with no health coverage."[111] So the prices are not cheaper for poor Mexicans whose incomes have declined relative to purchasing power.

Economists sometimes view remittances as the silver lining to the immigration cloud, but they are no substitute for real development policy. For one, they break up families, contributing to problems in communities and emotional hardships. For another, they are unreliable. The current slowdown in the U.S. economy has already affected remittances.[112]

When Vicente Fox came onto the scene, his rhetoric inspired hope that Mexico would put pressure on the United States and Canada to approach NAFTA differently. Although he was a candidate for the conservative National Action Party (PAN) in the Mexican presidential election of 2000, he had joined forces with leftist political parties to win the governorship in the state of Guanajuato. In his campaign for the presidency, he addressed NAFTA, declaring, "I feel we must go ahead with a new phase. We must begin to talk to Canada and the United States to include the free flow of people under NAFTA. What is needed—and I know it sounds a bit too strong now—is to have the three countries evolving into a common market, an association that, in the long term, will reduce the brutal wage differential among the three countries."[113] After his election, he sought EU-type "cohesion" funds from the United States for infrastructure development and a border policy that would allow the free flow of laborers from all three countries.[114] But the events of 9/11 intervened, and Fox's notions were brushed aside, although commerce involving money and goods ultimately was maintained despite the war on terrorism.[115]

Thus, in spite of the hope for a new direction in Mexico after the election of Vicente Fox, his background as a member of the same governing class as Salinas and Zedillo prevailed. Like Clinton, the Bushes, Mulroney, and Jean Chrétien, Fox remained loyal to his business supporters. When farmers harmed by NAFTA protested in late 2002, they were spurned by Mexican officials who claimed that the United States and Canada held the power. Indeed, the U.S. response was revealing: U.S. Agriculture Department officials advised Mexican officials to "focus on rural structural reforms and not

[on] constructing barriers to trade"—in essence, to move small farmers out of agriculture.[116]

Clearly, a global governing economic class was the true beneficiary of NAFTA—not any particular nation, and certainly not the poor or working class of the nations involved.[117] Some NAFTA promoters claimed that unrestricted trade with Mexico was like unrestricted trade between individual U.S. states. The problem with that analogy is that U.S. workers are covered by minimal, uniform employment protections involving wages, health and safety standards, and other benefits. No such uniformity applies among the NAFTA nations. The corporate investor across borders gains protection from the global economic structure of NAFTA, not the common worker who is restricted by the border. As a U.S. State Department official revealed, "When we negotiate economic agreements with these poorer countries, we are negotiating with people from the same class. That is, people whose interests are like ours."[118] Multinational corporations make up the protected collective institution, not the societies of each nation.[119] This global economic class is unified across borders, governing economic decisions from a class perspective rather than as representatives of different nation-states.[120] From that perspective, we have a better sense of who benefits from free trade in the name of eliminating protectionist policies.

A class-based lens also helps us better understand the impact that the WTO's policies have on the poor and working class of Mexico. Just a year after the United States approved NAFTA, Newt Gingrich and the Republican Party wrested control of the House of Representatives. Clinton joined forces with the Republicans, and Congress approved the WTO, which is essentially a global version of NAFTA.[121] Trade among non-communist countries had already expanded nicely after World War II under GATT, but the WTO gave more strength to transnational investors.[122] Governments could no longer require foreign investors to purchase supplies from domestic businesses or block certain products from entering their borders if they were considered unsafe or immoral (e.g., produced by child labor). Local laws relating to workers' rights, the environment, and public health could not be used to restrict corporations from buying, selling, or investing.[123]

By embracing the WTO, then actively encouraging China to enter the world market, the U.S. business economic class enhanced its profitmaking ability. Mexican businesses have complained that multinational businesses centered in the United States have abandoned a partnership vision of NAFTA in which Mexican businesses would supply low-wage workers and their U.S. counterparts would supply the capital. Bringing China into the world market—and U.S. trade talks with other Latin American countries—strikes at the heart of Mexico's low-wage strategy.[124] The per capita gross domestic product between Mexico and the United States has widened.[125] NAFTA becomes less about enhancing the competitiveness of North America than about easing constraints on private corporations that might otherwise be imposed by a particular country or even a continent.[126]

Mexico "bet the house" on export-led economic development tied to the U.S. economy.[127] This is scary, especially given the current economic crisis in the United States. Exports grew, but who really benefited? Only 1.2 percent of Mexico's 3 million registered businesses engage in non-oil exports. Even within this small group, benefits concentrate in a handful: 601 companies—1.6 percent of exporters and only .02 percent of all businesses, mostly transnationals—receive 76.3 percent of the export value, or $142 billion. To benefit this lucky few, Mexico gave up its right to adopt policies to support sectors that provide strategic services to the nation but are unable to compete on the world market.[128]

Government leaders pinned Mexico's future on the trade agreement, and in retrospect the results fell way short of the expectations. Unemployment and underemployment in rural and urban settings are destabilizing. As a result of little private or public investment in productive capacity, the Mexican economy today rests on four pillars: a non-renewable resource (oil), remittances from migrants, the informal economy, and the illegal drug trade.[129]

Conclusion

NAFTA has created a "seamless web of finance," as businesses, bankers, and brokers wheel-and-deal across borders. Food companies and automakers use and rely on supplies and markets in accordance with freedoms that they have under the international accord.[130] Mexico and Canada are now dependent on the U.S. market, with about 90 percent of their exports going to the United States.[131] To promote trade, eighteen U.S. states have offices in Mexico, compared with a dozen in Canada.[132]

The policy of giving multinationals access to cheap labor through trade agreements has contributed to a haunting U.S. trade deficit and massive foreign debt.[133] In the past, Europe and Japan have eased the pain that an overvalued dollar might have on U.S. living standards, in part because the U.S. market for imports was important, but also because of the need to support the United States for military security. But without a Soviet threat or a shared obsession on global terrorism, Europe and Asia may not be as helpful on the international financial stage. They are focused on their own economic growth, and their people may not be as willing to support the United States.[134] Yet to get out of debt and reverse the trade deficit, Americans simply have to "save more and spend less, export more and import less."[135] And crazily, in the 2008 stimulus package enacted by Congress and signed by President Bush, the hope was that rebates would send taxpayers on a spending spree to avert a recession. Given our trade deficit, some feel that all the spending will do is to help countries such as China that manufacture so many consumer goods for the U.S. public.[136]

A crisis tied to the value of the dollar is looming. If the value of the dollar begins to drop, the living standards for average Americans will fall. To ensure that employment does not fall, the U.S. government would have to increase deficit spending even more, with a concurrent rise in the level of debt. Pressure will rise to correct the U.S. trade imbalance; inflation will follow; American consumers and businesses will spend less; and income growth and wages will be slowed. This would be devastating for many American families who are already in debt, faced with mortgage payments and costs for health care, education, transportation, and insurance. Those expenses took up 50 percent of family income in the 1970s but now take up 75 percent.[137]

If in fact U.S. imports from the rest of the world decline substantially, capital in the developing world will decline. Transnational elites outside the United States could begin to reduce their support for trade agreements with the United States—especially those that allow government subsidies of U.S. agriculture. The EU will give priority to its own interests and resist large trade deficits outside its communities; China, Japan, and India will want to continue their successful export modes, but the United States may have to seriously consider import surcharges—tariffs—to stop the outflow of U.S. dollars.[138]

The fact that the economies of North America have become so integrated under NAFTA means that when the United States makes its financial readjustment because of debt and trade imbalance, Canada and Mexico could be severely affected.[139] As Chapter 2 shows, the Mexican economy cannot sustain much more pain. The poverty rate is high, and the border region is dependent on the U.S. market. A major shift in the economic relationship between Mexico and the United States could cause even greater pressure for undocumented migration and perhaps political upheaval.[140] The task is to figure out how to reduce the U.S. trade deficit without creating major crises in Mexico and Canada.[141]

A class view of NAFTA reveals that Mexico's economy has been vulnerable to the operations of the agreement. The poor and the working class of Mexico have borne the brunt of free trade without free labor movement. The much wealthier United States has been able to continue subsidizing its industries, while Mexico has not. Resulting undocumented migration from Mexico is not a surprise. As subsequent chapters on the EU system and Ireland show, this result did not have to occur. Much as Ireland, Spain, and Portugal were aided by serious investments and subsidies by wealthier EU nations, Mexico needed to be treated as a true partner so that its industries and workers could be successful as well. The EU was seeking success for all of its members, and the United States, Canada, and the entire region would be well served by thinking that way, as well.

2

Revolutionary Mexico

A Brief Economic and Political History

To understand the U.S.–Mexico immigration dynamic, policymakers must examine Mexico through a complex series of lenses. Obviously, Mexico's economic and political history directly affects its residents and thus the flow of immigrants into the United States. Certainly, the reasons that many Mexicans come to the United States to work are varied and not always simply because of a poor Mexican economy. However, without a doubt many Mexicans look to the north when jobs and wages in Mexico are suffering.

The rapid increase in immigration from Mexico to the United States over the past twenty years reflects a complex and struggling Mexican economic picture. Mexico represents a symbol for education reform and for political corruption, for revolutionary ideas and for the dangers of unchecked globalization. These representations reveal themselves in the dichotomy of statistical data. The Mexican economy has been growing at an annual rate of 3 percent for roughly the past decade, one of the worst rates in Latin America.[1] Contrast that number, however, with Mexico's 92.4 percent literacy rate, one of the highest in Latin America.[2] Mexico's economic woes could merely reflect what is happening in all of Latin America, a region struggling in a global economy with relaxed free-trade rules and stiffer competition with a growing Asian market. In Latin America, per capita GDP declined by .7 percent during the 1980s and increased by just 1.5 percent per year in the 1990s. During this period, Latin America's poverty rates did not change much, but the gap between rich and poor widened, a problem reflected in Mexico's economy.[3]

Mexico's current economic plight revolves around a series of multifaceted issues concerning infrastructure, globalization, trade, and politics. Simply attributing undocumented migration to the United States as a reflection of Mexico's stunted job growth overlooks the complexities and intricacies of the problem and the various relationships at work. The reasons behind slow job growth and large gaps between rich and poor are not as easy to understand and discern. The population increased in the mid-1970s, and residents matured and entered the workforce in the 1990s. Workforce participation of women also increased in the 1980s and 1990s, in part because the household needed help during economic downturns. The labor force expanded from 33.7 million immediately before NAFTA to 43.4 million in 2004, meaning that a million new jobs a year were needed to absorb the labor supply.[4] But the economy failed to generate the jobs needed to keep up with population growth. Plausible explanations are hard to find, given some favorable factors: high prices for crude oil, large remittances from Mexicans abroad, and a low inflation rate. Some analysts describe the problem as Mexico's failure to engage in "serious structural reform" of its rigid labor rules, poor tax collection, and government-controlled energy markets.[5] Mexico's infrastructure challenges remain a serious problem.

Currently NAFTA's structure represents the largest element in Mexico's economic quagmire and can be viewed as a direct "push" factor for Mexican migration into the United States. However, NAFTA cannot be viewed in isolation when examining Mexico's economic and political policies. How Mexico's present economic and political systems feed into the Mexico–U.S. immigration debate can be completely understood only after examining the past century of history and what led up to the current political situation. The stage for Mexico's current state of economic flux began to be set long before the country's entry into NAFTA in 1994.

The Mexican Revolution, 1910–1934

The Mexican Revolution of 1910 launched a widespread rebellion, changing the country's social, economic, and political structures and creating long-range impacts for Mexico and its position in the global economy. Poor working conditions, inflation, inferior housing, deficient social services, low wages, and a general sense of discontent led people of all classes to revolt against the dictatorship of Porfirio Díaz. During this time, a new generation of leaders began seeking far-reaching reforms to improve the lives of all Mexicans. The fundamental goals of the revolution (land redistribution, free and fair elections, and a democratic, accountable government) were incorporated into the 1917 Constitution. The constitution was predicated on the "social function"

of property, which required that even privately held property be used to benefit society as a whole. The constitution placed a number of restrictions on the
Catholic church, recognized minimum wages for workers, and established
a social-security system. With the election of Alvaro Obregón to a four-year
presidential term in 1920, political leaders embarked on implementing the
goals of the 1917 Constitution.

Despite Obregón's commitment to national reconstruction, his administration struggled with revitalizing the economy in the early years. The post–
World War I economic slump resulted in high levels of unemployment, hun-
ger, general unrest, and privatization. Indeed, only the price of and demand
for oil remained stable at the time. By 1921, Mexico had become the world's
third-largest producer of petroleum. So even without an adequate taxation
scheme in place, the country's oil reserves sustained the Obregón administration and allowed him to begin implementing the constitution.

Although positive reforms were sweeping across Mexico, their economic
benefits were slower to arrive. A combination of domestic and international
policy factors led to increased emigration to the United States. The United
States began rapidly expanding its agriculture, mining, and railroad industries at the turn of the century and continued to build steam in these areas
during the revolution. However, xenophobic ideology also gripped U.S. officials, and policies that focused on excluding Chinese and Japanese laborers,
such as the informal "Gentleman's Agreement of 1907–1908" in which the
Japanese government agreed to refuse to issue passports to Japanese citizens
who hoped to emigrate to the United States, grew in popularity. However,
American industry still desperately required large amounts of labor. As the
United States prevented flows of Asian immigrants through racist legislation,
it simultaneously recruited heavily in Mexico. At this time, Mexican laborers
were eager to escape the violence and economic upheaval of the revolution
and took advantage of relaxed policies to work across the border and earn
money for their families. This recruitment of cheap labor increased during
World War I, to the extent that the 1917 Immigration Act provided an exception to the head tax and literacy requirement for Mexican workers. In total,
experts estimate, two hundred thousand Mexicans fled to the United States
between 1910 and 1920.[6]

Obregón struggled to create the economic reforms he had hoped for,
but he did see success in implementing other goals of the revolution, mainly
broad educational reforms. The new constitution provided that education, an
area that heretofore had been run by the Catholic church and reserved for the
elite class, be secular and free. Initially, Obregón had difficulty implementing
this mandate in full because the Catholic church still dominated the educational field, and the state neither had funds nor teachers to educate children.

Despite its strong opposition, the Obregón administration had little choice but to allow the church to provide education under closely guarded conditions. Secretary of Education José Vasconcelos reformed the curriculum and started a nationwide literacy campaign. Armed with increased federal funding, he also set out to reform the curriculum, training teachers and sending them to rural communities armed with the basics of arithmetic, research, writing, geography, and history. More than a thousand rural schools were built between 1920 and 1924, more than had been constructed during the previous fifty years.

Thus, many economic factors contributed to the development of Mexico's complex relationship with the United States. However, no event affected the U.S.–Mexico dynamic like the discovery of oil. Although oil was discovered before the onset of the revolution, the true boom occurred during the height of turmoil, between 1910 and 1920. Obregón used this discovery to his advantage, cultivating good relations with the United States through the sale of Mexican petroleum in the U.S. market. While the rest of Mexico was reeling from constant upheaval and violence, oil became the one booming commodity keeping the fledgling democracy somewhat afloat. Obregón later leveraged this newfound discovery in dealing with the United States and becoming recognized as a legitimate leader. His presidential term coincided with Republican President Warren G. Harding's business-friendly administration, which reluctantly gave in to pressure from U.S. mining and oil companies that feared that the Mexican government would seize U.S.-owned assets. After a series of diplomatic meetings in 1923, Mexico and the United States reached an agreement: Mexico declared it would not seize the oil properties, and the United States, in return, extended Obregón diplomatic recognition.

Mexico's next president, General Plutarco Calles, inherited a more prosperous Mexico. The postwar economic slump had given way to sustained economic growth. For a full decade beginning in 1924, Calles increased land distribution, continued the emphasis on rural education, and built the government's health and sanitation program almost from scratch. For the first time in Mexico's history, the government undertook a massive vaccination campaign. A new sanitary code was established and designed to ensure cleaner markets, a safer food supply, and regular inspections of bakeries, butcher shops, and other similar businesses.

In 1928, Mexico's constitution was amended to limit the presidency to one six-year term. Before he left office, Calles threw his support behind the former president, Alvaro Obregón. Obregón was victorious but was assassinated by José de León Toral, who criticized his policies regarding the Catholic church. Charged with choosing an interim president, the

Mexican Congress selected Minister of the Interior Emilio Portes Gil. By the 1929 elections, Calles and Portes Gil had organized the Partido Nacional Revolucionario (PNR), Mexico's first official political party. Although the PNR would change its name on several occasions, its control over Mexico's political process would remain permanently intact.

Like those in all of Latin America, Mexico's economy suffered during the Depression of the 1930s. Important Mexican imports such as oil and metals decreased, and the value of the peso began to fall. Many industries either collapsed or were paralyzed by monetary deflation and tight credit. The entire treasury surplus, valued at about 30 million pesos in cash reserves in 1930, was used up in 1931. By 1934, however, the worst was over. Mexico had witnessed its last successful revolt, the political process had stabilized itself, and the social revolutionary movement found a new leader in Lazaro Cárdenas.

Final Years of Reform, 1934–1940

Under Cárdenas's presidency, Mexico focused on some of the original socialist goals of the revolution, such as agrarian reform, which dominated the first few years he was in power. Cárdenas also developed some of the revolution's more progressive goals, empowering the average Mexican worker, and helped Mexico assert itself in the international economy by nationalizing the country's oil companies. While the violent nature of the revolution ceased, the quest for true reform continued to develop and grow during this period, with varying success.

Despite the success of land-distribution programs that had parceled out more than 26 million acres of land, millions of Mexican peasants survived on minimal subsistence, and few owned land. Cárdenas sought to deliver on unfulfilled promises of greater land distribution. By the time his term ended, he had distributed 49 million acres, about twice as much as all his predecessors combined. Indeed, roughly one-third of the population had received arable land under Cárdenas's redistribution program by 1940. These lands, usually held by "*ejidos,*" or cooperatives, were sometimes used by entire communities. To sustain the *ejidos,* the administration established important infrastructure such as government-supported schools, social services, and modern hospitals. The Cárdenas administration also founded the Banco de Credito Ejidal, an agrarian bank that provided large-scale financing to *ejidos.* Cárdenas's dedication to agrarian reform spelled the demise of the hacienda complex that pervaded Mexican society and broke the type of servitude that had bound the lower classes to their *hacendados* for centuries.

By nationalizing foreign-owned oil companies, Cárdenas harnessed Mexico's petroleum industry, resulting in one of the most dramatic and celebrated decisions of his presidency. In 1936, Mexican workers within the petroleum industry went on strike, demanding higher wages and better working conditions. The oil companies, while extracting large profits from the country, refused to negotiate with union representatives in good faith. A series of bitter disputes arose, culminating in a decision by the Mexican Supreme Court ordering the companies to increase wages and improve welfare and pension benefits for workers. When the companies refused to obey the order, Cárdenas declared that they had flagrantly defied Mexico's sovereignty and signed a decree nationalizing their holdings. The nationalization of oil marked a critical moment in Mexico–U.S. relations, causing ripple effects in obvious and subtle ways throughout the following decades.

Shortly after this expropriation, Cárdenas decided to alter the structure of the PNR. Realizing that Mexico was embarking on difficult economic times, he felt it necessary to create a more broadly based national party with representation from the military, labor, agrarian, and popular sectors of society. Cárdenas established the Partido Revolucionario Mexicano (PRM), which became the new official party and, like the PNR, faced no serious opposition in either state or national elections.

While Cárdenas tried turning the idealistic goals of the revolution into real reform, he still governed over a nation in transition, with real problems. His last two years in office were marked by economic difficulties. Most wealthy Mexicans refused to invest in the Mexican economy for fear that a communist state would be established, and foreign capitalists looked to other countries for more lucrative investment opportunities. Oil revenues declined, rampant inflation set in, and land reforms were cut back in favor of promoting industrialization. In addition, while he increased federal expenditure for rural education to more than 10 million pesos, twice as much as any previous president, such spending did not curtail illiteracy among the masses. Although more Mexicans could read and write than ever before, inflation and high population growth resulted in a higher number of illiterates than there had been in previous decades.

Although Cárdenas's efforts brought tremendous growth and progress throughout the country, Mexico remained predominantly rural. Much had changed, however, in the lifestyle of those living in even the remotest rural communities. Rural schools became the focal point of village life. For the first time in Mexico's history, cultural programs were dominated by the school rather than the church. Cárdenas succeeded in fostering an impressive rural education program and reorganizing the labor movement into a more powerful union. With the extension and improvement of medical facilities and other social services, life expectancy improved. Indeed, much had improved in the daily lives of Mexican peasants, even though poverty still pervaded most of rural Mexico. By 1940, many believed most of the goals envisioned by the revolutionaries of 1910 had been attained under Cárdenas's leadership.

A Conservative Postwar Turn, 1940–1958

In 1940, Manuel Ávila Camacho succeeded Cárdenas to the presidency, ushering in a conservative vision for Mexico that was evident in the policy changes he made throughout his term. Ávila Camacho slowed the pace of land distribution, favoring small, private ownership over the more communal *ejidos*. He also shifted educational reforms away from the socialist bent demonstrated by prior administrations. Ávila Camacho's greatest success came from steering Mexico through the lean war years and leading it to renewed economic growth after World War II. Part of Mexico's success came through increased relations with the United States as the two countries developed more intertwined economic ties.

Ávila Camacho's educational programs departed from the socialist ideology of past presidents, placing greater emphasis on personal initiative. Under the slogan "Each One Teach One," the Ávila Camacho administration enacted a law calling on each literate Mexican to teach one or more individuals the basics of reading and writing. To encourage compliance, states enacted various types of incentive plans. Despite great fanfare and a genuine enthusiasm for the program, however, Ávila Camacho's private initiative approach failed to eradicate illiteracy, as the Catholic church and the government had also failed.

Like his neighbor to the north (although on a much smaller scale), Ávila Camacho was dragged into the global quagmire of World War II after two of Mexico's oil carriers were destroyed by German submarines in the Gulf of Mexico. Ávila Camacho declared war against the Axis powers on May 22, 1942, eventually leading more than fifteen thousand Mexican soldiers to fight in World War II. The most unusual, and ultimately the most controversial, contribution to the war effort was Ávila Camacho's decision to provide the United States with more than thirty thousand Mexican laborers to serve as agricultural workers to replace Americans who had left for the war under the Bracero Program.[7] The war greatly affected Mexico's development. Not only did relations with the United States improve but the country's economic growth and industrialization also accelerated.

Members of the U.S. agriculture industry pressured the Roosevelt administration to develop a Mexican immigration program to meet their labor needs during World War II. Roosevelt established the Bracero Program, permitting seasonal Mexican workers to legally work in the United States and guaranteeing the immigrant labor force certain quality controls. Under the Bracero Program, workers were guaranteed minimum wage, decent living and working conditions, and return transportation to Mexico. Although the program expired in 1947, the need did not. Undocumented workers continued to flood into the United States until the program was reauthorized in 1951, unfortunately without the previous qualitative controls. While the Mexican government protested the lack of oversight, Mexico desperately needed help with its own domestic unemployment crisis. While many immigrants entered legally through the Bracero Program, many others entered outside the limited legal and safety parameters of the program. The program was extended through five presidential administrations.[8]

The Ávila Camacho administration, seeking to increase national productivity and improve the standard of living for the masses, created the National Financiera, a government-owned bank created to provide loans and oversee the industrial process, ultimately fostering industrial expansion. Many industrialists believed that for Mexico to prosper, industries needed to be created, relying on Mexican raw materials, agricultural products, and the manufacture of fibers and chemicals. They argued that only with such targeted development would Mexico become completely self-reliant. This belief fueled the industrial revolution, which gathered momentum during the war years and gained massive support throughout the country. As industry leaders had hoped, the revolution generated new wealth. The national income almost tripled between 1940 and 1945, and per capita income jumped from 325 pesos to 838 pesos during Ávila Camacho's term.

From 1946 to 1958 the presidencies of Miguel Alemán and Adolfo Ruiz Cortines built on the postwar boom, doubling Mexico's gross national product and stimulating overall economic growth. With healthy dollar reserves, Alemán launched many laudable public-works projects to provide steady work to a growing labor force. These projects included improvements in communications, the modernization of the railway system, and the completion of the Pan-American Highway segment in Mexico. In addition, low taxes and high profit margins encouraged both Mexican and foreign investors to pour capital into the industrial sectors of the economy. Indeed, Mexico seemed a model of health and prosperity. However, behind the luster of industrial progress, many serious problems continued to prevent the realization of a fully self-sufficient nation. Problems in educational reform continued, for example, teachers' salaries were paltry, making it almost impossible to staff newly built primary and secondary schools with qualified professionals. School attendance also remained low, with fewer than 2.25 million of the 6 million school-age children attending classes on a regular basis.

Under Ruiz Cortines's presidency, the economy remained dynamic. However, a rapidly increasing population set the stage for renewed economic problems. When Cárdenas came into power, the population had remained steady at 16 million. But by 1958, the population soared to more than 32 million. Driven by this explosion and compounded by a concomitant trend toward urbanization, hundreds of thousands of Mexicans living in rural areas flocked to cities in hopes of a better life. Few, if any, found it. The industrial revolution required skilled labor, and many Mexicans lacked such training. Although most workers earned their living from industry, the labor force was growing much faster than the economy could provide jobs. At one point, things got so bad that Ruiz Cortines ordered the use of manual labor instead of machinery on public works to keep the staggering number of workers occupied.

The United States also began reacting negatively to increases in Mexican immigrants crossing the border. In 1954, more than a million Mexicans were deported under "Operation Wetback." By contrast, the Bracero Program quotas were raised from 1954 to 1959. This began a familiar dichotomy of stiff enforcement, on the one hand, and enticing and exploiting Mexican laborers, on the other. This conflicting paradigm persists today as recruitment of low-wage immigrant workers continues while interior U.S. Immigration and Customs Enforcement (ICE) enforcement remains a high priority.

The Next Wave, 1958–1964

Unlike his recent predecessors, President Adolfo López Mateos offered a much more liberal approach to governance reminiscent of the early leaders of the Mexican Revolution. López Mateos's policies markedly departed from those of Ávila Camacho, Alemán, and Ruiz Cortines. López Mateos decided to implement an oft-forgotten article of the 1917 Constitution that called for labor to share in the profits with management. Under López Mateos's leadership, a special commission was convened in 1962 to implement a profit-sharing plan. The complicated formula agreed on depended on the amount of capital investment and the size of the labor force within each industry. By 1964, many laborers were earning an extra 5–10 percent a year under the profit-sharing laws.

The López Mateos administration also placed renewed emphasis on rural schools. Education had become the largest single item in the Mexican budget by 1963, receiving twice the amount allocated for national defense. While illiteracy was cut from 77 percent in 1910 to less than 38 percent in 1960, explosive population growth virtually nullified these results; in absolute numbers, there were more illiterate Mexicans in 1960 than there had been in previous years. In response, López Mateos sought to rapidly increase the number of rural classrooms through an ingenious system of prefabricated schools. He also initiated a system of issuing free and compulsory textbooks, despite opposition from the Catholic church and other groups.

The economy remained relatively strong under López Mateos's watch. Growth in private industry catalyzed the construction of luxury hotels, and tourists started to flood the country. In addition, by 1964 Mexico had become self-sufficient in iron, steel, and oil. Local capital flooded the markets, and Mexican bonds were sold on U.S. and European markets for the first time in decades. Indeed, Mexico was still in its period of sustained economic growth.

Uncertainty and Tension between Development and Democracy, 1964–1976

By the 1970s, Mexico's strong financial outlook, while beneficial for industry and overall growth, began to unravel the developing nation's social and economic fabric. Rapid economic development had seemingly rattled societal stability, disrupting existing social structures and increasing the disparity between the wealthy and the masses. Rising literacy, exposure to mass communications, and other advances in technology placed further pressure on an already weak political system. Although the rate of industrial growth up to that point had been impressive, it rested on a foundation of protectionist policies. Mexican industry was not generally competitive in world markets; the country's imports outstripped exports by almost $3.5 billion in 1975 alone. Because of huge deficits in its balance of payments, Mexico's progress slowed. Other factors such as shortages of electric power, steel, and transportation facilities further hindered economic growth.

By the summer of 1976, rumors abounded that for the first time in more than two decades Mexico would have to devalue the peso. Despite the government's assurances to the contrary, nothing could quell the rumors or prevent the flight of huge amounts of pesos. Many members of Mexico's wealthy classes exchanged their currency for dollars and transferred their investments to the United States and Europe. The decision to devaluate came in September 1976, and the peso fell from 12.50 to 20.50 for every dollar, a 60 percent devaluation. The decision was accepted in most quarters because of assurances that the resulting reduction of imports and growth of exports would shore up the economy. These predictions were not realized, however, because policymakers had not allowed the peso to float long enough to reach stable levels. One month later, the government announced a second devaluation of an additional 40 percent, leaving no doubt that the country's financial institutions were very fragile and deeply flawed.

Mexico struggled in this period due to a foundation shaken by an uncertain and wavering sense of national identity. Since the 1940s, Mexican confidence had been bolstered by political stability and remarkable economic success. Indeed, Mexico had seemingly separated itself from the systemic problems of its neighboring countries. By the late 1970s, however, it became obvious that Mexico's fragile economic and political systems would be severely tested in the years to come.

Instability and the Deepening
Economic Crisis, 1976–1988

Voter apathy led to the election of José López Portillo to the presidency without any real opposition in 1976. López Portillo, a former finance minister, followed a program of economic austerity after taking office. The large discoveries of petroleum in southeastern Mexico greatly influenced his administration, often overshadowing many of its other successes in the early years. Despite attempts to resist pressures from the United States and other foreign countries to increase production rapidly, Mexican oil production more than doubled under López Portillo's watch. Production grew nearly 200 percent, from eight hundred thousand barrels per day in 1976 to about 2.3 million barrels in 1980. By 1981, Mexico had become the world's largest producer of petroleum. Such wealth greatly affected how Mexico related to the international community. Indeed, the country's newfound economic strength allowed López Portillo to adopt a more independent foreign policy, especially in his relations with the U.S. government.

Such economic success, however, was tempered by the dangers of being heavily dependent on petroleum, a capital-intensive, not labor-intensive, industry. By the late 1970s, the López Portillo administration faced an unemployment rate of almost 50 percent. Although continuing oil production absorbed roughly 150,000 new workers each year, it could not absorb the more than 800,000 Mexicans entering the labor force annually. Furthermore, the promise of wealth from oil revenues led to reckless government spending, corruption, and staggering foreign debt. Government construction, public works, social-welfare projects, and government subsidies of consumer goods meant increased government participation in the economy. Although national income was insufficient to cover spending, Mexico's vast petroleum reserves made the international banking community willing to extend huge loans with high interest rates. Massive deficit spending under the López Portillo administration was predicated on the notion that continued increases in oil prices would allow Mexico to generate new wealth and pay off its foreign debt. However, as oil prices sharply dropped in the early 1980s, Mexico's income from oil production significantly dropped, as well.

In no time, the nation faced a severe economic recession. As the business community and investors lost confidence in the economy, they began investing abroad and funneling money to offshore bank accounts. In a desperate attempt to stop the exodus of capital, López Portillo ordered the Central Bank to stop buying and selling dollars to stabilize the peso. Within a few days, the peso had lost a third of its former value, slipping from 26 pesos to 37 pesos for every dollar. By the summer of 1982, the value sank to 100 pesos, marking the peso's lowest value ever. Coupled with sharp price increases and tight currency controls, the devaluation of the peso created near panic in all sectors of society. The economic downturn of the 1970s combined with this freefall increased undocumented Mexican immigration into the United States. In response, the U.S. Congress passed the Immigration Reform and Control Act (IRCA) in 1986, creating an amnesty program for immigrants who had entered the United States before 1982, as well as for some agricultural workers who had entered after 1982.

López Portillo came under fire for mishandling the economy and demonstrating a lack of leadership. In response, he accused the country's private banks of looting, greed, and disloyalty, as demonstrated by their participation in the frenzied flight of Mexican capital. López Portillo also decided, without consulting any members of his cabinet, to nationalize fifty-nine of the country's banks in a last-ditch effort to stabilize the economy. The wisdom of the move was questionable, however, because many of the banks were in bad financial shape, and assuming their burden further weakened Mexico's financial institutions.[9] On leaving office, López Portillo left behind Mexico's worst economic crisis in the twentieth century.

López Portillo's immediate successor, Miguel de la Madrid, took over at a time of deepening economic crisis. The peso continued its freefall, plummeting to an exchange rate of 800 pesos to a dollar in the summer of 1986. The following year proved to be even more catastrophic: The peso opened at 950 pesos to a dollar and by December had fallen to 2,300 pesos to a dollar. Mexico's foreign debt also grew in geometric proportions, forcing de la Madrid to announce that the country had to postpone payments on its foreign debt.

Recognizing that domestic spending had to be reined in, de la Madrid not only curtailed new projects but also announced reductions in federal subsidies. He ordered the sale of inefficient state-owned enterprises and a freeze on federal employment, eliminating fifty-one thousand federal jobs and cutting back salaries. Under the de la Madrid administration, Mexico further attempted to stabilize its economy by renegotiating its foreign debt and accepting a $4 billion bailout loan from the International Monetary Fund (IMF) conditioned on the government's promise to raise taxes, cut public spending, and limit imports. De la Madrid's efforts, however, were simply not enough. The last years of his administration saw the country slip into deeper economic chaos. In addition to the collapse of the peso, inflation soared to new heights. Increases in the prices of gasoline, corn, wheat, and electricity exacerbated the nation's problems and added to the rapid growth of foreign debt. When de la Madrid left office, the Mexican government had an outstanding debt of $105 billion.

Growing Pains: Mexico in the Post-revolutionary Era, 1988–1992

The 1980s ushered forth a decade of democratization throughout Latin America. For most countries, this meant replacing military dictatorships with civilian governments chosen through relatively open electoral processes. In Mexico, however, democratization meant recognizing the systemic weaknesses of its political systems and working to be more responsive and accountable to its citizens. Mexico's democracy had largely been a one-party system, for all intents and purposes. Its official party, under different names, had won every presidential election since 1929. Indeed, the party (now known as the Institutional Revolutionary Party [PRI]) became synonymous with the Mexican government, commanding huge resources and patronage. Elections soon became a farce as citizens were denied the element of choice essential to their fundamental right to vote.

Mexico's political challenges were evident in the 1988 presidential elections. For the first time in recent memory, efforts were made to ensure fair elections, and antigovernment forces made a strong showing. The press gave extensive coverage to opposition candidates. Manuel Clouthier, a millionaire industrialist, articulated a conservative position and ran on a platform calling for close U.S. ties, a more limited government, and a stronger private sector. The leftist opposition found a leader in Cuauhtémoc Cárdenas, former president Lazaro Cárdenas's son. Although Cárdenas and Clouthier sharply differed on most issues, they agreed on the need to end the PRI's electoral fraud.

Economically and politically, Mexico was on the verge of change in the early 1980s, with a financial outlook promising strong economic growth, better income distribution, and a reduction in poverty. As a major oil producer,

Mexico was on a high, because most of the world expected oil prices to continue to rise. With that foundation, international banks were willing lenders
to the government and Mexican businesses. However, oil prices plunged in
the 1980s, and the peso followed, leaving Mexico with a mounting foreign
debt that was owed in dollars. The bottom fell out, and recession ensued.[10]

Carlos Salinas de Gortari, a third candidate with the PRI, stepped
forward with an answer. As President Miguel del la Madrid's minister of
planning and budget in the 1980s, he challenged the historical social commitment of his own party, the PRI, by advocating the privatization of state-
owned businesses, the deregulation of other businesses, and the breaking up
of the historical method of collective rural landholdings. Mexico's entry into
the General Agreement on Tariffs and Trade (GATT) in 1986 was a part of
the Salinas approach; Mexico became a part of the world trading system.[11]
Salinas had never held an elective office. Although he was a successful tech-
nocrat, he was unaccustomed to the demands of politics and adopted what
others saw as a lackadaisical approach to campaigning. Election day was
surprising: The election was close enough for all three candidates to claim
victory, although Salinas was ultimately declared the winner under a cloud
of fraud, barely receiving a majority of the votes cast.

Early in his administration, Salinas started criticizing the *ejido* system,
charging that it was unproductive, calling it a failure, and blaming it for poverty in the rural areas. For Salinas, land redistribution was a bankrupt solution to a problem rooted in Mexico's past. He proposed new laws providing
for private ownership of the *ejido* lands. For the first time in the twentieth
century, farmers received titles to their land and, with ownership, the right
to trade, mortgage, and sell their property.

Salinas also believed that the government should exercise a more constrained role in addressing societal issues. He attributed many of Mexico's
economic problems to an exaggerated statism that had seen the government acquire ownership and control of private companies. The Salinas
administration started privatizing these companies, selling back more than
85 percent of them to the private sector by 1992. Mexico's gradual shift
to a free-market economy enabled Salinas to lower inflation to 10 percent
by 1993 and greatly reduce Mexico's foreign debt. This also allowed the
government to foster a closer relationship with the United States. Salinas
believed Mexico's economic ills could be addressed by the conclusion of
NAFTA, which would bring in capital investment and higher-paying jobs
for Mexicans. Many critics disagreed, arguing that free trade would not
only place Mexico at an economic disadvantage but also signal the dilution of national sovereignty. The vision of a new, large, combined North
American market carried the day, however, and on December 17, 1992,

Salinas, U.S. President George H. W. Bush, and Prime Minister Brian Mulroney of Canada signed the historic agreement.

When Salinas was elected, his friends in Washington regarded him as a modern economic reformer. But by the time he left office in 1994, facts revealed that he had covered up a huge cut in Mexico's foreign reserves; Mexico was bankrupt, and he fled the country.[12] One of his brothers was murdered, probably by federal police, and another was jailed for murdering a rival politician. His entire family remains the target of numerous international money-laundering investigations.[13]

The Salinas-led path to financial ruin for Mexico involved high finance, investor greed, and U.S. protection of its own capitalists. As Mexico tried to pull itself out of recession prior to NAFTA, many U.S. financiers invested short-term money in Mexico, foreseeing a rise in the price of Mexican securities and other assets. These expectations fueled price inflation and attracted more investors. Interest rates soared, and right before NAFTA, speculators could "arbitrage"—that is, borrow money in the United States for perhaps 5 percent and buy Mexican bonds that paid 12 percent. The money trickled down to some urban areas of Mexico, painting a rosy picture that Mexicans would be good consumers of U.S. products under NAFTA. But things begin to crumble right after NAFTA was approved in 1994. Investors cashed in and looked for new investments around the globe. U.S. interest rates increased, narrowing arbitrage possibilities. In Mexico's southernmost state, Chiapas, an Indian peasant rebellion against rich farmers and NAFTA erupted. Political assassinations made matters worse. Luis Donaldo Colosio, the chosen presidential candidate of the ruling PRI, and the PRI's secretary-general were both victims of assassination. Interest in Mexican financial markets tumbled.[14] Timothy Canova criticizes this period of "liberalizing trade, capital, and current accounts prior to any significant investment in its public infrastructure needs" as part of a pattern that was promoted by the "Washington–Wall Street Consensus, . . . the IMF and World Bank" that was unwise for a developing economy.[15]

Before he left office, Salinas came up with a scheme that would enable him to maintain an image of fiscal soundness and position himself to head the World Trade Organization (WTO). He needed to keep the peso from falling so that Mexican consumers would continue to sense prosperity. Even though his handpicked successor, Ernesto Zedillo, won the elections in July 1994, Zedillo would not take office for five months, so Salinas kept borrowing money to buy pesos to maintain their value. To keep U.S. and other investors engaged, he issued special bonds—*tesobonos*—that would be repaid in dollars; thus, Salinas was buying pesos with loans that would have to be repaid in dollars. Mexico's trade deficit with the rest of the world grew, and by the end of 1994, its dollar reserves had fallen from $17 billion to $6 billion, with a looming repayment of $30 billion in debt due in 1995.[16]

Zedillo could not continue the charade. Salinas had selected Zedillo after Colosio's assassination, but Zedillo had little legitimacy to begin his presidency. After his inauguration in December, he announced that the government could not support the peso any longer through loans. Investors sold off their pesos, and within weeks the currency fell 50 percent against the dollar. The lack of confidence in the Mexican economy among international investors caused the stock market to collapse. Many businesses closed down, and banks began foreclosing on many urban and rural properties. Inflation rose, interest rates soared, and hundreds of thousands of workers were left without jobs. Mexican bank reserves dwindled, and new bank loans were halted. Interest rates skyrocketed from 15 percent to 130 percent in two months. Personal bankruptcies, business failure, and unemployment ensued.[17]

In the meantime, U.S. supporters of NAFTA were not going to be caught holding the bag as far as U.S. investors in Mexico were concerned. Lawrence Summers, the Treasury Department's chief economist, convinced Robert Rubin, who was about to be confirmed as President Bill Clinton's secretary of the treasury, that Mexico needed $25 billion to repay foreign holders of the *tesobonos* bonds that were coming due and to calm down creditors. They and Alan Greenspan, chairman of the Federal Reserve, warned Congress that if Mexico defaulted, a global economic crisis would follow. The Republican-controlled Congress would not help, so Rubin and Summers used $20 billion from a Treasury Department fund to defend the U.S. dollar. The IMF put up the remainder.[18]

The $25 billion calmed things down, but the purpose was not rooted in a selfless act of goodwill to salvage the Mexican economy. The money was not used to create jobs, to help small businesses, or to work on Mexico's infrastructure. The money was used to repay the Wall Street investors who held the *tesobonos* who had invested on the promise of high yields from Salinas. Mexican taxpayers were still on the hook for the funds their government had borrowed to pay off Wall Street and the other financial burdens incurred by Salinas. The $25 billion bailout simply put more financial pressures on Mexico.[19] As Jorge Castañeda, Mexico's secretary of foreign affairs in 2000–2003, put it, "The cost of that risk [which produced lavish returns for two or three years] has been transferred completely to the Mexican taxpayer. . . . Mexicans are left to pay, becoming more indebted and dooming our economy and that of our children to indefinite stagnation."[20]

Ordinary Mexicans were pummeled. The economy crashed. The GDP fell 9 percent; wages fell 16 percent; unemployment doubled; and domestic consumption dropped 10 percent. Business investments were curtailed by a third. Funds for social services, education, and health care were decimated. As Mexico's poor (half the population) got poorer, the middle class was crushed, as well. Soon after NAFTA, members of the middle class had taken out variable-interest-rate loans for cars, house, and businesses, but their monthly interest payments spiked along with consumer prices.[21] The poor and the middle class of Mexico were victims of Salinas's excessive borrowing, which had inflated the Mexican economy in the early 1990s, enabling purchases of U.S. goods and even creating a U.S. trade surplus for a while.[22]

Corruption and fraud became commonplace, preserving the positions of certain members of the higher economic class in Mexico. Mexico's private banking industry had contributed to crisis a dozen years earlier, in 1982, by facilitating flight of capital, so President López Portillo nationalized the banks and left President de la Madrid to rationalize and administer the resulting chaotic mess. But Salinas sold the banks back to the private sector beginning in the early 1990s.[23] For example, Roberto Hernández Ramirez organized a group with little banking experience to purchase Banamex for $3.2 billion. One new banker, Carlos Cabal Peniche, used two banks to make loans to himself, and after the banks went bankrupt in the wake of the peso crisis, he fled the country.[24] Salinas sold Mexico's privatized telecommunications company, Telmex, to his friend Carlos Slim, essentially facilitating a private telephone monopoly. After raising rates 170 percent, Slim became the wealthiest person in Latin America.[25] Today, he may be the richest person in the world.[26]

The $20 billion U.S. loan did help slow further devaluations of the peso and helped the Zedillo administration stabilize the economy. As economic and political pressure abated, Zedillo was able to embark on a series of domestic reforms that included the overhaul of Mexico's social-security system and the continued privatization of state-owned enterprises.

Revolution Retrospective and the New Age of Democracy, 1992–Present

By the 1980s, the government had again become repressive. Social priorities such as land redistribution had given way to economic development, and exploitation in the form of multinational corporations became even more pervasive in the mining and petroleum industries. Poverty still abounded, with the lowest 20 percent of the population sharing only 3 percent of the national wealth and the upper 20 percent controlling 54 percent of the wealth. Indeed, the manifestations of this skewed distribution of wealth were evident throughout society. Millions were still illiterate, wages were low, and unemployment was high. Social services and housing were still grossly inadequate, especially in the rural areas. Only one-third of the population had access to running water in their place of residence. As inflation consistently outran increases in the minimum wage, real income declined until the 1990s.

Arguably, while the gap between the rich and the poor was as wide as ever, Mexico was no longer a country of two social poles; a burgeoning middle class had been created. Infant-mortality rates had fallen from thirty deaths per hundred to about five, and life expectancy soared. The overarching goal of the revolution had been to ensure a better life for Mexican citizens. In large part, despite multiple flaws in Mexico's system, this goal had been achieved. More Mexicans were living better in the 1990s than ever before. Although the degradations of poverty would most likely continue to manifest itself in Mexican society, undeniably Mexico had lifted itself up from its deep malaise and turned itself into a economic and social force with years of progress and growth in its horizon.

Enter NAFTA

In contrast to the wealthy, little farmers in Mexico were disfavored by NAFTA and deserted by their own government. Many have charged that Salinas and Zedillo wanted small farmers off the land because they were inefficient. The best use of these farmers, in these presidents' view, was as part of the cheap labor pool for foreign capital. In fact, parts of the Mexican Constitution that protected land distribution rights were rescinded under Salinas.[27] Under NAFTA, tariffs against foreign corn were steadily decreased, and small Mexican farmers did not have a chance against subsidized U.S. and Canadian agribusiness. U.S. corn was being exported up to 30 percent below production cost. In contrast, the Mexican government reduced subsidies and technical assistance to farms from $2 billion in 1994 to $500 million in 2000. Of the subsidies that continued, 85 percent went to larger Mexican farming enterprises. Small farms tried to concentrate on the home production and barter, but the government did not support those efforts.[28] These farmers' vociferous protest of their abandonment by the Mexican government have fallen on deaf ears.[29]

Mexico also has suffered from a post-NAFTA depression in domestic manufacturing in part because credit for small and medium-size firms has been reduced. The fact that foreign banks such as Citibank have come in has not helped. In theory, they have more money to lend and are not influenced by local politics. However, multinational banks compete with local banks for the good business found in the hands of the rich or multinational businesses. Hurting small banks in turn hurts the little guy, because the local banks do not have as much revenue from the profitable ventures to cover the risks associated with the smaller firms. The multinational banks thus are skimming the best business and do not have much commitment to long-term development. Ownership of about 90 percent of Mexico's banks has been transferred to U.S., Spanish, and other foreign banks, and lending to the private sector has fallen to 10 percent of GDP.[30]

While we tend to view Mexican workers as vital to the U.S. economy, we tend to forget that they are vital to the future of Mexico, as well. Mexican authorities share much of the blame for the condition of the country's workers. Incidents of exploitation, suppression of wages, and violations of civil rights are well known.[31] Organizing of independent unions has not been strongly endorsed by the government.[32] Those who come to the United States are ambitious and hardworking, and if forced to remain in Mexico, they are likely to become restless, with a middle class experiencing little progress and the poor getting poorer. Yet if Mexico is to develop, the ambitious and the industrious will be needed. If they are lost to the United States, Mexico has in effect subsidized the United States with the cost of their education and training.[33] Many who have migrated to the United States maintain social, economic, and political influence back in Mexico.[34]

The Mexican political system's culpability in the country's economic woes has a sinister side. The Mexican marijuana business blossomed during the de la Madrid and Salinas administrations. Mexican narco-traffickers also became big cocaine providers in the United States. By the time Salinas left office in 1994, drugs provided $30 billion in foreign exchange for the Mexican economy. Violence and government corruption associated with the drug trade reached new heights, and free-trade provisions under NAFTA actually stimulated illicit narcotics trafficking.[35] Today, U.S. law-enforcement officials are unhappy with NAFTA's easing up on commercial trucks coming from Mexico because of the flow of methamphetamine across the border.[36]

As noted in the context of maquiladoras,[37] wages in Mexico fell in the 1980s. One reason was the undervaluation of the peso to the dollar.[38] Combined with wage ceilings, wages for Mexican workers decreased. The wages of a maquiladora worker earning $7 per day in 1980 saw wages drop to a daily rate of $3.13 within ten years.[39] But Mexico's financial restructuring also had a significant effect. The government is the largest employer in Mexico, and by cutting its budget in response to fiscal deficits, it reduced public employees' wages. When the financial crisis struck in 1982, companies paid debts by restructuring and freezing wages.[40] One commentator even attributes lower wages to the "ineffectiveness and corruption" of organized labor in Mexico.[41]

Of course, contextualizing the decision to pursue NAFTA within Mexico's history is important. Manuel Pastor and Carol Wise point out that Mexico's rise to liberalization of trade has been a unique journey. Even back in 1984, the country's exposure to international trade was unthinkable. They offer four broad explanations for change in policies: global political economic structures; factor endowments, sectoral concerns, and related interest group politics; national political institutions; and leaders' values and beliefs.[42]

Global Political-Economic Structures

Rather than follow the conventional path of strict policies in relation to not reducing tariffs, Mexico steered clear of this economic orthodoxy back in 1983. This could have been due to pressure from international creditors and financial institutions, but it was more connected to domestic than to foreign pressures and politics. Between 1975 and 1985, industrial exports based on advanced technology, such as computers, office machines, and automobile engines, displayed dynamic growth. Such growth was important because intra-industry and intra-firm traders tend to push liberalization on the grounds that such a policy reduces the costs of their imported inputs. In the same vein, trade protection puts them at a competitive disadvantage both at home and abroad. Over time, these large, internationally oriented capitalists—represented by business lobbies such as the Confederation of Chambers of Industry (CONCAMIN), which consists of large manufacturing firms; the Employers' Confederation of the Mexican Republic (COPARMEX); and the Confederation of National Chambers of Commerce (CONCANACO)—supported Mexico's participation in GATT. By 1986, these large businesses had gathered enough strength to support the liberalization of Mexico's trade policies. Thus, stronger intra-industry trade links is one reason Mexico responded to the worsening international economy by opening rather than closing its borders.

Factors, Sectors, and Interest-Group Politics

Pastor and Wise also argue that landed agribusiness interests persuaded their rural-labor allies to push for a more competitive exchange rate and an end to import restrictions on manufactured goods, while organized urban workers sided with small and medium-size industrialists in an attempt to preserve high tariffs. In this struggle, the automobile-engine, microcomputer, and pharmaceutical sectors were the winners, and industries such as textiles, shoes, basic metals, and wood furniture were the losers.[43]

That fact that concentrated interest groups were better able to overcome the usual collective problems associated with realizing common objectives also is relevant. The winners (big industrialists) were for liberalization, while the bulk of the population had less incentive to support free trade, because the costs from foreign competition are tangible and immediate. Part of the answer to this contradictory result stems from the fact that, in the wake of the debt crisis and first wave of unilateral commercial opening, some of the protection-ist opposition decreased, allowing the "winners" to lobby for free trade. The adamantly protectionist Camara Nacional de la Industria de Transformación (National Chamber of Transformation Industries; CANACINTRA) was now a weak lobby. Thus, the political weakening of the "losers" is another way to explain why Mexico opened itself to free trade.

National Political Institutions

Pastor and Wise also suggest that an organizational overhaul, particularly at the state level, played a strong role in facilitating the successful implemen-tation of Mexico's trade reform. Trade policy was taken from its traditional location in the Trade Ministry and placed within more insulated state agen-cies, such as the Secretariat of Finance and Public Credit and the Secretariat of Programming and Budget. This helped neutralize protectionist demands, decreasing the pressure from protectionist groups to continue Mexico's con-servative approach to trade.

Leaders' Values and Beliefs

In Mexico, a massive shift in the ideological orientation of key political and economic actors during this crucial time occurred. For the first time during the postwar era, "Mexico's most powerful leaders share[d] a consensus con-cerning past excesses of statism and protection and seem[ed] unequivocal in their commitment to free trade."[44] Moreover, Mexico's highly presidential, low-accountability political system made it easier for the president and his U.S.-trained advisers to instill their own free-trade preferences. The anti-pro-tectionist leanings of President de la Madrid and President Salinas comple-mented those with a more international view of the economy.

An Alternative Explanation

The NAFTA negotiations were initiated not by the United States but by President Salinas. Therefore, Pastor and Wise argue, one must consider that trade policy originated inside Mexico rather than focusing solely on external factors. The debt crisis of 1982 called into question the country's long-standing political ties based on state patronage and domestic markets. The de la Madrid administration responded by marginalizing the nationalist-populist forces that had earlier thwarted liberalization. Under Salinas, economic management became highly presidential, and he further concentrated policy decisions in the hands of liberals.[45]

The reconstitution of the government party, the PRI, was also important. The economic crisis no longer made it possible for the PRI to maintain its level of widespread social benefits. Development financing was decentralized away from Mexico City and toward regions in an effort to create new constituencies that could replace the weak pack of uncompetitive workers and industrialists. As a result, private representatives, led by the Business Coordinating Council (CCE) and its public-sector counterparts, including executive-level appointees from the PRI and highly qualified technocrats from the Ministry of Trade and Ministry of Finance, set key price targets and then announced them to labor and small-business interests. This new alliance became so powerful that the PRI base was largely a bystander to a process that helped firm up a new alliance between a highly insulated executive, his technocratic corps, and representatives of Mexico's powerful business conglomerates. This alliance filled the vacuum left by PRI's dismantling to Mexico's traditional corporatist policymaking structure, providing a forceful impetus for NAFTA.

Outside NAFTA, Mexico currently faces other complex growth, industry, and trade problems in the new global market. Specifically, Mexico faces what many analysts call the "China problem." Many of the issues presented by the China problem can be traced back to a failure to buffer infrastructure and a consistent missing of key opportunities. For example, Mexico has long dominated the U.S. textile market as a supplier of cheap basic goods. However, textile quotas on China expired in 2004. That year, China produced 17 percent of basic textile goods in the global market, and it was expected to supply half of the global market within a year.[46] Mexico compounds this problem by failing to install the infrastructure necessary to remain competitive. For example, when a textile plant in Mexico runs out of thread or buttons, it must order from a supplier that is often outside the country, delaying production for weeks. When a Chinese textile plant runs out of buttons or thread, it often has access to a supplier just a few meters away and is back on schedule within hours. In addition, Mexico has consistently missed opportunities to remain competitive. Mexico has international trade agreements with many countries across the globe—but not China. "For years, China has been considered an enemy that must be defeated, not a potential ally."[47] Only recently has Mexico begun to make an effort to reach out to China in any significant way regarding trade.

In 2000, Vicente Fox, a prosperous rancher and former chief executive of Coca-Cola de Mexico, won the presidency. He made political history when he defeated the PRI's candidate. It was the first time the PRI had lost the presidency since the party was formed in 1921.

Fox was fully aware that one-quarter of the Mexican population lived in extreme poverty. As a member of the conservative National Action Party (PAN), Fox believed that market forces alone were insufficient. He called for "selective and temporary" state intervention to battle the causes of persistent poverty. In particular, Fox paid close attention to the plight of Mexico's Native Americans, who were among the most impoverished groups in the nation. In an effort to combat high mortality rates, low life expectancy, and systemic discrimination suffered by these groups, Fox created a cabinet-level office to address discrimination and launch Mexico's first affirmative-action program for the country's minority populations.

Although Fox took bold steps in calling for a reexamination of NAFTA, labor migration, and greater investments in Mexico, his efforts were thwarted by the events of September 11, 2001, when these issues took a back seat to the U.S. war on terror.

The Calderón Era

After a controversial election, Felipe Calderón, secretary of energy under President Fox, assumed the presidency in late 2006. He has exercised troubling loyalty to NAFTA, without the type of critique and call for reexamination demonstrated by Fox. Calderón maintains that NAFTA has generally "been beneficial for Mexicans because it has given consumers access to a greater range of high-quality products at better prices, [while allowing] us to export more Mexican products."[48] The biggest opposition to NAFTA has come from poor peasant farmers, who have condemned the provisions of the trade pact.[49] Throughout NAFTA's history, Mexican farmers have suffered the adverse consequences of the free-trade agreement. Calderón, however, insists that he will not renegotiate NAFTA; instead, he believes that he can address the issue by implementing policies that mitigate the negative economic impact of having to compete with agricultural imports priced below market from the United States. Ironically, he also plans to eradicate tariffs, which in turn will hurt the already struggling subsistence farmers even more. Calderón's critics charge him with "ignoring the plight of poor, subsistence farmers." They say he has "had to pass legislation placing a ceiling on [the] price of tortillas (which are made of corn) so that the Mexican poor could continue to eat, [and he] doesn't care if poor families are displaced and leave so long as U.S. products are in the supermarkets for those who can afford them."[50] The unfair competition between Mexico's subsistence farm products and subsidized U.S. agriculture, coupled with the abolition of the *ejido,* has increased poverty rates in rural Mexico, which in turn has led to a rise in immigration to the United States.[51]

Calderón's economic decisions do seem to be based more on promoting corporate profit than on protecting the interests of the poor. Yet he has overhauled the Mexican tax system to increase taxes on corporations and to expand public spending. His decision not to add a tax on medication and food, however, was largely a practical measure to ensure that his legislation would be approved by the Mexican Congress.

NAFTA

President Calderón is pro-NAFTA. During his campaign, he explained: "In the coming two decades, I envision the whole North American region . . . as a single region with a free market, not just in goods and services and investments, but also a free labor market. . . . The region could be like the European Union [EU]."[52] This call to turn NAFTA into something like the EU echoed President Fox's statements that he wanted to develop NAFTA along the lines of the EU.[53]

Calderón won the presidency in 2006 by less than 1 percent of the vote through what many still regard as a fraudulent election.[54] Andrés Manuel López Obrador contends that he was the actual winner of the election, and a large portion of impoverished Mexicans tend to see it the same way. Calderón's controversial win is to some extent due to his stand on NAFTA.[55] After Calderón was announced as president, leftists protested his presidency in part because of the devastating effect of NAFTA on Mexican farmers.[56]

Calderón believes that NAFTA has a positive effect on the Mexican economy and wants to open up Mexico even more.[57] He points to his home state of Michoacán as an example of the positive effects of NAFTA. The pact has enabled Michoacán to become a large exporter of avocados, which in turn has attracted foreign investment to the state and created jobs.[58] In a speech in January 2008, Calderón reiterated that he believes that NAFTA is beneficial to the Mexican economy and to Mexican farmers.[59] He stated that because of NAFTA, nations in the region now buy five times as much from Mexican farmers as they did in 1994.[60] He also claimed that greater economic integration between the countries would lead to greater economic growth for Mexico.[61]

Increased poverty rates among Mexican subsistence farmers actually has led to "illicit farming," a phenomenon in which farmers who can no longer survive by growing traditional crops, such as maize or corn, have turned to growing illegal agricultural goods, such as marijuana and opium, to survive.[62]

Illicit farming, increased immigration, and the perception that NAFTA has hurt more blue-collar workers in the United States has increased tension between the United States and Mexico and was a significant issue during the U.S. presidential elections in 2008.[63]

Despite the pact's negative impact on subsistence farmers, Calderón presumably does not want to renegotiate NAFTA in light of the economic incentives Mexico has seen since its passage.[64] Richard Vogel explains one of these economic factors: income inequality. Compared with its North American neighbors, Mexico has the highest level of economic inequality to this date. However, as Vogel points out, the inequality of household earnings fell significantly for Mexico in the decade following NAFTA. Vogel attributes this drastic change to the transfer of industrial jobs from the United States and Canada to Mexico under the trilateral free-trade agreement. Not surprisingly, income inequality has risen at a steeper rate in both the United States and Canada since the passage of NAFTA. Vogel cautions, however, that despite the significant fall in income inequality in Mexico since NAFTA, Mexico's levels of income inequality and poverty remain staggeringly high.[65]

Presumably, Calderón fears that in light of the recent post-NAFTA economic progress, the impact of the current economic meltdown in the United States will have painful effects on Mexico's economy if NAFTA is renegotiated. As Vogel explains, the current recession has already reduced the demand for goods produced in Mexico and has decreased the need for Mexican workers in America. Presumably, a new NAFTA agreement would make it even more difficult for Mexican industries to sell their goods to their northern neighbors. Mexico also has been losing out on remittances from emigrant workers. Remittances constitute a significant source of income for Mexico and have contributed hugely to the Mexican economy in the past few years.[66] However, according to Mexico's Central Bank, remittances fell 3.6 percent in 2008, to $25 billion, apparently because of the crackdown on undocumented immigration and job loss among migrants caused by the U.S. recession.[67]

Despite the pitiful plight of Mexican workers, NAFTA has been beneficial not only to capitalists in the United States and Canada but also to the "Mexican ruling class that [has] externalized [its] underdevelopment problems by both opening [its] depressed labor markets to foreign capitalists and by encouraging [its] unemployed to emigrate."[68]

CALDERÓN AND NAFTA DURING THE BUSH ADMINISTRATION

Calderón's dealings with the Bush administration indicate that he is not looking out for the best interest of farmers or other poor segments of the population and that he seems most concerned with protecting corporate profits. In August 2007, Calderón, Bush, and Canadian Prime Minister Stephen Harper met in Canada to discuss the second phase of NAFTA. The public was worried about the secrecy of the talks. People were most concerned about the influence the Security and Prosperity Partnership (SPP) was exerting on these talks.[69]

Tellingly, important issues that would benefit the Mexican poor were not discussed. Calderón reportedly expressed concern about harsh new sanctions on employers who hired undocumented workers in the United States and the "void" left in the immigration law following the failure of the U.S. Congress to pass reforms that effectively deal with the estimated 12 million undocumented U.S. residents.[70] Calderón, however, made no mention of measures to reduce deaths and human-rights violations on the shared U.S.–Mexican border, provide compensation funds to Mexico's displaced sectors, or regularize Mexican immigrants in American communities.[71]

Another taboo subject was the total elimination of tariffs on corn and beans in Mexico, which was slated for January 2008 under NAFTA's agricultural chapter.[72] Mexican small farmers had demanded renegotiation of the chapter, charging it would drive them out of business and increase out-migration. According to government representatives, however, the three governments decided not to take up the issue.[73]

Calderón, Bush, and Harper met again in April 2008 in New Orleans. This time, the three leaders "appeared to be on the defensive, doing their best not to advance the SPP agenda but to save NAFTA itself."[74] They spent their time trying to persuade their respective national publics that NAFTA has been good for the economies and for workers, and that it is necessary for the future of North American economic growth. Calderón publicly stated that changes to NAFTA would "provoke considerable damage on the economy" and would condemn North America "as a region to compete from a position of backwardness in today's world."[75]

CALDERÓN AND NAFTA DURING
THE OBAMA ADMINISTRATION

In his first meeting with a foreign leader since his election, President Barack Obama told Felipe Calderón that he wants to "upgrade" NAFTA.[76] However, Calderón continues to strongly urge against any effort to renegotiate the deal.[77] He warns that anything that curtails trade will hurt his economy and push even more workers to cross the border illegally in search of jobs.[78] Even as numerous reports of job loss, wage declines, inflation, and capital flight surface—and even as one report shows that the public opposes NAFTA two to one—Calderón maintains his view that NAFTA is beneficial to the Mexican economy.[79]

President Obama has repeatedly criticized NAFTA and the adverse effects it has had on U.S. jobs. Obama's insistence on renegotiating NAFTA may be beneficial to protecting jobs in the United States, but jobs may be lost in Mexico. As Vogel posits, Mexico's already high levels of unemployment will be worsened with a renegotiation of NAFTA and may even lead to a total collapse of the Mexican economy and a "resurgence of an open class struggle in Mexico—Calderón's nightmare come true."[80] Fortunately, however, President Obama has acknowledged the need for investment in Mexico's economy and understands its relationship with undocumented migration:

At a national level, our diplomacy with Mexico must aim to amend NAFTA. I will seek enforceable labor and environment standards— not unenforceable side agreements that have done little to curb NAFTA's failures. To reduce illegal immigration, we also have to help Mexico develop its own economy, so that more Mexicans can live their dreams south of the border. That's why I'll increase foreign assistance, including expanded micro-financing for businesses in Mexico.[81]

Since the meeting with Obama in January 2009, Calderón and Harper have been in communication to join forces against his "protectionism stance."[82] Canada's and Mexico's leaders are concerned about the "Buy American" provisions in Obama's massive stimulus package.[83] The U.S. stimulus bill included the "Buy American" language; however, the provision was softened with the clause that the rules "must be applied consistent with U.S. obligations" under trade agreements such as NAFTA and the WTO.[84]

Drug Trafficking

Felipe Calderón has made fighting drug trafficking the centerpiece of his administration.[85] Calderón's strategy is not to eliminate drug trafficking from Mexico, as that seems to be an impossible task, but to fragment the drug cartels and reduce the violence—a goal that "is at least possible."[86] During his campaign for the presidency, Calderón expressed his desire to work with the United States to fight drug trafficking and declared, "I'm going to work on the side of the offer, but the United States has to work more on the side of the demand."[87]

Calderón has made substantial efforts to fight drug trafficking. Since December 2006, he has sent more than thirty thousand troops into eight Mexican states and cities in an attempt to quell drug violence.[88] But the violence continues to increase.[89] More than three thousand people were killed in drug violence in Mexico in 2008.[90]

In June 2008, Mexico accepted a $400 million anti-narcotics aid package from the United States.[91] The aid was controversial because President Bush and Calderón negotiated a deal without consulting legislators in either country.[92] The Democratic U.S. Congress then redrafted the package by shifting more funds from Mexico to Central America and insisting that Mexico meet certain human-rights conditions to get access to all of the money.[93] Mexican officials reacted angrily to these changes and hinted that they might turn down the assistance unless the conditions were removed.[94] In subsequent negotiations, the U.S. Congress toned down the language of the conditions, and Mexico accepted the aid.[95]

Mexico is also facing a growing drug-addiction problem within its borders. To address this problem, Calderón proposed legislation that would decriminalize the possession of small quantities of cocaine and other drugs for addicts who agree to undergo treatment.[96] However, the legislation will probably be too controversial at home and in the United States.[97] Similar legislation was proposed by Vincente Fox in 2006 but was eventually dropped.[98]

U.S. officials have commended Calderón for his crackdown on Mexico's drug cartels,[99] and President Obama recently praised Calderón for his "extraordinary courage and leadership" in dealing with the cartels.[100] Calderón's assault apparently has disrupted the cartels' business in the United States, as reflected in the rising price of cocaine: By the end of 2008, the price of cocaine was up 41 percent since 2006, from $87 to $123 per gram; purity is down 16 percent.[101] To aid in the fight against Mexican drug cartels, the Obama administration pledged to spend $700 million in 2009 and more in the future on a wide variety of bilateral security programs, including improving cross-border interdiction, upgrading intelligence-gathering methods, and establishing corruption-resistant police agencies and courts.[102]

Changes to the Legal System

In June 2008, President Calderón signed legislation designed to fundamentally change Mexico's justice system. Mexico adopted a U.S.-style legal system that will include public trials and a presumption of innocence for criminal defendants. Under the constitutional amendment creating these changes, closed legal proceedings, in which judges relied almost exclusively on written briefs and evidence, will be replaced by prosecutors and defense lawyers arguing cases in court. Calderón had also wanted the legislation to allow for warrantless searches, but that provision was dropped after human-rights organizations complained. A compromise was created that includes a special class of judges who have the power to speedily grant warrants.

The changes have also sought to close loopholes that allow criminal suspects to evade justice on technicalities and improve the failing public-defender system that is currently in place. The most controversial aspect of the legislation is that authorities are now able to hold suspects for eighty days without charges and, some say, without probable cause. These changes to the justice system are seen as a great improvement for Mexico overall; however, the eighty-day provision has been criticized as the longest in any kind of Western democracy.

The sweeping measures require state and local police departments to purge their ranks of corrupt officers. The measures also grant those agencies the power to investigate organized crime, an authority that had previously been the exclusive domain of the states. Calderón sees these changes as another crucial tool in his battle against the drug cartels.[103]

Energy Reform

In May 2008, Calderón pleaded with the Mexican Congress to approve his energy reform proposals after figures showed that oil production had slumped to a nine-year low.[104] The rate of decline in oil production in spring 2008 was much quicker than had been anticipated by the Mexican government.[105] Moreover, the situation for Mexico, which relies on oil revenue for about 40 percent of total government income, was made worse by the fact that proven reserves have been deteriorating so fast that the country could become a net oil importer within a few years.[106] Calderón argued that his proposal would "make Pemex stronger, more transparent, with greater operational and tech-nological capacity and, importantly, stop falling production."[107] One of the main ideas was to give Pemex greater flexibility to associate with third parties and, at the same time, to give private companies working with Pemex finan-cial incentives linked to performance.[108]

In October 2008, the Mexican Congress approved part of Calderón's energy-reform proposal that allows the state oil monopoly Pemex to offer service contracts where payments are linked to the success of the project.[109] The approved reform plan did not allow Pemex to sign production-sharing agreements with outside firms.[110] At the Davos World Economic Forum in January 2009, Calderón met with chief executives of multiple oil companies and stated that Mexico is looking to make important changes based on these approved reforms.[111] Moreover, Pemex officials have said the company has maintained close contact with Statoil and Petrobras on potential oil projects under the company's new legal framework.[112]

Tax Overhaul

In September 2007, President Calderón won his first major legislative victory when the Mexican Congress passed a comprehensive tax bill aimed at one of Mexico's biggest economic problems: its meager tax take and miserly public spending.[113] When Calderon took office, the country had one of the lowest tax rates in Latin America, collecting only about 10 percent of its GDP. About 40 percent of the government's revenues came directly from Pemex. But Pemex's contributions are declining as its on-shore fields mature, and Pemex lacks the technical capacity to explore its offshore reserves. Without major reform, the oil giant will weaken further and bankrupt Mexico.[114]

Calderón's reform proposal targeted Mexico's biggest tax evader: the business sector. The plan proposed a 19 percent flat tax on all companies, along with taxes on large cash deposits to prevent smaller cash-based businesses from operating below the tax radar. In addition to closing tax loopholes, a flat tax simplified the highly complex tax code, making it harder for companies to avoid taxation.[115] The bill also gives back more money to the country's cash-short oil monopoly and imposes a gasoline tax that will go to state governments.[116]

The Calderón tax plan was criticized by more conservative elements for not going far enough because it did not call for the addition of value-added tax (VAT) on food or medication. Calderón's decision to avoid VAT changes was pragmatic.[117] Proposed and highly controversial additions to VAT killed the reform plans of former President Vicente Fox because of their potential effects on Mexico's lower-income population.

Pension Reform

A week after taking office, Calderón started working to rein in the out-of-control spending on pensions for civil servants. Calderón personally lobbied for the bill, and the Mexican Senate voted to cut pension spending by raising the minimum retirement age for civil servants from 49.5 in 2010 to an average of 59 by 2028. The bill also increases workers' contribution to the pension system to 6.125 percent of their salaries by 2012, from 3.5 percent in 2007. This was the first major piece of economic legislation passed in Mexico since a tax increase was enacted in 1995 under Fox.[118]

Immigration

During his campaign and since taking office, Calderón has harshly criticized the United States for its treatment of undocumented immigrants.[119] When the Bush administration stepped up raids on factories and farms suspected of hiring undocumented workers, Calderón criticized the raids as persecution of undocumented workers and a failure to acknowledge their contribution to the U.S. and Mexican economies.[120] Calderón has stated that "immigration is not solved by a wall," and when discussing the border fence, he has joked, "We'll jump it anyway."[121] During his campaign, Calderón also promised to fight for the right of Mexicans working in the United States to be paid pensions to which they have contributed if they return to Mexico.[122] And in his meeting with President Obama in January 2009, Calderón reasserted the need for the United States to undertake comprehensive immigration reform.[123]

Criticizing the United States for its treatment of undocumented immigrants has become routine for most Mexican politicians, including Calderón.[124] Because Mexican immigrants send home more than $25 billion a year, and because the yearly migration of more than four hundred thousand people relieves Mexico of masses of poor, one could argue that the government has little incentive to stem the migration northward. The money from remittances is Mexico's second-largest source of foreign income after oil revenues.[125]

Education

In May 2008, Calderón launched his Alliance for Educational Quality education-reform program. The document he signed was not a new law but, rather, an agreement with Elba Esther Gordillo, head of the national teachers' union. Gordillo is a powerful political figure in Mexico. Her critics contend that she is more of a politician than an educator and say that her union has long been an obstacle to improving education. But Calderón is by nature a pragmatic dealmaker, and ignoring the union would only have led to a hopeless stalemate.

The need for good teachers is glaring, and one of Calderón's goals is to develop a million qualified teachers within a generation. The main problem lies not with salaries for teaching, which are competitive with other jobs in Mexico, but with the quality of teachers. The government has been trying to solve the problem since 1992, when it introduced annual bonuses linked to teachers' participation in training courses and their scores on tests. This system is far from perfect. A study by the American think tank Rand Corporation found that the tests given to teachers required only low-level cognitive responses, and the criteria for evaluation were fuzzy and subject to manipulation.

The new agreement between Calderón and Gordillo has two aims. First, there is a promise to improve the fabric of the twenty-seven thousand schools—about one in eight—that are in poor repair (though no new money was allocated to this as part of the agreement). Second, it seeks to break the hold of the union over teachers' careers. Under the agreement, teachers would be hired and promoted according to how they fare in a set of tests devised and marked by a new independent body.

The reaction of educational experts to the deal has been muted. Many find it hard to believe that the union will concede its power over hiring and firing in a meaningful way. They also note that Gordillo has a knack for co-opting reforms to serve her own ends. Yet Minister of Education Josefina Vásquez Mota is one of Calderón's more able political operators. If she can make the agreement stick in practice, the quality of Mexican schooling should gradually improve.[126]

Effect of the U.S. Financial Crisis

Although Mexico's economy was once thought to be relatively immune to outside financial slowdowns, the country has been seeing some unfortunate trends in finance that can be attributed directly to the financial crisis in the United States. The U.S. recession has been pulling down fiscally disciplined Mexico. As is the case with most countries, Mexico attempted to be prudent with economic policies that reduced debt and tamed inflation, but this did not save the country from the effects of a global recession. Exports account for almost a third of Mexico's GDP, so the country is undoubtedly affected when American consumers suddenly stop buying and the market for "Mexican-made big-screen televisions, auto parts or expensive winter fruit" shrinks.[127]

The effects are felt across the board. Unemployment levels in Mexico are at their highest in eight years. The peso has fallen 25 percent, leading to a spike in the price of imports, which in turn hurts consumers and businesses that rely on imported goods. The economy has especially hit exports, industrial production, and retail sales. Private analysts have predicted that Mexico's economy will not grow at all in 2009. In the worst case, the economy could even contract as much as 1.7 percent, according to BBVA Bancomer, Mexico's largest bank.[128]

The financial crisis has created a large-scale destruction of wealth across the entire American continent. Claudio Loser, former Western Hemisphere chief at the IMF, predicts that 40 percent of Latin American's wealth was wiped out in the first eleven months of 2008 by stock losses and currency depreciation. Gross domestic products (GDPs) across the region, including Mexico's, were severely reduced in 2008.[129]

In early January 2009, with the decline in commodity prices as well as a sharp decline in consumer spending, President Calderón announced that an additional $150 million would be put into Mexico's export industry to stabilize the sector. While the Canadian government was able to keep its export industry afloat by promising U.S. automakers in Canada part of an auto-industry-support package with conditions to keep 20 percent of North America's auto industry within Canada's largest province, Mexico has had a harder time striking a deal. Mexico's $150 million investment in its export industries is far short of the investment dollars needed in one particular industry. Mexico's export-oriented economy is directly influenced by the health of the U.S. economy, so it is likely to be substantially affected by the ongoing financial crisis in the United States.[130]

However, any boost for the U.S. economy will positively affect the Mexican economy, since the country sends about 80 percent of its exports to the United States. For example, when the United States provided aid for American banks to ease some investors' concerns, Mexico's peso firmed up. The optimism offset concerns about growth after Mexico's central bank slashed borrowing costs in an effort to prevent a recession.[131]

Analysts in Mexico predicted trouble for Mexico when the Mexican stock market sank 6.4 percent in the last week of September 2008. Rogelio Ramirez de la O, a well-respected economist in Mexico City, predicts tough times for jobs. Mexico may record a million jobs lost in 2008 and 1.5 million more in 2009. Furthermore, tough economic times in America mean that Mexican migrants to the United States will send less money to Mexico, indirectly affecting the Mexican economy. Ramirez predicted a fall of 20 percent, taking $5 billion out of the Mexican economy.[132]

The silver lining, however, is that even though the Mexican economy will slow down due to the U.S. financial crisis, Mexico's financial system is somewhat insulated because the banking system is healthy and does not seem to depend on foreign credit.[133]

Conclusion

The economic and political history of Mexico reveals a country that has gone through tremendous social and economic upheaval. Its citizens have suffered through the effects of inconsistent economic policies and political battles that have left them at the mercy of inconsistent governance, all the while subject to the influence of its more powerful economic neighbor to the north. For the past century, emigration and seasonal work have been part of the Mexican response to social and economic phenomena, and that movement now flies in the face of U.S. immigration policies that do not accommodate the movement.

The historical pressures to immigrate from Mexico, exacerbated by the more recent effects of NAFTA, are manifested in a population of undocumented Mexicans residing in the United States that is estimated to be in the millions. Without sufficient visas to accommodate the demand to migrate and, at least in better economic times north of the border, the corresponding demand for cheap labor, the migration north becomes illicit. In determining how to address the so-called undocumented immigration problem, we would be well served by a better appreciation of Mexico's political and economic history, the plight of displaced Mexican workers, and the role that the United States has played in Mexico.

3

Canadian Stability and Responsibility

I n contrast with Mexico, Canada, the other NAFTA partner of the United States, has done well, benefiting from the agreement. Even in the face of the recent global economic crisis that has presented severe challenges to the United States and the rest of the world, Canada's economy has stood out as remarkably strong. Given its strategic alliance with North American countries as well as its partnership with the United States in NAFTA, Canada also shares a special responsibility for assisting Mexico in its path toward political and economic stability. Understanding Canada's strengths helps us understand its ability to help with the challenges of the Mexican economy and Mexican migration.

How has Canada avoided the trade imbalance, currency devaluations, and employment problems suffered by Mexico under NAFTA? Why has the NAFTA framework not hampered Canadian industries? What we find in an examination of Canada is a country that came to the agreement with a stable economy from the start that featured a strong manufacturing sector, a small agricultural sector that did not stand to lose from competition with U.S. farm subsidies, and a willingness to challenge the United States when terms of trade agreements appeared to be breached.

The national economy of Canada historically has been closely linked with that of the United States. Proximate physical geography and generally friendly government relations have resulted in the largest bilateral trading relationship in the world. In recent years, the Canadian government has publicly recognized the need to diversify its trading relationships, especially in light of the economic slump experienced in the United States. Steps toward doing so, however, have yet to trigger any substantial change, and the overwhelming majority of Canadian trade continues to be conducted with the United States.

Political Background

In many fundamental respects, the structure of the Canadian government parallels that of the United States. The federal government of Canada comprises three branches: executive, legislative, and judicial. The legislative branch consists of a Senate, which is entirely appointed by the prime minister, and a House of Commons, which is entirely elected.[1] There are ten Canadian provinces and three territories, each with a local government system. Under federalist form, however, matters of defense and regulation of international trade and commerce between the provinces are left to the federal government.[2]

Brian Mulroney served as Canada's prime minister from 1984 to 1993. A member of the Conservative Party,[3] he negotiated the Canada–United States Free Trade Agreement (CUFTA) in 1988 with President George H. W. Bush. Mulroney later resigned while flirting with single-digit approval ratings following, among other things, the enactment of the highly controversial Goods and Services Tax (GST).[4] Two more recent former prime ministers of Canada, Jean Chrétien and Paul Martin, have been members of the Liberal Party. During Chrétien's term, from 1993 to 2003, NAFTA was signed, superseding the CUFTA. Although there has not been any economic recession since the end of Mulroney's tenure, both Chrétien and Martin have resigned amid investigations into the so-called Sponsorship Scandal.[5]

Canada's current prime minister, Stephen Harper, was sworn in on February 6, 2006. He is the first Conservative prime minister since 1993; he and his finance minister unveiled an economic agenda entitled *Advantage Canada: Building a Strong Economy for Canadians*. Their priorities were reducing the national debt and attracting greater foreign investment. Designed to "create the right conditions and opportunities for businesses and organizations to succeed,"[6] *Advantage Canada* describes plans to reduce both entity taxation rates and government market regulation. The plan, however, has been characterized by some as "so vague that it is unlikely that major progress will be reached."[7]

Overview of the National Economy

Canadians maintain a standard of living that is similar to that enjoyed in the United States; the Canadian economy ranks eighth in the world.[8] The service sector has become more prevalent in both countries, although the U.S. economy is much larger than the Canadian economy.[9]

The Canadian Department of Finance claims that Canada is the only Group of Seven (G7) nation in surplus, recording a budgetary surplus of 1 percent of GDP in 2005, and has the lowest debt burden of any G7 country.[10] The Canadian economy has recorded strong numbers recently, primarily led by its service sector, and the U.S. Central Intelligence Agency (CIA) describes Canadian economic prospects as "solid" and taking particular note of "top-notch fiscal management" producing "consecutively balanced budgets since 1997."[11]

Major Sectors

While Mexico has retained its agricultural focus, since World War II Canada has moved definitively away from being an agriculturally based economy.[12] Currently, the service sector accounts for an appreciable majority of both annual output and national employment.[13] In recent decades, investment and services within the Canadian market have increasingly dominated economic productivity. However, international trade in service-sector industries has been slightly hindered by various trade barriers. Meanwhile, international trade of goods constitutes a significant element of the national economy, and the manufacturing sector continues to record relatively stable performance. Containing many export-oriented industries, the manufacturing sector stands to gain from increased access to foreign markets facilitated by trade agreements.

MANUFACTURING
As Mexico struggles to develop its manufacturing sector, the Canadian manufacturing sector accounts for 17 percent of total GDP and 13 percent of total employment in Canada.[14] It is an increasingly export-oriented sector, and as of 2004, 70 percent of Canadian manufactured goods were bound for export. This is in stark contrast to the 1980s, before Canada had entered into any of its current free-trade agreements, when only 25 percent of manufactured goods were sent abroad.[15] Manufactured goods account for about 60 percent of all merchandise exports coming out of Canada.[16]

Despite an overall upward trend in the economy, the Canadian manufacturing sector has experienced a net 2.7 percent loss of jobs since November 2002.[17] These losses come largely from the textile and food and beverage industries.[18] Like Mexico, Canada attributes some of the recent difficulties experienced by the manufacturing sector to greater competition from China and India, as well as to the appreciation of the Canadian dollar.[19] Because the Canadian economy is closely integrated with the United States, recent slower growth in the United States also has caused decline in some Canadian manufacturing industries.

Key industries in this sector are automotive products, food, chemicals, and fabricated metal products.[20] Southern Ontario is the center of Canada's manufacturing sector, and it is where almost all of Canadian transportation-equipment plants are located, as well as many food-processing plants.[21] The automotive industry is especially important to this sector, and since the creation of the Auto Pact in 1965, trade in automotive goods with the United States has constituted a significant part of the sector's productivity.[22] The transportation-equipment industry continues as a primarily export-oriented industry and has recently anchored productivity of the manufacturing sector as a whole, holding the position of the second-most-important net national export.[23]

SERVICES

The service sector dominates Canadian economic productivity, constituting two-thirds of measured productivity in 2005.[24] In addition, 80 percent of new jobs created in 1992–2005 were in the service sector.[25] Included in the definition of the service sector are notable industries such as financial, health-care, educational, legal, and accounting services.[26] Despite the predominance of service industries within Canada, only 12 percent of Canada's international trade is in services.[27] In 2005, Canada exported services valued at $51 billion and imported services valued at approximately $62 billion.[28]

The financial-services industry is a key industry within the services sector. This industry includes investment and securities services, banks and insurance companies.[29] A significant percentage of income realized by Canadian banks and insurers is from foreign sources.[30] Internal regulation of foreign investment within Canada is a responsibility shared by three government departments: finance, foreign affairs and international trade, and Industry Canada.[31] The World Trade Organization has called Canada's trade and investment regime "one of the world's most transparent."[32] However, the Organization for Economic Cooperation and Development (OECD) has suggested that Canada has "the highest level of explicit curbs on foreign-equity ownership among the G7 industrial countries."[33] All direct acquisitions of control of a Canadian business by a non-Canadian must be revealed. Such acquisitions over certain monetary limits are also subject to government review.[34]

The Canadian Services Coalition and Canadian Chamber of Commerce speculate that a significant barrier to international trade in Canadian services is the presence of non-tariff barriers. Such barriers include restrictions on international movement of personnel, investment, and ownership.[35] They note that even the NAFTA nations have not followed through in facilitating movement of personnel across the international borders.[36]

AGRICULTURE AND ENERGY

Canada is second only to Russia in geographic size and owns a variety of natural resources. Agriculture was once the cornerstone of the Canadian economy.[37] The importance of this sector has diminished greatly, however, in terms of national employment and productivity, accounting for merely 2 percent of the Canadian GDP in 2005. Industry Canada estimates that more than half of this productivity is exported.[38] This figure, however, masks variations within the sector. Industries such as timber and energy are highly export-oriented, while industries such as dairy and poultry are focused primarily on the Canadian market. Within Canada, and absent a trade agreement stating otherwise, food and animal commodities are subject to some of the steepest duties.[39] Even under the terms of NAFTA exceptions are carved out for selected agricultural items.[40]

The timber and forestry industry remains a relatively small component of the national economy, making up less than 1 percent of the GDP, but is also very export-oriented. Canada is the world's largest exporter of timber, pulp, and newsprint.[41] The export of Canadian softwood to the United States has recently been a point of contention between these nations under NAFTA, as discussed in more detail below. In addition, export to the United States has contracted recently due to slowing housing demand.[42]

The production of energy-related resources is very important to some Canadian provinces. Energy from all sources of production contributed 5.9 percent to the national GDP in 2004. Distribution of energy among the provinces is non-uniform. Alberta, a province with economic activity valued at less than half that of Ontario, produced 64 percent of total national energy in 2004. That same year, Ontario, the nation's industrial center, accounted for merely 3 percent of production.[43]

Importantly, in contrast with the United States, Canada, like Mexico, operates as a net energy exporter.[44] In fact, some of Canada's top net exports are energy goods, including natural gas and oil.[45] Trade in energy is significant, particularly with the United States, which was the destination for 99 percent of all Canadian energy exports in 2004.[46] This is mostly in the form of petroleum, natural gas, and electricity, and the importance of this energy-trading relationship is further demonstrated by linkage of the national energy grids.[47]

Recent History

Until the current worldwide economic crisis, Canada had experienced two economic recessions in the past thirty years.[48] The most recent was a recession during 1989–1992.[49] The United States was experiencing a recession at the same time, and that contributed to the depth and long recovery period of the Canadian recession.[50] In 1981–1982, Canada experienced an even worse recession. Again, that period coincided with an economic downtown in the United States.[51]

Before fall of 2008, the fact that the Canadian economy had avoided a recession for more than a decade was remarkable,[52] given its intimate integration with the U.S. economy and its southern neighbor's slowdown. Trade surpluses were recorded by Canada for most of the past decade. The Economist Intelligence Unit, however, noted that "although Canada's overall trade position is healthy, this is only because it runs a huge trade surplus with the United States. Canada runs a deficit with its other major trade partners, the European Union, Japan, Mexico and China."[53]

As a proportion of the U.S. economy, Canadian GDP peaked around 1980 and dropped somewhat after that but held steady. In terms of proportional growth, however, the OECD reports that Canadian economic growth, both actual and per capita, has kept pace with the United States over the past decade.[54]

When the global economic crisis struck the United States and the rest of the world in the fall of 2008, the common wisdom was that Canada somehow avoided being pulled down. The main reason was Canada's highly regulated banking system. The World Economic Forum has rated Canada's banks as the world's soundest, ahead of banks in Sweden and Luxembourg.[55] Canada experienced no subprime-mortgage or home-foreclosure mess. Canadian banks are more tightly regulated, more liquid, and less highly leveraged. The concept of an investment bank is for all purposes nonexistent in Canada, as the major Canadian financial institutions are all-round organizations providing services to both individuals and businesses. Few Canadian banks got caught holding large numbers of toxic American mortgages.[56] They tend to operate in a more traditional manner, with large numbers of loyal depositors and a more solid base of capital. Strict rules also govern mortgage lending. By Canadian law, any mortgage that will finance more than 80 percent of the price of a home must be insured. Two-thirds of all Canadian mortgages are insured by the quasi-governmental Canadian Mortgage and Housing Corporation. As a result of the tough standards for insurance, borrowers tend not to take out mortgages that they cannot afford. Defaulting on a loan is also more difficult in Canada than in the United States. For Canada's seven biggest banks, the percentage of mortgages at least three months in arrears was .27 percent in July 2008, close to historic lows.[57]

Of course, Canada's economy has not escaped unscathed. The Toronto Stock Exchange is down. The appreciation of the Canadian dollar has harmed exports. The slowdown in the United States has a direct impact. The Canadian economy is dependant on exports for 45 percent of its GDP, and 76 percent of those exports are based on trade with the United States. Canada's trade surplus has been dropping.[58] In particular, U.S. housing troubles have hurt because much of the wood in new U.S. houses comes from Canada.[59] During the first two months of 2009, 240,000 Canadian workers lost their jobs. Losses from November 2008 to February 2009 were the steepest since the 1981–1982 recession. The federal government reported a budget deficit of $40 billion in fiscal 2009. Yet relative to the United States and other industrialized nations, Canada has fared well. On the eve of a Group of 20 economic summit in early 2009, Prime Minister Harper told a business audience in Ontario: "Canada was the last advanced country to fall into this recession. We will make sure its effects here are the least severe, and we will come out of this faster than anyone and stronger than ever."[60]

International Trade

International trade is highly important to the Canadian economy. The value of trade, as a percentage of GDP, for 2005 was nearly 60 percent.[61] Since 1990, Canada has experienced growth in both imports and exports, averaging 7 percent annual growth in value of international trade. In 2003, international trade made up 59 percent of the national GDP. The United States has largely facilitated this rapid growth in trade by absorbing 93 percent of the increase in exports during this time while supplying 58 percent of the increase in Canadian imports.[62] International trade plays an increasingly important role in the Canadian economy; so does the importance of relations with foreign trading partners.

Tariffs imposed on goods imported into Canada vary widely according to country of origin and nature of the commodity. The most heavily burdened goods are animal products and prepared foods.[63] The default status provided by Canada to its trading partners is that of most favored nation (MFN). Goods from MFNs are subject, on average, to the highest duty rates within Canada.[64]

Trade Agreements

Canada is currently a member of four bilateral free trade agreements. In addition, Canada has been actively pursuing agreements with its other significant trading partners. These agreements, while not entirely uniform, have the common goal of eliminating tariff and other trade barriers between the parties. The most prominent example is NAFTA. Mexico has many trade agreements beyond NAFTA, as well. However, unlike Canada, Mexico has not been able to protect its manufacturing and agricultural producers while participating in these new markets.

NAFTA

The first free-trade agreement between Canada and the United States was the Canada–United States Free Trade Agreement (CUFTA), effectuated in 1989.[65] The CUFTA was the result of negotiations between Brian Mulroney and George H. W. Bush and provided, generally, for liberalized trade between the two nations. Most prominently, the agreement provided a schedule by which tariffs on goods from both countries were to be eliminated.[66] The manufacturing sector was most affected by the agreement, particularly in light of the lack of any provisions affecting trade in services.

The CUFTA has since been superseded by and incorporated into NAFTA.[67] NAFTA was the result of negotiations between Jean Chrétien and Bill Clinton and is a much broader agreement than its predecessor in that it includes Mexico as a party to the agreement and its scope far exceeds that of the CUFTA. Trade sectors previously excluded from the CUFTA, such as investment, trade in services, intellectual property, and government procurement, are included in NAFTA. Under the scheduled terms of NAFTA, almost all tariffs have been removed on goods and services traded between the party nations since 2004. A few exceptions to this duty-free treatment remain, mostly for agricultural products.

Other important features of NAFTA are the supplements that were negotiated parallel to the primary agreement. These supplemental agreements are the North American Agreement for Environmental Cooperation (NAAEC) and the North American Agreement on Labor Cooperation (NAALC).[68] The agreements set baseline standards for environmental and labor conditions in the member countries and promote effective enforcement of environmental and labor-related provisions. They were primarily designed to address fears that unusually low standards would be used to attract business.[69]

The terms of NAFTA also provide a dispute-resolution framework for its parties. Chapter 11 addresses disputes over equal treatment of investors and provides four possible mechanisms for resolution. One of them—a particularly notorious one—allows foreign private corporations to sue a host government for compensation pursuant to allegations that a federal, provincial, or municipal law is a threat to present or future corporate profits.[70] Chapters 19 and 20 provide for panel review of disputes arising thereunder.[71] Panel decisions are published in commercial databanks such as Westlaw, although they are binding on the parties only under Chapter 19. This process has been used in a handful of instances and is discussed more fully below.

OTHER BILATERAL FREE-TRADE
AGREEMENTS AND NEGOTIATIONS

Canada has entered into three free-trade agreements in addition to NAFTA: the Canada–Chile Free Trade Agreement, Canada–Israel Free Trade Agreement, and Canada–Costa Rica Free Trade Agreement.[72] In addition to these bilateral trade agreements, Canada gives unilateral trade preferences to developing nations in the form of a General Preferential Tariff and Least-Developed Country Tariff.[73]

Discussions and negotiations regarding possible trade agreements are currently under way between Canada and a number of nations, among them Iceland, Norway, Switzerland, and Liechtenstein—collectively referred to as the European Free Trade Association. This region represents the eighth-largest destination for Canadian exports, and the focus of these negotiations is primarily on the mutual elimination of tariffs rather than on new policies for investment or services.[74] Within the Americas, Canada has been actively pursuing regional trade agreements. Negotiations with the Central American Four (CA4)—El Salvador, Guatemala, Honduras, and Nicaragua—began officially on November 21, 2001, with the tenth round of negotiations taking place in Ottawa on February 16–20, 2004.[75] Canadian and CA4 negotiators met again on February 23–27, 2009, when further progress was made. Preliminary discussions have also been initiated with the Dominican Republic regarding the potential benefits of a trade agreement.[76] Exploratory discussions, prior to engaging in formal negotiations, began in Ottawa on January 11, 2007.[77]

Trade negotiations are under way among the thirty-four democratic governments of the Americas, aptly named the Free Trade Agreement of the Americas (FTAA).[78] A number of obstacles, particularly concerns regarding the social consequences of such a trade agreement in Central America, have delayed this regional agreement. These negotiations have moved slowly and have been met with significant resistance.[79] In many ways, the recent bilateral trade agreements that Canada has been pursuing with the CA4, the Dominican Republic, and Costa Rica can be viewed as a back-up plan in the event that the CUFTAA negotiations fail.[80] Currently, the status of the CUFTAA remains unsettled, and the most recent meetings, in Miami in 2003 and Argentina in 2005, failed to yield an agreement.[81]

Finally, Canada announced in November 2004 that it would begin exploring the possibility of a free-trade agreement with South Korea.[82]

Negotiations began formally in 2005 and have continued into their ninth round, in Vancouver, January 29–February 1, 2007.[83] In the meantime, absent a trade agreement to the contrary, Canada will continue to trade with Korea on an MFN basis.

Trade Partners

Foreign trade is vitally important to the Canadian economy, with such import and export traffic totaling C$836 billion in 2006.[84] The majority of Canadian import and export activity takes place with its NAFTA partners.[85] Canada has also made efforts to forge trade relationships with Asian nations. In particular, China, though still sometimes listed in the "other" category for reporting, has been quickly gaining in importance to the Canadian economy. Discussed below are the five largest trading partners of Canada, including its NAFTA partners, the European Union, China, and Japan.

UNITED STATES
The United States is by far Canada's largest trading partner, and the flow of two-way trade between these two nations is in fact the world's largest.[86] In 2007, 81.6 percent (C$358.7 billion) of Canadian exports went to the United States, and 54.9 percent (C$217.6 billion) of Canadian imports came from its southern neighbor.[87] Most trade between Canada and the United States is done under NAFTA. A few exceptions to the duty-free treatment of goods provided by NAFTA are dairy and poultry.[88] Important items of trade between the United States and Canada are automobiles, machinery, minerals, and oil.[89]

Trade disputes sometimes arise between Canada and its largest trading partner. Goods that recently have been subjects of contention are beef, softwood lumber, and wheat. All three goods have been the subject of post-NAFTA trade barriers within the United States. Recall that concerns regarding bovine spongiform encephalopathy (commonly known as Mad Cow Disease) caused the United States to ban Canadian beef for a period of two years beginning in 2003. Because the vast majority of exports of Canadian beef and live cattle go to the United States, this action hit the industry very hard.[90] The United States has since been the first nation to ease restrictions on beef imports from Canada.[91]

Additional and more contentious conflicts have arisen over trade in softwood lumber and wheat. Contrary to NAFTA's provisions, the United States has burdened both goods originating in Canada with duties. In 2002, the United States implemented a steep anti-dumping duty on Canadian lumber imports.[92] Canada took this issue to both the World Trade Organization

(WTO) and the NAFTA dispute-settlement board.[93] The party governments reached a new agreement over softwood-lumber in August 2006.[94] Under this agreement, the United States would remit a large portion of the duties it had collected on softwood lumber since 2002. Canada would then be allowed free access to the American market, provided that prices for its lumber were kept above a certain level.[95]

More recently, a conflict erupted over tariffs imposed by the United States on Canadian wheat. In 2003, the United States began to impose duties on the wheat, claiming that the Canadian Wheat Board (CWB) provides unfair subsidies to the industry in the form of government financing and transportation.[96] The CWB appealed to a NAFTA panel that concluded there was not substantial evidence to support the U.S. tariff. As a result, the tariff was lifted.[97]

MEXICO

NAFTA has increased trade between Mexico and Canada. Mexico is Canada's fifth-largest trading partner, and such trade with Mexico is growing.[98] Similar to the situation with the United States, dairy, poultry, and eggs, however, continue to be burdened by tariffs imposed by Canada at the MFN rate.[99] Notable exports to Mexico included motor vehicles and parts and oilseeds, while top imports included electrical machinery and motor vehicles and parts.[100]

During 2006, Mexico imported goods from Canada valued at C$4.4 billion, making it the fifth-largest recipient of Canadian goods. That same year, Mexico was Canada's fourth-largest source of imports, which were recorded at a value of C$16.0 billion. In 2006 and over ten years, Canada has consistently recorded a trade deficit with Mexico.[101]

EUROPEAN UNION

When taken on the basis of individual countries, the United Kingdom plays the largest role in Europe in the Canadian trade.[102] Aggregating the constituent nations of the European Union, it becomes the second-most-important Canadian trading partner overall, after the United States.[103] Since 2006, the European Union has absorbed 6.3 percent of Canadian exports, and 11.7 percent of all imports into Canada originate in the EU.[104] Canada has been maintaining a moderate trade deficit with the EU over the past decade.[105] Exports to the EU nations included precious stones and metals, as well as mechanical machinery. Notable imports from the EU during 2005 included mechanical machinery, mineral fuel and oil, and pharmaceuticals.[106]

Without a free-trade agreement, Canada trades with the EU on an MFN basis. Efforts to establish a Canadian–EU free-trade agreement have been under way since 1998, although a formal agreement has yet to be reached.[107]

Instead, the EU–Canada Trade Initiative (ECTI) and Joint Political Declaration on Canada–EU Relations and the Canada–EU Action Plan describe a number of goals and initiatives that are to guide trade between the nations.

CHINA

As in the United States, Canadian consumers purchase volumes of products made in China. During 2006, China was Canada's third-largest source of imports, with trade valued at C$34.4 billion. That same year, China was the fourth-largest destination for Canadian exports, which were valued at C$7.6 billion.[108] Thus, the Canadian trade deficit with China in 2006 was C$26.8 billion. Major exports to China included organic chemicals and wood pulp, and goods typically imported from China consisted mostly of equipment.[109]

Trade with China has greatly increased in importance recently. Statistics Canada reports the view that a trading relationship with China is important not only for Canadian interests but also for "encouraging China's further integration into the global economy." Trading with China is done on an MFN basis, and although negotiations are currently under way regarding a foreign-investment agreement between the nations, the negotiations do not address trade agreements.[110] In coming years, as the Chinese market continues to mature, this trading relationship is set to become an even higher priority within the Canadian economy.

JAPAN

Although it remains a significant trading partner, Japan's relative importance to Canada has declined with the assent of China on the world market. In 2008, Japan took approximately 2.1 percent of Canadian exports, valued at C$9.44 billion, and held the position of third-largest importer of Canadian goods. Japan is also the fifth-largest supplier of imports to Canada, valued at C$15.3 billion, following closely behind Mexico; Japan supplies 3.9 percent of all goods imported by Canada. Canada recorded a trade deficit of C$5.9 billion with Japan in 2005.[111]

Generally, Canada exports resource goods to Japan, including wood, meat, and grains. From Japan, Canada tends to import manufactured goods such as automobiles and machinery.[112] There is currently no trade agreement between Japan and Canada. Since 2005, though, steps have been taken toward creating a more informal Canada–Japan Economic Framework.[113]

Ten-Year Trading History

In the past decade, Canada has managed to consistently record a trade surplus. This is entirely due to the trade relationship that it maintains with the

United States. The United States continues to be Canada's dominant trading partner, and trends in this economic relationship are directly reflected in the state of the Canadian economy in total.

Future Forecast

Prior to the global economic meltdown in 2008, steady national growth in the Canadian GDP was predicted. In 2009, the outlook for countries such as Japan, Italy, and Great Britain was poor, but by comparison Canada's prospects were brighter. Canada's relatively small financial sector and its large commodity-based export industries made the country more stable.[114] The relative strength of the Canadian dollar and lagging demand for construction and manufactured goods within the United States are predicted to hinder these export industries in the near future. Such market contraction may be offset by increased exploitation and export of Canada's mineral goods.[115] However, some observers have cautioned that Canada will need to change the way it produces and handles its natural resources if it is to maintain the economic benefits from their exploitation beyond the short term.[116]

Further enhancement of trade relations with the United States is also of high importance to the Canadian government. Toward that end, improvements are planned for the Windsor–Detroit corridor, through which 28 percent of all shipments of goods between Canada and the United States pass.[117] More important, though, Canada is recognizing the need to diversify its trade relationships. Export Development Canada characterized 2006 as "a rough year." Decline in export activity to the United States during 2006 was reflected in markedly lower growth in exports for the Canadian economy as a whole.[118] However, during that time period, exports from Canada to the European Union increased, as they did for many of the emerging global markets.[119] As the export market for Canadian goods and services has contracted in the United States, Canadian exporters have begun to, and will need to continue to, diversify their target markets.[120]

Domestically, the Harper government has made the reduction of Canada's national debt a high priority. Before the effects of the global financial crisis, the national debt was being reduced from its high point of C$562.9 billion in 1996–1997,[121] and the government aimed to eliminate the entire national debt by 2021.[122] The Department of Finance also reported a C$9.5 billion budgetary surplus in the first ten months of 2007,[123] predicting a budget surplus for at least another next five years.[124] Obviously, the recession has slowed this process. Along with the elimination of the national debt, the Canadian government seeks to reduce national taxation. Mostly this affects taxation of low-income individuals and entities.[125] The *Advantage Canada* economic program promoted by the Harper government equates taxes with barriers to investment.[126] The interest savings due to national-debt reduction will ostensibly be used to finance reductions in taxation.

Mexican Migration to Canada

Mexican migration to Canada has been soaring since the passage of NAFTA and in response to the mounting challenges the United States is posing to Mexican immigration. Between 1991 and 2001, the number of permanent and temporary residents from Mexico in Canada nearly doubled, to almost forty-three thousand. Canada's Seasonal Agricultural Workers Program currently takes in twelve thousand Mexican workers. The program matches workers from Mexico and the Caribbean countries with Canadian farmers who need temporary support during planting and harvesting seasons. In addition, the number of Mexicans studying in Canada has been steadily increasing.[127]

As U.S. immigration officials were ramping up enforcement and tightening regulations on Mexicans in the United States, the Canadian government was encouraging increased immigration from Mexico. In 2007, Prime Minister Harper met with Mexican President Felipe Calderón to discuss increased labor mobility between the countries to deal with chronic labor shortages in Canada. Many Mexicans see Canada as a more attractive immigration destination than the United States.[128] In an effort to encourage immigration from Mexico, the Canadian government has been relaxing and simplifying its immigration rules over the past few years. Mexican tourists enter Canada just by showing a passport, and the process of applying for either permanent or worker status is far easier and usually cheaper than the process of getting a U.S. visa.[129]

The more welcoming atmosphere is a draw for thousands of Mexicans. Between 40,000 and 50,000 Mexican-born Canadians were living legally and permanently in Canada by 2005, while 10,000 continue to enter each year to study, and 200,000 more visit every year as tourists. The biggest growth, however, has been in the number of Mexican temporary workers going to Canada. The number of legal, temporary workers in Canada from Mexico rose almost 69 percent, to 22,344 from 13,261, from 1998 to 2003. By comparison, 110,075 legal, temporary workers were admitted to the United States from Mexico in 1998, and 130,327 were admitted in 2003, an 18 percent rise.[130] The Canadian immigration expert David Rosenblatt has observed that very few Mexicans overstay their visas or come illegally to Canada: "They go back home to their families with a lot of money in their pockets, secure that they can easily return the next year if they please."[131] Officials at the Mexican

Ministry of Labor, which handles the paperwork for this workforce, agree, saying that 80 percent of the temporary workers come home, are rehired, and return to Canada the following year.[132]

Conclusion

Canada has benefited from NAFTA. Trade has increased and, overall, so has job growth. In contrast to Mexico, Canada came into NAFTA with a strong economy and a strong dollar. Its manufacturing sector has been able to maintain steady growth. Although agriculture was once a major part of the Canadian economy, long before NAFTA that sector was small; although it accounts for only 2 percent of GDP, more than half of this productivity is exported. When necessary, Canada has stood up to the United States in conflicts over duties imposed on such products as softwood lumber and wheat.

The Canadian economy has established itself as a reliable entity, consistently recording surpluses of trade and balanced budgets over the past decade. The Canadian government has made paying down the national debt a public priority and projects its own success within the next fifteen years. Canada's economic prospects are solid, and its financial management is sound. The agricultural sector has been replaced by the services sector as the driving force behind Canadian economic productivity. In addition to services, exploitation of energy-related resources promises to play an important role in Canada's economic future.

International trade constitutes a very significant portion of total economic activity in Canada. The United States has been, and continues to be, Canada's primary trading partner. Thus, NAFTA and WTO provisions continue to be significant contributors to Canadian economic policy on the whole. In the past several years, Canadian industry has responded to the need to diversify target markets and has actively pursued additional trade relationships. Trade agreements with Central American and Asian nations have evolved; trade with the EU has increased. But both the United States and Mexico remain important forces within Canada's national economy.

Canada is well positioned to help take North American integration many steps further. Canada has played a key role in the evolution of NAFTA and has the economic strength and credibility to partner with the United States in key investments in Mexico. Canada has an experienced-based understanding of how Mexican migration can be beneficial to its economy. Given the market forces that have brought the three nations of NAFTA together, Canada, along with the United States, now must seriously step up to assist

Mexico develop its own infrastructure and economy to strengthen the entire continent. Canada, the United States, and Mexico are much more than simple trading partners in the NAFTA framework. Even without NAFTA, they owe one another mutual responsibility.

4

The European Union Strategy

In contrast to the failure of NAFTA to incorporate labor migration and development assistance to poor members in its vision, the European Union (EU) evolved with rigorous commitment to the economic stability of all members and freedom of travel. The EU approach permits open labor, engages in development assistance to poor nations to reduce migration pressures, and maintains border control.[1] The EU approach appears to be working without massive flows of workers from poor nations to wealthy nations. In fact, poor nations do not seem so poor any longer. For those reasons, looking to the European experience for instruction—or, at least, illustration—is appealing in reviewing NAFTA and the challenge of undocumented Mexican migration.

The EU started in 1951 when Belgium, Italy, Germany, France, Luxembourg, and the Netherlands, all devastated by World War II, formed a partnership in the hope of forging economic progress.[2] The Treaty of Rome of 1957, which established the European Economic Community, developed a plan for free movement of people, goods, services, and capital among the member states.[3] The Schengen Agreement provided for the free movement of citizens between the member states beginning in 1995, while the Treaty of the European Union (Maastricht Treaty of 1992) enhanced the process by creating the notion of European citizenship.[4]

Thus, within the EU a central component of economic integration is the mobility of people. This is done with a commitment to "harmonizing" labor standards in terms of wages, the workweek, and other labor-cost factors.[5] Economic-development aid was provided to poor countries such as Spain, Portugal, and Ireland to enhance broader economic opportunities throughout the region and lessen pressure to migrate, although meeting labor needs through movement also was contemplated.[6] To enhance the mobility of workers, a European Social Fund provides vocational training and retraining. This facilitates adaptation to business needs in different member countries.[7] The idea is that to really integrate the member nations' economies, the free movement of workers is necessary, and the workers should have the right to accept employment in any member nation.[8] The workers' families have the right to follow and establish new residence with the workers.[9]

Labor migration within the EU is not a hard sell to those who understand what is happening to the workforce in many parts of Europe, particularly in Western Europe. The EU approach to labor migration and investment has been thoughtful and deliberate. At the outset, leaders and planners knew that, as open migration was contemplated, a necessary underpinning was the reduction of economic difference between various regions of Europe. Beginning with the enlargement in 1973 to include Denmark, Ireland, and the United Kingdom, the British pushed for an approach to aid poor regions. When Greece (1981) and Portugal and Spain (1986) were added, all three nations, as well as Ireland, received infusions of capital and assistance with institutional planning. This shared-responsibility model was based on "a commitment to the values of internal solidarity and mutual support."[10] To gain political support in the rich countries, funds were provided for impoverished "areas," not poor countries, so that needy areas in rich countries could qualify, as well. Of course, most of the "adhesion" funds went to Spain, Portugal, Greece, and Ireland.[11] The poor nations had suffered from significant levels of underemployment and weak safety nets, so new investments focused on capital investment and infrastructure such as roads and technology and boosted job creation. The new member countries also enacted social legislation aimed at assisting the unemployed.[12]

The adhesion-fund approach worked. The gap between the poor and rich nations narrowed. By the beginning of the new millennium, Ireland's economy had transformed, and its per capita GDP was above the EU average. Incredibly, Ireland—a nation that for years had been a constant source of emigrants—began attracting immigrants.[13] The feared "mass migration of the unemployed" fizzled. People stayed in their own countries because work opportunities were created. Only 2 percent of EU citizens looked for work in other EU countries.[14]

The EU also has adopted measures in response to some members' concerns that nationals of certain countries might move to countries with better welfare systems. To move, individuals must demonstrate the financial ability to support themselves through work or other financial ability. Migrant workers are not automatically eligible for welfare benefits. For example, unemployment benefits are not available unless the worker has paid into the system. In short, workers and their families are not eligible for benefits in another EU country until a definite work history has been established.[15]

Inter-EU Migration

The ability of EU residents to freely migrate among member states has been a hallmark of the union. However, this right has been extended with much forethought, especially as the EU expanded at different periods of time.

Border Controls

Everyone concerned knew that the new EU members would undergo a period of transition before meeting all EU standards, even with significant financial-assistance measures in place. The EU has added twelve new countries in the past several years, which represents the biggest enlargement in its history. This "fifth" enlargement took place in two parts. Part one allowed Cyprus, the Czech Republic, Estonia, Hungary, Latvia, Lithuania, Malta, Poland, Slovakia, and Slovenia into the EU on May 1, 2004. Part two of the enlargement led to Bulgaria and Romania joining the EU on January 1, 2007.[16] The EU therefore allowed for certain transition period policies to alleviate concerns over the fifth enlargement.

One of the major transition-period policies concerned open borders. Acceding countries, such as Poland, feared a brain drain to the EU-15.[17] EU-15 countries worried about a potential overflow of migrants from new member states. The EU therefore created a transition period during which the freedom of movement of workers from acceding countries to the EU-15 would be limited.[18] A similar policy had been adopted earlier, when Spain, Greece and Portugal joined the Union.[19]

EU members could choose to restrict the free movement of labor for up to seven years, and many of the EU-15 opted to impose such restrictions. Germany and Austria opted to use the full seven-year period, and France and Belgium opted for two years. The United Kingdom never had any restrictions against workers from the first ten countries; however, in October 2007 the United Kingdom did renew its restrictions for another year for workers from Romania and Bulgaria. Only Finland and Sweden of the EU-15 have opened their labor markets fully to the two newest members.[20]

After 2011, no restrictions will be allowed.[21] In the meantime, these restrictions on labor movements are supposed to help curb mass migration and a "brain drain" from newly acceded countries.

Even with the major financial-assistance measures that were intended to help enhance the candidate countries' economies to meet EU standards, certain precautionary steps were taken to curb immigration into the EU-15. That was a lesson relearned from the entry of Poland. When Poland was allowed into the EU in May 2004, most of its development aid had not yet arrived. Before the bulk of that aid arrived in 2007, about eight hundred thousand Poles had emigrated. Thus, making sure that the investments are made before opening borders was the lesson to avoid labor shortages in the poor country.[22]

More Consequences of the Fifth Enlargement

Despite some political and public backlash against migration within the EU in countries such as Italy and the United Kingdom, the fifth enlargement and the resulting migration within the EU has benefited all individual countries, as well as the union as a whole. The open labor market has allowed jobs to be filled by young foreign hands and improves the EU's economy overall. The Trades Union Congress (TUC) reported that jobs are filled in host countries, and employed individuals send money home that allows their native economies to grow.[23] Thus, both host and home countries gain from migration.

After a period of transition, the boost in the economies of the new EU countries is expected to draw their natives back home. In this way, immigration from East to West will regulate itself. Adam Roberts of the *Economist* asserts that in the near future, more young Poles and Hungarians in the West will be tempted back home by rising wages.[24] The financial assistance the EU has provided allows the economies and income levels of the most recent members to meet those of the EU-15 after a transition period. People from the new member states are therefore expected to remain in place or return home as income levels rise and economies grow in their native countries.

Moreover, Roberts predicts that the labor market will further self-regulate with an open-border policy, and inter-EU immigration will be an overall benefit. He explains: "The human tide will ebb and flow. As housing booms end in countries which have seen lots of migrants—Ireland, Britain, Spain, Greece—young east Europeans may turn elsewhere. Germany faces severe shortage of skilled hands, and may see bigger flows."[25] An open labor market is highly advantageous for both host and home countries, and for the EU as a whole. An open labor market allows individuals to cross borders to find employment; therefore, migration patterns adjust based on job demands. The labor market therefore becomes more efficient with open borders.

An open-border policy within the EU, which will be fully realized in 2011, is welcomed in most quarters. Open labor markets are largely self-regulating. The EU has taken sufficient precautionary measures and has provided enough financial support to new members that a mass migration to the EU-15 has not occurred. Moreover, the migration within the EU that does take place has proved to be beneficial to host and home countries and should continue to help the economy.

Adhesion Funds

Understanding the adhesion-fund approach in the EU can be useful in considering possible approaches to the Canada–United States–Mexico relationship. The European approach was fueled in part by concerns that nationals from poor countries would stream into wealthy nations if something was not done to help the economies of the poor nations. The financial assistance that the EU provided to the countries that had become members most recently is a good example. The financial support consisted of both pre-accession and post-accession assistance, which aims to help candidate countries achieve certain EU political, economic, and social standards. Given this financial assistance, a full open-border policy, which will be realized in 2011, is not expected to lead to mass migration and is viewed as a positive development for the EU.

The EU has established criteria for candidates to join the community. To join the EU, an applicant country must meet the following political standards, known as the Copenhagen Criteria, established by the European Council in 1993. The applicant country must have (1) stable institutions guaranteeing democracy, the rule of law, human rights, and respect for and protection of minorities; (2) a functioning market economy as well as the capacity to cope with competitive pressure and market forces within the EU; and (3) the ability to take on the obligations of membership, including adherence to the aims of political, economic, and monetary union.[26]

To help candidate countries meet these standards and join the union, the EU has developed pre-accession and post-accession financial assistance. This funding targets certain regions or economic sectors, allowing candidate countries to implement programs to develop their laws, infrastructure, and economy to become a competitive EU member.

Pre-accession Assistance

As countries contemplate how to meet the Copenhagen Criteria for EU membership, they can access assistance through the process.

The New Instrument for Pre-accession Assistance

The EU has developed a system of assistance measures to help candidate and potential-candidate countries meet their criteria for eligibility and more easily integrate into the community. The overarching assistance program for countries not yet part of the EU is the Instrument for Pre-accession Assistance (IPA). On January 1, 2007, the IPA came into force, bringing all pre-accession support into one single, focused instrument. The IPA covers the countries with candidate status (currently Croatia, the former Yugoslav Republic of Macedonia, and Turkey) and potential-candidate status (Albania, Bosnia and Herzegovina, Montenegro, and Serbia).[27]

The IPA has several components. It focuses on giving candidate countries transition assistance and helps them with institution building. The program aims to foster cross-border cooperation between its members. In addition, the EU uses the IPA to promote regional development, human-resources development, and rural development in candidate countries.[28]

The five major pre-accession assistance programs included in the IPA today are (1) Poland and Hungary: Assistance for Restructuring Their Economies (PHARE); (2) Instrument for Structural Policies for Pre-accession (ISPA); (3) Special Accession Program for Agricultural and Rural Development (SAPARD); (4) Community Assistance for Reconstruction, Development and Stabilization (CARDS); and (5) the Turkish Pre-accession Program.[29]

POLAND AND HUNGARY: ASSISTANCE FOR
RESTRUCTURING THEIR ECONOMIES (PHARE)

As its name suggest, PHARE was created in 1989 to help Poland and Hungary accede to the EU and was later expanded to cover other joining countries. PHARE's main objectives are to (1) strengthen public administrations and institutions to function effectively inside the European Union; (2) promote convergence with the European Union's extensive legislation (the acquis communautaire) and reduce the need for transition periods; and (3) promote economic and social cohesion.[30] PHARE contributed €5.7 billion to ten candidate countries between 1999 and 2006 to help them achieve these objectives.[31]

PHARE primarily involves two areas of action and funding: investment and institution building. Institution-building projects are intended to strengthen the economic, social, regulatory, and administrative capacity of candidate countries. Assistance is given to various professional organizations, trade unions, government agencies, and nongovernmental organizations.[32]

PHARE institution-building assistance is provided specifically to implement the acquis communautaire (EU law) and to prepare for participation in EU policies, as well as fulfill the requirements of the Copenhagen Criteria. PHARE investment provides supports for key regulatory institutions whose equipment or infrastructure needs to be upgraded to monitor and enforce the acquis communautaire effectively.[33] By funding programs in candidate countries that aim to achieve PHARE's objectives, the EU fosters cross-border cooperation with candidate countries and economic and social cohesion within the EU. It also generally helps the potential members reach EU economic, social, and political standards.

INSTRUMENT FOR STRUCTURAL POLICIES
FOR PRE-ACCESSION

The ISPA also now falls under the IPA. Launched in 2000, the ISPA provides assistance for infrastructure projects in the EU's high-priority fields of environment and transport. The ISPA has three principal objectives: (1) to familiarize candidate countries with the policies, procedures, and funding principles of the EU; (2) to help them catch up with EU environmental standards; and (3) to upgrade and expand links with the trans-European transport networks.[34]

Candidate countries are eligible for ISPA grants until they accede to the EU. Once the countries join the EU, they become eligible for the Cohesion Fund, described below. The new members' ISPA projects then become Cohesion Fund projects.[35]

During the ISPA's first four years of implementation (2000–2003), its grants aided more than three hundred large-scale infrastructure investments in the ten candidate countries of Central Europe and Eastern Europe (Bulgaria, Czech Republic, Estonia, Hungary, Latvia, Lithuania, Poland, Romania, Slovakia, and Slovenia). Assistance amounted to €7 billion for an investment value of more than €11.6 billion (current prices).[36] After the enlargement of the EU in 2004, the remaining ISPA beneficiary countries were Bulgaria and Romania, the other beneficiary countries having become eligible for the Cohesion Fund.

ISPA projects focus on funding environmental and transport infrastructure projects to accomplish their objectives. Environmental projects fall under the categories of water and sewerage; water or wastewater, including treatment; solid waste collection; and air quality. Transportation projects include building infrastructure for roads, for rail, for airports, and for inland waterways.[37] Transportation projects seek to build, upgrade, and repair transport infrastructure, as well as create a link to the EU transport networks.[38]

Beneficiary countries are responsible for the implementation of the ISPA. However, as long as decentralized implementation procedures are not in place, the European Commission exercises close control over all stages of project implementation.[39]

SPECIAL ACCESSION PROGRAM FOR AGRICULTURAL
AND RURAL DEVELOPMENT (SAPARD)

SAPARD finances agricultural and rural development for candidate countries.[40] Its financial assistance is designed to help candidate countries structurally adjust their agricultural sector and rural areas. SAPARD also helps candidate countries implement the acquis communautaire concerning the Common Agricultural Policy (CAP).[41]

CAP is responsible for improving the EU agricultural sector. It aims to provide farmers with a reasonable standard of living and consumers with high-quality food at fair prices. It also aims to preserve rural heritage. CAP is increasingly focused on food safety, preservation of the environment, and crops for fuel programs.[42] To meet CAP's goals, candidate countries therefore have to improve their agricultural and production standards and implement certain changes in legislation and agricultural policy. SAPARD funding helps candidate countries to achieve these goals.

Financial assistance to candidate countries under SAPARD is substantial. In 2003, the annual budget for the ten candidate countries of Central Europe and Eastern Europe was €560 million. In 2004, the SAPARD budget for Romania and Bulgaria was €225.2 million.

Programs funded under SAPARD are divided by sector within a given candidate country. In Bulgaria, for example, projects financed by SAPARD fell under categories such as "improving processing and marketing of agricultural and fishery products." Funds were distributed based on projects that fall into these groups, such as "adapt establishment to EU standards on hygiene and food quality" and "improve storage capacity."[43]

SAPARD comes under the authority of the Directorate-General for Agriculture of the EU.[44] Its implementation is preceded by the approval of the European Commission of a National Plan for agriculture and rural development, the accreditation of a SAPARD agency, and multi-annual and annual financing agreements.[45]

Financial assistance under SAPARD allows candidate countries to improve their rural and agricultural sectors to meet the CAP standards. SAPARD aims to make these sectors more efficient in candidate countries to boost the economy and create a more sustainable life for farmers and rural workers.

COMMUNITY ASSISTANCE FOR RECONSTRUCTION, DEVELOPMENT, AND STABILIZATION (CARDS)

CARDS is the financial instrument for the western Balkans. The Stabilization and Association Process (SAP) is the most important element of CARDS and is the cornerstone of the EU's policy toward the region. CARDS, through SAP, seeks to promote stability within the western Balkan region while facilitating closer association with the EU.[46]

Through SAP, €4.6 billion was provided to the western Balkan region in 2000–2006 for investment, institution building, and other measures to achieve four main objectives: (1) reconstruction, democratic stabilization, reconciliation, and the return of refugees; (2) institutional and legislative development, including harmonization with EU norms and approaches, development of the rule of law, human rights, civil society and the media, and the operation of a free-market economy; (3) sustainable economic and social development, including structural reform; and (4) promotion of closer relations and regional cooperation among the EU and the candidate countries of Central Europe. CARDS financed hundreds of projects across all sectors, countries, and regions to help the western Balkans meet these goals.[47]

TURKISH PRE-ACCESSION INSTRUMENT

The Turkish Pre-accession Instrument is geared specifically toward helping Turkey meet the economic, political, and social requirements of joining the EU.[48] The program did not give financial assistance to the countries that joined the EU in the fifth enlargement.

Post-accession Assistance

After admission into the EU, new member states are provided with further accession assistance.

Post-accession Transition Facilities

Post-accession Transition Facilities provide funds to countries that have recently joined the EU. The ten new member states that joined the EU in 2004 received this assistance until 2006. Romania and Bulgaria began benefiting from a Post-accession Transition Facility in 2007. This post-accession financial assistance is implemented by the Extended Decentralized Implementation System and provides new members with continued financial support in a number of core areas previously financed by the pre-accession assistance measures.[49]

Cohesion Fund

Programs financed under the ISPA are funded under the Cohesion Fund once the candidate country becomes a member of the EU. The Cohesion Fund, as described by the European Commission, is a structural instrument that helps member states reduce economic and social disparities and stabilize their economies. The Cohesion Fund finances up to 85 percent of eligible expenditure of major projects involving the environment and transport infrastructure.[50] This financial support is intended to strengthen cohesion and solidarity within the EU.

Eligible countries are the least prosperous member states of the EU. Countries supported by the Cohesion Fund have per capita gross national products that are below 90 percent of the EU average (Bulgaria, Cyprus, Czech Republic, Estonia, Greece, Hungary, Latvia, Lithuania, Malta, Poland, Portugal, Romania, Slovakia, Slovenia, and Spain since January 5, 2004). The Cohesion Fund's budget was €15.9 billion for the years 2004–2006. More than half of the funding is reserved for new member states.[51]

Common Agricultural Policy (CAP)

CAP funds help new EU members who received SAPARD funds as candidate countries further modernize their agricultural and rural sectors. When the EU was enlarged in May 2004 and January 2007, the number of farmers in the EU increased first by 55 percent and then by 53 percent. Farmers and food processors in the new member countries face particular challenges when competing with agriculture in the rest of the EU. CAP therefore provides a special funding package to new member states tailored specifically to the needs of these farmers. A €5 billion budget provides help for early retirement, impoverished areas, environmental protection, forestation, semi-subsistence farms, producer groups, and programs for compliance with EU food, hygiene, and animal-welfare standards.[52]

The new EU countries also have access to benefits provided to all EU member states under CAP. The 2004 entrants into the EU have immediate access to price-support measures (export refunds and intervention buying). Direct payments are phased in over ten years (2004–2013), starting at 25 percent of the rate paid to existing countries in 2004, and 30 percent in 2005.[53] CAP funds therefore provide continued financial support to rural and agricultural development in new EU member states.

The substantial amounts of EU aid to the acceding countries was intended to increase reform measures, boost the candidate countries' economies, raise income levels, and ultimately make Europe more democratic and stable.[54]

After providing this financial assistance, the EU was able to welcome new members into the union without fear that the new countries would have a long-term detrimental effect on the overall economy or the EU's political and social systems. The assistance the new members obtained from the EU have for the most part been successful and have allowed the countries' economies and political and social infrastructure to develop. The pre-accession and post-accession assistance therefore has been a key to helping new EU members achieve economic growth.[55]

EU Funding Sources

Adhesion funds for candidate and new member countries are taken out of the EU budget. Revenue for the European budget comes from payments from member states. The EU budget is mainly financed from three resources:

- Own resources: Taxes obtained on behalf of the EU, mostly customs duties on imports into the EU, agricultural duties, and sugar levies. These are collected by the state where the importing occurs and are passed on to the EU. States are allowed to keep a proportion (25 percent) of the revenue to cover administration. The European Commission operates a system of inspectors to investigate the collection of these taxes in member states and ensure compliance with the rules.
- VAT-based resources: Taxes on EU citizens derived as a proportion of VAT are levied on exchanges in each member country. Every member state charges VAT on the consumption of goods and services. Some of these revenues go into the EU budget. This contribution is calculated by applying a flat rate to the VAT base, which is the total value of a member state's consumption of goods and services. The contribution must not exceed .5 percent of the member state's VAT base.
- Resources based on gross national income (GNI): GNI-based resources currently form the largest contribution to EU funding. A simple multiplier is applied to the calculated GNI for the country concerned. This is the last recourse for raising funding for a budget year, so the actual figure is adjusted within predetermined limits to obtain the budget total required. Revenue is currently capped at 1.24 percent of GNI for the EU as a whole.

Approximately 1 percent of the EU budget comes from other revenue. This part of the general budget, which is not financed by own resources, includes taxes and other deductions from staff remunerations, bank interest, contributions from non-member countries to certain community programs (e.g., research), repayments of unused community financial assistance, and interest on late payments.

The EU Experience and NAFTA

Robert Pastor provides this list of lessons that the NAFTA countries can learn from the EU experience:[56]

1. A declaration of goals is needed. EU leaders defined mission in terms of community and solidarity; the goal was for people of Europe to cooperate in new ways to bring peace and well-being to all.
2. A few solid institutions are needed for guidance.
3. Economic convergence is essential. The spectacular reduction in the income gap between the rich and poor countries was achieved in a relatively short period (since 1986). Among the factors responsible were the establishment of a single market, foreign investment, and massive EU aid programs. The EU also insisted on democracy as a criterion for membership.
4. Reduction in disparities will reduce pressures to emigrate. The effect of convergence in incomes and social policies was to reduce the level of emigration from the poor countries and regions in the EU. Although the gap within the EU was narrower than that within NAFTA, the result is indisputable.
5. Reducing volatility is vital. First, sustained growth remains the most effective way to reduce disparities, and national policies are at least as important as the EU's regional policies. That is why Ireland did so much better than Greece, although it received a third as much aid. Second, the single market and foreign investment may have contributed as much to the development of the poor countries in Southern Europe as aid. Third, regional aid helped in significant ways: by encouraging governments to maintain good macroeconomic policies, by targeting bottlenecks in the economy, and by multiplying investments. Of all regional aid projects, the two most effective ways to stimulate growth and reduce disparities were infrastructure and education. Rich countries need to find ways to cushion the swings that poor economies suffer. Opportunities and dangers of integration are much more serious for weak countries than for more advanced ones. Cohesion

countries outperformed the EU average in the boom years and did worse than the average during recessions.

6. Growing inequality within the successful poor countries can occur. Monitoring the progress of all regions of poor countries is needed.

7. Politics and bureaucracy have to be balanced. The right balance is needed to keep democracy at the core of deliberations as an organization deepens.

8. The magnitude of commitment must be great. The EU appropriated truly significant funds to reduce disparities between rich and poor governments and regions. When the EU first decided on a regional policy, its funds were scarce, but with each enlargement, it expanded the resources for poor regions to a point at which the sheer magnitude of investment helped lift some and gave a sense of community to all.[57]

The EU and Schengen Area Failures

The EU is not, of course, perfect, and it would be naïve not to acknowledge some real problems that have arisen, especially with respect to North African and Sub-Saharan African migrants who are not from EU countries. I have highlighted the strengths of the EU's more integrated approach. However, when it comes to those countries that are not part of the integration, the results are horribly similar to those at the U.S.–Mexican border.

Background on the Schengen Area

The Schengen Agreement, first signed by Belgium, Germany, Luxembourg, and the Netherlands in 1985, defined the European border regime. The agreement allowed for the elimination of systematic border controls between the participating countries. Simultaneously, it created a common, external Schengen border. The agreement set guidelines by which the Schengen border would be defined, implemented, and monitored. It also set up border patrols, visa procedures, cross-border police cooperation, and information sharing among all signatory states.[58]

In the 1990s, programs were launched that invested military resources in border surveillance and created an EU-wide border-control authority.[59] Since then, the EU has set up an increasingly militarized European border control agency, called FRONTEX, to apprehend Africans and other non-Schengen migrants. FRONTEX had a €45 million budget in 2008. It has developed a surveillance system, Eurosur, to monitor immigrants' movements via satellites and aerial drones, as well as via Rapid Border Intervention Teams.[60]

In addition, as national borders within the Schengen Area disappear, national border guards focus their resources on guarding against African and other non-Schengen Area migrants. As countries signed the Schengen Agreement with all their neighboring states, their traditional border guards seemed to appear obsolete. Interestingly, in the case of Germany, instead of reducing its forces the government gave its border guard a new mission. It created new legal areas of operation by reclassifying train routes and train stations, interstate highways, and big public plazas as strategic transit areas and as de facto internal extensions of the border. In addition, the German federal border guard began to cooperate with new partners, such as local police and private security contractors, and to support regular police units during special events such as political rallies and soccer games. National border guards are now also put to the task of guarding Schengen Area borders against non-Schengen migrants.[61]

Today, the Schengen Agreement has been signed by thirty countries, including all EU member states and Iceland, Norway, and Switzerland. In addition, the Schengen Agreement has become part of the acquis communautaire, which means that future EU candidates will have to meet Schengen criteria and adopt the European immigration and border policies.[62]

Moreover, by means of supranational European programs and bilateral agreements, EU member states routinely export European border standards to states outside the EU. The border standards are written into European financial, technical, and administrative aid. Border-control measures become an explicit component of the law-enforcement training and assistance offered by the EU in humanitarian-aid packages.[63]

Schengen Area border policies has created a "Fortress Europe," making legal migration into the EU virtually impossible for Africans and others coming from outside the Schengen border, and undocumented migrants make life-threatening attempts to cross into the Schengen Area.[64]

Euro-African Ministerial Conference on Migration and Its Consequences

In July 2006, fifty-eight European and African states convened in Rabat, Morocco, for the Euro-African Ministerial Conference on Migration and Development. The conference was prompted by the large number of undocumented migrants from Africa attempting to enter the EU, coupled with their rising body count. In the first half of 2006, an estimated nine thousand undocumented migrants had arrived at the shores of the Spanish Canary Islands, which was more than the number for all of 2005. A week before the conference began, two Africans died after falling off a six-meter fence at the

Spanish enclave of Melilla, which is part of the external border of the EU. In the fall of 2005, five Africans were shot dead by Moroccan border police while trying to cross the fence at the Ceuta enclave along the coast.[65]

As Gregor Noll explains, since the 1990s governments in the global South had pushed for a UN conference on world migration and sought to link migration to development. European countries "could hardly [have been] less interested," as the EU wanted to improve migration control first.[66] Only after the EU could no longer ignore the large numbers of undocumented migrants and the increasing fatalities did the European governments decide to take part in such a conference.

The Rabat conference was a failure for two main reasons. First, it established the "Rabat Plan of Action" that trades African cooperation in restricting migration for European development assistance. Europeans offered Africa the annual sum of €2.5 billion in return for their cooperation on immigration enforcement. Although this measure was largely welcomed, Noll points out that this is not a realistic solution to curbing migration flows. Remittances to less-developed countries—money immigrants send home to their families—amounted to €60 billion in 1999. Such figures emphasize that emigrant-producing countries in the South would be foolish to prevent their citizens from traveling to and working in the EU.[67] Moreover, the sum dwarfs the amount of aid promised to Africa by the EU.

The other significant outcome of the Rabat conference focused on repressive measures, including (1) a comprehensive reinforcement of border control by air, naval, and police forces (African included); (2) "readmission agreements" between target, transit, and source countries to facilitate the return of undocumented Africans; and (3) enhanced registration of African migrants. In Noll's view, African governments sold out to Europeans at the conference in return for conditional development assistance. He concludes that the result is a Mediterranean "Berlin Wall" made of water and razor wire that will persist and proliferate on the African continent.[68]

Even in an attempt to reform its border policies as the death toll of migrants rose, the EU focused on ineffective and detrimental enforcement measures with regard to countries outside the Schengen Area. The year 2006 ended with new records all along the Schengen Area border for tragedy.[69] Spanish authorities reported that six thousand refugees had drowned in the Atlantic Ocean while trying to reach the Canary Islands.[70] Hundreds more had suffocated in containers, trucks, and cargo boats in the ports of London, Dublin, and Rotterdam or had frozen to death in Eastern Europe. Others who had been locked in the 224 internment camps spread over the heart of Europe and North Africa desperately took their own lives.[71] At the same time, Europe reported the lowest rate in years of people who were officially seeking asylum. The criteria and procedures for securing legal refugee status have become so restrictive that most migrants no longer bother to apply for it.[72]

The Schengen Area's border policies vis-à-vis Africa thus are strikingly similar to the U.S. policies toward Mexico, and they have similar results. The militarized Schengen Area border focuses on enforcement rather than effectively dealing with the causes of migration. This policy accounts for a mounting death toll of African migrants. Moreover, Europe's conditional aid to Africa is insufficient and, as some say, a mere "loud-sounding nothing" remedy to African poverty.[73] Tongkeh Fowale has summarized the shortfalls of European aid:

> It does not take a professional economist to realize that African economies are predominantly agricultural and that European (and American) policies are increasingly suffocating and asphyxiating the continent. These subsidies leave African markets flooded with cheap European and American goods. Chicken, tomato paste, onions, fruit and vegetables and other agricultural products from the EU now flood the African market. African farmers are left with what Fidel Castro would call "starvation salaries" [and] have little options but to "employ their feet" in this desperate attempt at survival.[74]

Conclusion

EU adhesion funds to poor regions within the EU have been effective. The investments have financed infrastructure, job creation, local development, retraining of displaced workers, rural development, and aid to farmers. In contrast to the failure of NAFTA to incorporate labor migration and investment in its provisions, the development of the EU proceeded with the movement of workers and the interests of poor members clearly in mind. The EU approach appears to be working, without massive flows of workers from poor nations to wealthy nations. In fact, poor nations do not seem so poor any longer. The EU's public infrastructure investment has created a "climate that draws in private investment [and] raises living standards."[75]

The EU's failures with respect to North African and Sub-Saharan African migrants also serves as a good lesson for the U.S.–Mexico challenge. When bad policies supported by the World Bank, the International Monetary Fund, and the World Trade Organization destroy an industry overnight,[76] the EU should not be surprised when African farmers come knocking at their door.

If Europe wants migration from Africa to slow, the EU will have to change its economic policies and invest more wisely in that region.

Unfortunately, instead of contemplating more expansive and intelligent assistance to African development, the EU continues to implement greater and more militarized immigration-enforcement measures. As with Operation Gatekeeper along the U.S.–Mexican border, this has only led to a higher death toll. As one border area is further secured, people look toward more dangerous routes in the hope of successfully entering the Schengen Area.[77] Moreover, as larger numbers of migrants are being apprehended and detained, human-rights organizations are voicing greater concern about their treatment in immigration detention centers. For many migrants, "The ordeal they encounter on their way to Europe is either similar or equal to the environment of despair back home."[78] Both the Schengen Area and the United States can learn from the benefits of symbiotic economic policies, coupled with open borders, that have been implemented to an important extent within the EU.

5

Celtic Tiger

The Irish Example

Taking a closer look at Ireland gives us a good sense of the benefits of the European Union's investment approach to a formerly poor, emigrant-exporting country. Ireland developed into an economically successful country that attracted immigrants. While the analogy between Mexico and Ireland may be imperfect, important lessons can still be retrieved from this example.

Not long ago, Ireland was an immigrant-sending nation. That changed when Ireland became part of the EU. The Great Famine of 1848 launched a century of continual emigration, culminating in more than four hundred thousand nationals fleeing Irish shores in the 1950s. The vast departure of labor forced Irish policymakers to examine their economic policies. Slowly, Ireland shed its protectionist economic policies and, with the aid of foreign investment and EU membership, became an international economic heavyweight. Ireland made the transition from an economy based on agriculture to an exporting powerhouse in areas such as technology. Entering the new millennium, Ireland produced almost one-third of all personal computers sold throughout Europe and was vying for the top position in Europe's e-commerce broadband markets. The effect of adhesion funds in Ireland exemplifies how such investments have helped a poor country and affected migration patterns.

Every Irish tourism brochure touts Ireland as "the Emerald Isle," playing on the clichéd ideas of a rural and lush landscape filled with simple farmers singing ballads about the Great Famine and drowning their sorrows in Irish whiskey. While focusing on the lush landscape draws in tourists, Ireland's heavy focus on agriculture hindered its economic growth. This struggle caused the Irish people to obsess about leaving their native land and seeking fortune in far-flung countries. The problem of migration in Ireland has been felt by many generations of Irish people. In the 1840s, Ireland suffered a huge and devastating famine that killed almost a third of its population, leading to the emigration of another third of the population to Australia, the United Kingdom, and the United States. The powerful appeal of the prosperity in those countries continuously draws large numbers of young Irish people. This constant flow of Ireland's youth depleted Ireland's labor and intellectual resources, limiting the improvements that the country could achieve. This trend continued into the twentieth century, even after Ireland achieved freedom from the English in the war of independence of 1922. Ireland's economy suffered greatly due to this trend and only recently began to turn around.

Few young people desired to remain in Ireland. Old farmers continued to run their farms in the west and south of the country, clinging to often ineffective methods of farming. The Irish engaged in far more importing than exporting, and causing serious problems for the economy; whatever was exported relied far too heavily on the English market. The situation in Ireland was bleak.

The Irish stopped abandoning their green hills because they finally had a reason to stay. Ireland's greatest export for decades has been its population. But when economic growth began, the Irish began to stay to take part, fueling even greater growth and development.

Until the global economic crisis began at the end of 2008, the Irish economy had become one of the strongest in the world. Ireland is one of the world's most highly educated nations, and the Irish have one of the highest standards of living in Europe. The upswing in the Irish economy began in the late 1950s and took a huge leap when Ireland joined the EU in 1973. The path was not all plain sailing, and the Irish economy took a serious and almost fatal dive from 1977 to 1987. However, due to EU investment and the fact that EU membership opened the Irish economy to a huge European market of 500 million people, the economy rebounded and became as strong as ever. This led the Irish into a period of unprecedented growth and a time in which the "Celtic Tiger's" roar could be heard all over the globe.

How Ireland Changed Its Economic Luck

After joining the EU, Ireland became a hugely prosperous and vibrant economy. The number of young Irish leaving the country dropped dramatically. Indeed, many older Irish people returned home. And incredibly, Ireland experienced a completely new phenomenon: immigrants from abroad moving into the country.

Several factors contributed to the Irish turnaround. Certainly, no single factor could lead to such an amazing overhaul of a seemingly desolate economy. As recently as 2007, it did not take much effort to see the immense and immeasurable impact of the EU on Ireland. From investment in agriculture, infrastructure, and tourism to the development of more effective and lucrative trade links, the effect of the EU could be seen and felt throughout the country.

The drop in the number of Irish emigrants was understandable. People move to where they believe they can make the best lives for themselves. Many had chosen America—the land of opportunity—in search of a new life filled with promise. But as the Irish economy improved, the Irish no longer perceived a need to go abroad in search of a better life; the economy on their doorstep offered opportunities equal to, or often even better than, those in other countries. As faith in the Irish economy grew, and the fear of another collapse was dispelled, the Irish began to remain at home and reap the benefits of what EU investments and generations before had sown.

Ireland was no longer the peripheral, rural, weak country in Europe. It was always an island with great ports, fishing, and agricultural land. But now a foundation had been laid for those assets to help build success. After centuries of nothing more than reliance on the English market, Ireland stepped out of the shadow long cast by the British Empire, a step that many Irish believed should have occurred after the war of independence that took place almost ninety years ago. The transition from the old, rural Ireland into the economic and technological hub began a decade before Ireland succeeded in attaining membership in the exclusive EU club. The story began in the late 1950s and continued to move in stages until 2008.

Before the 1960s, Ireland's entire economy depended on the often unstable and unreliable agricultural sector. During this period, the Industrial Revolution, which had hit England more than a hundred years earlier, began to see a slight revival as Ireland began to develop and invest in new industries. Ireland's watershed moment came inn 1958, when T. K. Whitaker, the Irish economist and secretary of finance, wrote a report on the economy and the opportunities in Ireland. He argued that the time was right for Ireland to make changes, invest money, and use its own resources and advantages. His influential report spoke of policies to attract international investors, industrialization, and the development of an export-oriented trade economy. The 1960s were an optimum time for Ireland to finally seek this development, given a boom in Europe that facilitated some of the changes within the country. The report spurred action, and growth began.

The economic growth in the 1960s helped Ireland gain acceptance in the EU, creating the opportunity to benefit from membership and involvement with other European nations. Ireland attained EU membership in 1973, following two previous failed attempts in 1961 and 1967. The idea of Ireland's joining the EU was very favorably received by the Irish population, who viewed membership as the vehicle to open doors in a way that the Irish could not have dreamed possible without the assistance of the EU. With membership in the union, foreign investors would be attracted to Ireland as a gateway to Europe. The EU also served as a catalyst for change and development in Ireland's agricultural industry.

Changes in the Roman Catholic church have also seeded change in Ireland. The church always had, and continues to have, a strong influence on all matters in Ireland. With the ascension of Pope John Paul II in 1978, the strict and immovable policies of the old Catholic church and previous popes began to lessen. Although John Paul II may not be considered a liberal pope in contrast with others, he did place fewer constraints on the lives of the Irish people, who, despite every stereotype, do live in a truly religious nation. In 1979, Ireland lifted the ban on importing and exporting contraceptives, a culturally and practically symbolic event. Culturally, it epitomized the shift toward a more liberal form of Irish Catholicism, even though the church did not officially sanction medical birth control. Practically, it helped Ireland control its population and its constant problem of a flooded labor supply. The more modern approach to Catholicism meant that the Irish could develop and broaden their horizons without losing their religion, which is key to their ethnicity.

The 1960s witnessed a remarkable 50 percent increase in the standard of living in Ireland. The young now had a choice: They could remain in Ireland and get jobs. The number of emigrants slowed as many decided to stay and raise families in Ireland. The marriage rate increased by 9 percent, resulting in an increased birthrate, as well. The number of children in primary-school education surged from 496,000 in 1960 to 554,000 in 1973. This represented a growth of 9.68 percent in just thirteen years. The average marriage age also fell.

For the first time in 140 years, Ireland experienced the entry of more immigrants than the exit of emigrants in the 1970s. Prior to that point, and since the 1840s, the large number of emigrants leaving Ireland each year had been a serious social problem. The 1970s ended this concern, at least for the moment. The reasons for the slowdown in emigration centered on Ireland's entry into the EU in 1973. The Irish gained confidence because entry into the EU meant membership in the European Economic Area (EEA) and Common Agricultural Policy (CAP) funding that would support Irish agriculture for a five-year transition period. Ireland received huge amounts in support and investment money almost immediately. During this period, many Irish nationals returned to Ireland, with families and children. Slowly, new immigrants began to arrive in Ireland, as well.

However, emigration from Ireland experienced a huge increase once again in the 1980s. The reversion was due in large part to huge public debt. Following the Irish elections in 1977, the government fulfilled its promise to slash taxes, and public coffers were left empty. Massive debt ensued. The resulting recession affected every part of social and economic life for the citizens of Ireland. The EU was in the midst of reworking CAP, and Ireland had initiated an industrial-restructuring program. The hopes and faith of the 1970s began to crumble, leaving the Irish people with little confidence in the stability of their economy. Many looked abroad again. Most new Irish emigrants went to the United Kingdom, just as they had since independence in 1922.

By the 1980s, Irish nationals were traveling beyond the United Kingdom to other parts of Europe and to the United States. In the United States, the growing numbers of undocumented Irish became an issue, as many overstayed their visitor's visas. Some estimates placed the number of undocumented Irish as high as 100,000. The problem gave rise to legislative responses by the U.S. Congress in the form of diversity programs that allotted extra visas for Irish nationals. In a new phenomenon, many emigrants traveled to continental Europe in the 1980s, as well. No one had predicted this huge outflow of emigrants, given Ireland's success in the 1970s. The exact number of people who left Ireland in the 1980s is not known; the best estimate, however, is about 250,000.

Although it was not as huge as in the 1980s, Irish emigration in the 1990s still remained relatively high, at about forty thousand people per year. The numbers decreased toward the end of the 1990s, when the Celtic Tiger began to boom. The economic climate in Ireland became more appealing to young Irish generations, as well as to the Irish abroad. The main change was in the destination of emigrants. Although the United States and the United Kingdom remained key destinations, continental Europe gained in importance. In 1994, 22 percent of Irish emigrants went to Europe. The climate in Europe became more inviting; when the Berlin Wall was pulled down at the end of the 1980s, Germany began to reunify, creating a booming market. Many Irish were enticed to mainland Europe to take advantage of the new growth.

Great change was taking place in Ireland in the 1990s. Many companies began to invest in the country again, including in high-skill technological firms and pharmaceutical and computer companies. The highly educated, skilled workforce was a draw for these companies. These trends, coupled with new EU investment in agriculture, tourism, and infrastructure, turned around Ireland's emigration rates.

In sum, Ireland has experienced many economic and social changes since it joined the EU in 1973:

- The population has increased by almost a million.
- Life expectancy has increased significantly; the average life expectancy of an Irish woman is now 80.3 years.
- Birthrates have decreased due to the tendency to have smaller families.
- Trade and investment have increased.
- By 2007, there were almost 750,000 more people in the workforce.
- The number of women in the workplace increased to more than 460,000, accounting for 42 percent of the working population (compared with 27 percent in 1973).
- The price of housing increased until the 2008 bubble burst.
- Property values have boomed, and the construction sector has seen huge growth.
- Average incomes have increased markedly, which has led to a higher standard of living and more discretionary income that the population can spend on travel, dining out, and entertainment.
- The number of people working in the primary sector—especially in the agricultural industry and the fishing industry—has decreased, and significant growth has occurred in the tertiary, or services, sector.
- The number of people attending college has increased almost five times, to about 130,000, giving Ireland a much more highly qualified workforce.

Education became an even bigger priority after Ireland joined the EU in 1973. All children must receive compulsory education from age 6 to 15. In 1973, the requirement to pass an examination in the Irish language to receive a second-level certificate was dropped. English is the primary medium of instruction at all levels, except in Gaelscoileanna, or schools in which Irish is the working language and which are increasingly popular. Universities also offer degree programs in diverse disciplines, taught mostly in English, with a few in Irish. Some universities offer some courses partly in other languages, such as French, German, or Spanish.

Higher (third-level) education was made free in 1996. Critics complained, however, that undergraduate education in Ireland was starved of funds, especially as the number of students started to grow rapidly after 1996. That is, colleges had to educate far greater numbers of students without a corresponding increase in funding, leading to a dilution of the quality of lecturing and tutorial support that each student receives. In a controversial decision, fees for higher education were restored in late 2008.[1] A year earlier, Ireland had been ranked very low in its expenditures on children's education, even though it was one of the wealthiest countries in the world. Teachers' salaries are relatively high, and Irish spending on primary and post-primary pupils between 1995 and 2004 increased by 74 percent—the second-highest increase in twenty-four countries—but it was not enough to keep pace. On average, industrialized countries spend 6.2 percent of their GDP on education, but Ireland spent 4.6 percent in 2007, down from 5.2 percent in 1995.[2]

Changing Irish Perspectives on Immigration

Despite the fact that Ireland had suffered huge loses of population due to emigration since the 1840s, the Irish people and the Irish government remained closed-minded about the idea of immigration. When a council was held during the late 1950s to discuss the falling population and the role that allowing immigrants into the country might play in alleviating some of the problems, the Irish government made clear that immigrants were not wanted. As Ireland began to focus on economic development. the attitude toward immigration evolved, and Ireland's borders began to open to meet new labor-force demands.

From 1996 to 2000, approximately 250,000 people immigrated to Ireland. This represented about 7 percent of Ireland's population. About 50 percent were returning Irish or of Irish decent. The number of asylum seekers also increased significantly. The number of applications for asylum in 1992 was 39; by 2001, that number had grown to 10,325. The number of work permits sought during this period also began an unprecedented rise, from 1,103 in 1993 to 40,322 in 2002.

Ireland struggles with one of the Celtic Tiger's biggest side effects: a new multicultural society. The economic success resulting from entry into the EU has attracted many immigrants to Ireland, both to shore up the labor market and for asylum seekers and refugees seeking to immigrate to a country on the rise. One common criticism directed at Irish society as a whole is that the country institutes hypocritical policies toward these newcomers. On the one hand, Ireland welcomes immigrants, viewing them as an economic commodity to stimulate the Celtic Tiger. On the other hand, Ireland struggles to integrate immigrants and institutes contradictory policies in this vein.

Ireland instituted several campaigns to raise awareness about immigration issues and curb increasing levels of racism. At the same time, however, support for legislation that restricts immigrant rights, such as barring groups of immigrants from third-level education, continues to grow. While the Irish economy remains stable, Ireland will continue to struggle integrating immigrants drawn to their shores.

Ireland's Economy: A Closer Look at the EU Role

The history of Ireland's economy for more than two centuries has included elements of mass emigration and relatively high unemployment. This changed radically in the early 1990s when employment began to grow rapidly—more rapidly even than employment growth in the United States.

The extremely high growth levels of the Irish economy in the 1990s, described as the Celtic Tiger, include 67 percent growth in employment between 1998 and 2004. This growth, the first since independence in 1922, was brought about largely, though not entirely, within the European Social Model. The end of involuntary emigration, net immigration, and rapidly rising living standards accompanied the growth to a level slightly above the European average. Ireland's per capita income had languished around twenty-fourth place in Europe for many decades but is now slightly above the EU average.

When Ireland joined the EU in 1973, the country was backward, run down, and poor. High unemployment, low levels of income, and high levels of emigration reigned. In statistical terms, the average income was 62 percent of the European average. This meant that the whole country qualified as a high-priority black spot in need of EU funding. In EU terminology, the country was designated an "Objective 1" European region for the twenty-four years between 1975 and 1999. This designation meant that Ireland's economy met the criteria of those countries most in need of economic assistance because their annual GDP was at least 75 percent below the EU average.

Attributing Ireland's economic turnaround solely to EU funds may be an overstatement. However, Ireland's accession into the EU in 1973 was a decisive milestone in opening the country to a global economy and reducing its economic dependence on the United Kingdom. Some of the factors related to the EU that helped facilitate the economic boom included

1. Billions of Euros in EU funding over thirty-three years, which enabled Ireland to upgrade its road networks, education and training, and productive sector
2. A single European market established among the EU members

3. The break-up and privatization of national monopolies
4. The deregulation of the marketplace across Europe
5. The encouragement of free and fair competition among EU countries
6. Unrestricted trade among EU member countries using common rules
7. A large and growing market of consumers as more countries joined the EU

Some internal factors also greatly aided the change, including

1. Low corporate taxes introduced within Ireland (12.5 percent)
2. A stable Irish political system
3. A young, educated population
4. High levels of foreign direct investment flowing into Ireland

The European economic and political climate therefore presented the opportunity. Ireland's national taxation policies and the development of the EU made Ireland an attractive location. And the EU's funding made it all possible.

EU membership has had great benefits. One obvious benefit has been the unhindered access to a market of some 460 million people. Membership has contributed to rapid progress in a range of areas, including the development of agriculture, industry, and services. Some seven hundred thousand jobs have been created in Ireland during the years of membership, and trade has increased ninety-fold. In addition, the levels of foreign direct investment in Ireland have increased dramatically as a result of membership. In 1972, a mere €16 million was coming into the economy from foreign investors. Thirty years later, with full access to European markets, foreign investment is measured in billions. Investments have exceeded €30 billion, and the economy was transformed, with more than 128,000 people employed in more than a thousand companies in the foreign-owned sector.

Apart from the economic benefits to the nation, EU membership has had a major impact on social and cultural life in Ireland. Every Irish citizen is also an EU citizen. As we have seen, subject to certain limitations EU citizens have the right to move, work, and reside freely within the territory of other member states.

The EU embodies the principle of economic and social cohesion. This means that the less prosperous regions in the union are helped to reduce disparities between their levels of development and those of the more prosperous regions. This principle was reinforced in the Single European Act (1986) and again in the Maastricht Treaty (1992). In 2000–2006, Ireland was given more than €3.9 billion from the Structural and Cohesion Funds, as well as billions since it joined what was then the European Economic Community in 1973.

Ireland's membership in the EU has drastically affected the country in several key areas, including trade, employment, agriculture, and living standards. Ireland has gone from having a huge emigrant population to an ever growing immigrant population. This turnaround has resulted from the economic gains facilitated by membership in the EU.

Economy and Trade

The Irish Development Authority (IDA) attracted large foreign companies that wanted to locate and invest in Ireland to take advantage of its access to a large, competitive market of millions of people. EU funding ensured that improvements in road and broadband networks facilitated their installation in any county.

Transport Networks

Underdeveloped transport links often inhibit economic development, so improving Ireland's transport infrastructure was vital to its economic development. Transporting freight speedily from port to city without costly delays through small towns and villages is essential. Much of the massive investment in Irish route infrastructure has been financed by EU Cohesion Funds. Cohesion Funds are aimed at upgrading and improving transport infrastructure.

Up to the end of the 2000–2006 funding period, Ireland spent the largest share of the Structural Funds on road projects rather than on railways or airports. Improvements were also made to the seaports in Cork, Killybegs, and Rosslare to allow them to handle bigger ships with bigger loads. Public transport networks were not ignored. Intercity train and extended local lines were all partly financed by the EU.

Foreign Industries and Exports

Export goods from Ireland changed under the EU. Before joining union, Ireland's main exports were food and drink, and most of this consisted of meat and dairy products. Ireland's main industry was agriculture and farming. After joining the EU, Ireland's industrialized sector shifted dramatically from farming and agriculture to new software, pharmaceutical, and chemicals industries. Companies were attracted to locate in Ireland in the 1990s, including Dell, Microsoft, Pfizer, Wyeth, Intel, Google, and eBay. Foreign banks such as Citibank opened offices offering financial services, and America Online opened a customer-support call center. Ireland became a European high-tech base, and this trend is likely to continue as the EU enlarges further.

The level of exports also increased. In 1973, Ireland imported more than it exported and had a trade deficit of €340 million. By 2006, this situation had changed radically. The value of exports was 43 percent higher than the value of goods imported, generating a positive trade balance of €26.2 billion.

Trade beyond the British Isles

Ireland's main trading partners have also changed. Before EU membership, Ireland's entire economy was dependent on agricultural exports to the United Kingdom. In 1973, more than half (55 percent) of Irish goods went to the United Kingdom or Northern Ireland. By 2006, this figure had dropped to just under 18 percent. The United States has now overtaken the United Kingdom as Ireland's most important trading partner. Ireland's trade with the United States and other EU countries has doubled since 1973.

Employment

From 1973 to 2008, the Irish workforce increased by more than 70 percent. Women contributed greatly to that growth. Women are now 42 percent of the workforce, up from 27 percent in 1973. The unemployment rate was low—just 4 percent in 2008, compared with the EU average of 7 percent. Young Irish people had opportunities at home and the option to remain in their homeland. According to the Eurobarometer Spring 2007 public-opinion report prepared by the European Commission, Ireland has the fifth-highest level of confidence in the economy at 89.[3] Emigration has been greatly reduced.

Prosperity

Ireland has experienced tremendous growth in wealth, fueled by intense direct foreign investment, the expanded workforce, and the increase in exports. Per capita GNP, a useful indicator of domestic economic affluence, by 2008, was more than three times the 1973 equivalent in Ireland. Ireland's growth in wealth lured British retail chains onto every main street. The fruits of wealth were apparent: expensive properties, new restaurants, foreign travel, high-performance cars, electronic gadgets, penthouse apartments, and designer-label goods.

Agriculture and Fishing

Agriculture and the fishing industry experienced different fates after Ireland's entry into the EU.

Farmers

The Common Agricultural Policy (CAP) served as a savior to Irish farmers after 1973. CAP maintained higher than average prices for agricultural products sold within the EU and compensated farmers when goods were sold on the world market at prices lower than those of the EU. Assured of a steady income, farmers were lifted out of poverty, and consumers could be confident that food prices would not fluctuate wildly according to scarcity. Indeed, many Irish farmers depend on CAP funding for a livelihood.

Irish farmers did well with CAP. The more they produced, the more they earned. Sometimes they produced more than was needed, flooding the market with excess food. When Ireland joined in 1973, the EU was a large market of nine countries, and the CAP prices for beef and dairy products—Ireland's forte—were 20–30 percent higher than the world price.

In June 2003, CAP reform provided more opportunities for farmers. The reforms introduced a single farm payment to replace most of the direct subsidy payments to farmers. The new single payment is no longer linked to what a farmer produces. The amount of the payment is calculated on the basis of the direct subsidies farmers received in a reference period (2000–2002). A major aim of the single payment is to allow farmers to become more market-oriented and to release their entrepreneurial potential. Management decisions that in the past have been influenced by what the CAP offered in subsidies can now be made on the basis of market requirements. When a particular production activity is profitable, farmers will continue to follow the market. The reformed CAP is designed so that farmers can take advantage of such opportunities. Since 2005, farmers have received the annual single payment on the condition that they maintain their land in good agricultural condition, comply with EU standards on public health, and meet environmental and animal-welfare standards.

Subsidizing farmers using CAP prices used to account for 70 percent of the entire EU budget. Today, the EU devotes 40 percent of the budget to this program.

Fishermen

Irish fishing fleets are under pressure and in decline. Because of the global decline in fish stocks, the EU's total catch allowance has been reduced, and some fishing zones have been closed.

Population

Ireland's economic success has led to a much more diverse population. Ireland has needed immigrant workers to satisfy the needs of the economy. Thus, Ireland has experienced a very sharp increase in immigration within a very short period. Many of the immigrants are returning men and women of Irish descent. Many more are from the new EU member states.

Irish women have benefited from the country's membership in the EU. European legislation guarantees rights to equal pay, rights to maternity leave, rights for part-time workers, and rights against discrimination in the workforce. Governments that fail to enforce EU laws may be summoned before the European Court of Justice. Where a violation of the European Convention on Human Rights is involved, an application can be lodged with the European Court of Human Rights in Strasbourg, which is a Council of Europe body.

Since EU membership, Irish nationals find it easier to travel, study, live, work, and even retire in other EU countries. Students can avail themselves of EU-funded study schemes such as Erasmus Mundus, an EU cooperation and higher-education mobility program that promotes the union as a center of excellence in learning around the world. The program's overall aim is to enhance the quality of European higher education by fostering cooperation with third countries to improve the development of human resources and to promote dialogue and understanding between peoples and cultures. The program's specific objectives are to (1) select high-quality integrated master's courses that are offered by a consortium of at least three higher-education institutions in at least three participating countries; (2) give scholarships to highly qualified graduate students and scholars from third countries to follow or participate in the selected master's courses; (3) select high-quality partnerships between selected master's courses and third-country higher-education institutions; and (4) select projects of at least three institutions in at least three participating countries aiming to improve accessibility and enhance the profile and visibility of higher education in the EU. The program provides a whole different perspective on life lived abroad for EU students, as well as the opportunity to learn a foreign language.

Results of the EU Assistance in Ireland

As the Irish economy grew and the Irish people themselves began to return to Ireland, those from other nations also were attracted to the country. Ireland became a land of opportunity and wealth that attracts many Eastern European nationals.

Ireland had suffered huge losses in population since the 1800s due to famine, poor opportunities, and a weak economy. Its population fell from 4.2 million in 1861 to 2.8 million in 1961. By 1996, driven by economic success, Ireland had reached a position of net immigration. Now Irish nationals are returning, and Ireland has become a center for asylum seekers and Eastern Europeans seeking a better life. With a boom in development until 2008, Ireland relied heavily on immigrants to shore up its labor force. Unemployment dropped from 15.9 percent in 1993 to a historic low of 5.7 percent in 1996.

While residents of other EU member states migrated to Ireland, the greatest number of immigrants comes from non-EU states. The non-EU migrants represent 50 percent of all immigrants to Ireland since 2000. The largest category of non-EU immigrants come to work, while the second-largest class is seeking asylum, followed by students and dependents. Today, Ireland has one of the highest net immigration rates in the EU.

As a member of the EEA, Ireland permits free movement of workers into the country from other members of the EEA. Any citizen of an EEA country has the right to move freely between these countries and seek work. The member states of the EEA include all EU member states, as well as Lichtenstein, Norway, and Iceland.

Ireland made an important policy choice related to immigration in 2004. Ireland, Sweden, and the United Kingdom agreed to allow open access to the newly accessioned states in terms of work rights. However, in Ireland and the United Kingdom, these immigrants cannot claim social-welfare benefits from the state.

Ireland's Approval of the Lisbon Treaty

In October 2009, Irish voters voted in favor of adopting the Lisbon Treaty, which will provide more uniform rights and policies within the EU. Sixteen months earlier, Irish voters had rejected the treaty, but in a stunning about-face spurred by economic turmoil, the "yes" votes won by a margin of two to one. Signed by European leaders in 2007, the Lisbon Treaty is the result of years of painstaking negotiations among countries trying to retain their national identities and hang on to power while ceding some control to an ever more integrated Europe. The prior rejection by the Irish electorate was particularly troubling to many observers, who believe strongly that Ireland has benefited so much from its EU membership and, of course, from EU funding. A second no vote by Ireland would have buried the Lisbon Treaty, creating institutional chaos for the EU.[4]

The economic downtown that began in 2008 greatly contributed to the change in voter sentiment. Soaring unemployment and a step decline in real estate were, of course, great concerns for the citizens of Ireland. Almost universally, Irish voters felt that the economy was kept from imploding largely because of EU support, in the form of liquidity from the European Central Bank. The drafters and proponents of the Lisbon Treaty argued that 495 million Europeans would benefit. Ireland has benefited from €32 billion in EU handouts, helping to transform it from one of the poorest countries in the European Economic Community in 1973, when it joined, to the second-richest per capita. Jobs have been created, and Dublin has been transformed from nearly a Third World city into a cosmopolitan metropolis, complete with cafés, space-age trams and Chanel shops.

Downturn in the Irish Economy

Since the financial downturn in the United States and its impact worldwide, Ireland's economy has been adversely affected. A deteriorating trend had been noticeable since the start of 2008: Sales volumes declined by 5.7 percent in the third quarter of that year.[5] The housing sector has been hit the hardest. A number of factors have contributed to the weakening of consumer sentiment and activity, the most noticeable change being a sharp downturn in the labor market.[6]

The recession started in Ireland earlier than it did elsewhere, and its effects have been deeper.[7] Housing prices have fallen by as much as 50 percent, and bank shares have plummeted by more than 90 percent. Unemployment rates are high, at 10 percent.[8] The roots of Ireland's fall can be traced back twenty years. Despite a booming economy that was caused by government policy that cut taxes, reduced import duties, and embraced foreign investment, a housing bubble had already begun to form. Low interest rates, a wave of inward immigration, and a bank-lending spree drove housing's share of the economy from 5 percent to 14 percent.[9] Irish policymakers were also "seduced" by the economy and did not pay attention to rising interest rates in the rest of Europe. However, despite a downturn primarily caused by the bursting of the housing bubble, some economists do not envisage an Irish recession.[10] The country's financial sector has mostly steered clear of sub-prime lending, and most of the population has behaved more prudently than their counterparts in the United States. Ireland's savings rate has remained high, and the withdrawal of housing equity is still low. This should reduce the pain of falling housing prices. The new generation in Ireland also has stayed in the country and demanded higher standards of public life rather than emigrating, in contrast to the past.[11]

Irelan's slump in many respects is a microcosm of the challenges facing countries such as the United States, Britain, and Spain. It is not just about the global credit crunch, weak banks, or bearish stock markets. Rather, Ireland is at the tail end of a housing- and consumer-fueled boom—similar to that of the United States—and finds itself at the mercy of global trends such as inflation, wage-scale gaps, and increased competition from emerging economies.

Ireland's membership in the EU is effectively keeping the country afloat economically during the downturn. Without the implicit guarantee of EU loans, it is doubtful that the Irish government would be able to raise the €400 million weekly that is necessary to pay teachers' and nurses' salaries, and all the rest. In those circumstances, many Lisbon Treaty voters were understandably reluctant to risk transforming Ireland's relationship with Europe.

Most economists agree that the economic outlook for Ireland is good. Robert E. Kennedy of the University of Michigan predicts that Ireland's economy will bounce back from the credit crunch and start to outperform its major European rivals over the next ten years.[12] Rossa White, another economist, foresees the Irish economy returning to growth in 2010 and an expansion of 4 percent in 2011. Consumer spending could increase 1.5 percent as real incomes stabilize and precautionary saving eases, and export growth is likely to quicken as Ireland feels the effect of a worldwide economic recovery.[13]

Conclusion

EU funding essentially helped to stop—and, indeed, reverse—the hemorrhaging of people out of Ireland by aiding the economic turnaround. Certainly, other factors contributed to the transformation of the Irish economic climate: a youthful population and rapidly expanding labor supply; substantial inward investment inflows; the pursuit of pragmatic and innovative government policies; a social-partnership approach to economic development; an openness to international trade in goods and services; and an emphasis on education and technological innovation. But the significance of strategic deployment of EU Structural Funds and Cohesion Fund cannot be understated. The EU funding provided the scaffolding for the rest of the investment framework.

The Irish people have a strong allegiance to their country and their heritage. Had there been more prosperity in Ireland in the past, emigration would not have been such a major phenomenon. Today, young Irish are staying home. They took part in the economic growth of their country, and they found work in many sectors of the economy. Despite the worldwide economic crisis, economists predict that Ireland will rebound well.

The NAFTA countries have something to learn here. The Irish experience suggests that basic investments in education, training, and infrastructure are critical for the poor countries that have been brought into partnerships for strategic and economic reasons. Any redesign of NAFTA or rethinking of North American relations needs to make room for such policies.

Addendum: A Young Irish Voice

As the body of the chapter text discusses, for generations Ireland was more of an emigrant country than an immigrant country, watching its population decline. The Irish diaspora flowed to the United Kingdom and the United States, and then to other parts of Europe, always in search of better economic opportunity. As the benefits of EU membership took hold, emigration slowed, then ended. The attitude of one young Irish adult who visited the United States during the 2007–2008 academic year is illustrative:

There is a term used in Ireland to describe my generation, and that is "the Celtic Tiger cubs." This term is often very accurate because the majority of my generation has felt the benefits of Ireland's recent successes and economic boom.

I come from a large family. I am one of five children who grew up in Dublin in the late 1980s and 1990s. My family was not the typical Irish family, as both of my parents had been to college, and all of their families had been to college. Both sides of my family had come from a relatively wealthy background, and so they had all been sent to private school and then on to college. As such, we were not part of the stereotypical Irish poor families. We were lucky enough to have all been well educated and to have been given far more opportunities than many others in Ireland around that time.

I am the third of five children in my immediate family. My parents have been married for twenty-five years, and the eldest in my family is 23 years old. We are all very close in age, and as a corollary to that, we fought a lot when we were younger but now are extremely close due to our close ages. My sister Jenny is in London doing a master's in competition law; my brother Ross is in Dublin studying hotel and catering management; I am in America for the year through the international program of my law degree in University

College Dublin; and my younger brother and sister, who are twins, are both in the middle of their leaving certificate, the exams that gain one admittance into university. They are aiming for architecture and medicine, respectively. All of my family attended private secondary schools in Dublin and have benefited from this sacrifice that my parents made for us. We all actively engaged in sports and were involved in much more that just the classroom work. My school in particular had so many extracurricular activities that it would have been more difficult only to attend school and participate in none of them than to take part. My brothers attended a school that my dad's family has been attending for the last 150 years, and they both loved that school.

I believe that we were and still are very lucky children, as my parents are very open to us trying new things and to traveling the world and they have given us every opportunity possible to enjoy ourselves while we are young. I have never been stopped from reaching my goals, and I think that my parents' readiness to help us to achieve our best is in part due to the fact that they, too, had the opportunities that we have today, but as I said, they were not in the majority of the country in their generation who could say that. However, I believe that as a result of my generation being more prosperous and being enabled to travel more and learn more and live more, that will trickle down to our children as it did in my family, and the next generation will have the opportunities to travel and see the world and become more enlightened and well-rounded people.

I am abroad this year in California, and many people have asked me if I think I will return to America after I finish my degree. The honest answer is that while I want to travel a lot, I could not live outside of Ireland indefinitely. My sister is also out of Ireland this year. However, the fact that I come from such a close family has led all seven of us to conclude that we all want everyone to live in Ireland—even more specifically, in Dublin. This is a choice, and a viable choice, that is open to us but would not have been years ago. We are lucky enough that we can create lives for ourselves in Ireland. However, I am enticed by the idea of moving abroad for maybe four or five years and working very hard for those years and then returning to Ireland. All of the intentions to stay in Ireland may not hold strong forever, but I do not believe that I will live outside of Ireland indefinitely. The quality of life is too good; the people are the people I grew up with, and while the weather is not great, it is "Irish" weather. Being away from home seems only to reinforce one's sense of patriotism, and that has definitely occurred with me. Among my closest friends, none of them plan to move out of Ireland. Many have the same plans to travel and see the world before they begin to work in earnest, but they have the ultimate goal of settling in Ireland. While the climate may seem not so strong economically, the housing market in Ireland is still so strong that this is a major concern for most young people in my generation. There is a real concern that they will not be able to buy their own homes, as the price of houses seems to continue to skyrocket. And yet I do not believe this concern is enough to make my generation to leave.

None of my family moved away from Ireland, and as such that makes my family quite a rare family in Ireland. A lot of my parents' friends moved to America, Hong Kong, Singapore, and even Australia in search of better lives. However, while they did all make their fortunes abroad, they have all more recently returned to Ireland, as it not only is their homeland but also has become a lot more advanced and welcoming than when they left. Many of these people who did leave Ireland have sent their children back to Ireland to be educated, as they wish to instill a sense of their Irish heritage in them from an early age.

Growing up in Ireland in the 1980s and 1990s for a lot of people meant that if they were close to Northern Ireland, they would have been directly affected by the troubles in the north. I can honestly say that I never noticed the troubles in the north at all; maybe that was due to where I lived or due to my own ignorance and the fact that as a child I lived entirely in my own world. The only time I became aware of the troubles would have been in school when our teachers would bring certain events to light and ask us to discuss them. I was fortunate in that respect, but I know that many people from my generation felt the troubles affect them in many ways. There were border patrols between the Republic and Northern Ireland, and if one intended to go to the north, [he or she] would be searched by men with guns and have to pass through several stations before [he or she was] allowed to continue the journey.

The effect of the Irish economy on my generation has been profound. Of the twelve cousins on one side of my family, not one of them has any intention to leave Ireland. A few have already set up their families in Dublin, as the quality of life is as good as, if not better than, they can find abroad. There is, however, a large difference in my generation in relation to travel. My generation spends much of its earlier years traveling the world. It is now a phenomenon in Ireland that each year of college must be followed by a summer of travel in the United States, Canada, Europe, or Asia, while leaving the larger task of Australia until they have finished their undergraduate degree.

The Celtic Tiger's effect on the young people in Ireland can be seen in most areas of life, and one example that shows this change most is in the rates of people who now attend university. Of my friends' parents, only a very few attended college, but not one of my friends today is not in college or in a training course of some degree. The mentality of the Irish has changed in this respect. Many more people do attend college; the workforce is more highly educated and has traveled more, leading to a more diversified work-force. While university is free in Ireland, there are obviously many other costs associated with attending university, and those costs in the past would have prevented many people from seeking higher education. But due to the . . . increased wealth of the majority of the population, attendance levels in universities has increased hugely.

In saying all of this, it cannot be forgotten that all this prosperity has had an effect on my generation that cannot be described as beneficial. There is selfishness among my generation, the generation that has had it all too easy and has never had to work for what they get. The older generations always say that the younger generations have it easier; however, it is very true of my generation. There is a mentality among many in my generation that it is OK not to aim for anything, not to work hard, and not to try too hard because at the end of the day "Daddy" will help them. This has led to a huge number of my generation being idle and becoming even more spoiled due to the fact that their parents continue to work so hard to give them what they want and so never see that all their work is in vain. Now, that is not to say that all Irish people of my generation are lazy. On the contrary: Many people feel a pressure to emulate the success of their parents and to . . . prove that they are also capable of making a success of their lives.

The prosperity in Ireland can be seen everywhere you go, whether it . . . is [in] better public transport, or that more people in your university drive cars, or that more go abroad on their summer holidays. Wherever you see it, it is undeniable that my generation, the "cubs," have benefited from all this success. However, we can only hope that this does not ruin the chances of the cubs by having created greedy, spoiled, lazy cubs. I, for one, am very aware of all that we have that generations before us did not and am painfully aware that this boom in Ireland has slowed down, and that it may not last forever. As such, I am committed to working hard to give the next generation the wonderful opportunities the generations before mine worked so hard to create for us.

6

The Failed Enforcement Approach

"There Ain't No Reason to Treat Them Like Animals"

Instead of addressing the contemporary causes of undocumented Mexican migration that are linked to NAFTA and globalization, the United States has addressed the symptoms of the challenge by adopting an enforcement-only approach. That approach has failed miserably, because the social and economic forces behind undocumented migration are stronger than even the militarization of the border can withstand. Instead of trying to understand why the flow persists, the phenomenon has been answered with more fencing, expanding the Border Patrol, and stepping up U.S. Immigration and Customs Enforcement (ICE) raids.[1] While more border crossers have died and more families have been separated as a result of these policies, the tide of undocumented migration has continued. In the process, the United States has spent billions of dollars on this enforcement-only approach. Along with the increased number of undocumented immigrants, smuggling, trafficking, and sales of fraudulent identity documents have surged. The failure of the current U.S. immigration-enforcement approach to undocumented migration demands that we consider alternative solutions.

Hard Dollars Spent

In response to the outcry over undocumented migration, billions of dollars have been poured into enforcement in recent years. The Immigration Policy Center of the American Immigration Law Foundation, has itemized several of these expenditures:

- The annual budget of the U.S. Border Patrol, $1.6 billion, represents an increase of 332 percent between 1993 and 2006. The number of Border Patrol agents in 2007 was about fifteen thousand, an increase of 276 percent since 1993, and the number is to increase to twenty thousand by 2009.
- U.S. Customs and Border Protection (CBP), the parent agency of the Border Patrol within the Department of Homeland Security (DHS), has seen its budget grow from $6 billion in 2004 to $9.3 billion in 2008. Its expected budget in 2009 is $10.9 billion.
- The budget for the ICE has grown from $3.7 billion 2004 to $5.1 billion in 2008; its expected budget in 2009 is $5.7 billion.
- The DHS has completed 670 miles of fencing along the U.S.–Mexican border by the end of 2008. The fencing was facilitated in part by the REAL ID Act of 2005, which authorized the DHS to waive any and all "legal requirements" such as environmental laws that might stand in the way of fence construction. The Secure Fence Act of 2006 directed DHS to build 850 miles of additional fencing along the southern border. The construction of this fencing is tremendously expensive yet questionable in its effectiveness. The U.S. Army Corps of Engineers estimates that the cost of construction—not counting the cost of buying the land on which to build the fencing—is about $1.3 million per mile, although the first 9.5 miles of San Diego fence cost about $3 million per mile. Maintaining the fence for twenty-five years would cost from $16.4 million to $70 million per mile, depending on anticipated damage. So a fence along all 2,000 miles of the southwestern border would cost at least $2.5 billion to build, plus another $32.8 billion to $140 billion to maintain for twenty-five years.
- The DHS's Secure Border Initiative (SBI) relies heavily on so-called smart technology (such as thermal imaging, ground radar, and motion detectors) to detect unauthorized border crossings. The first stage was Project 28, a $20 million contract with Boeing Corporation to secure twenty-eight miles along a section of the Arizona border. But in March 2008, the U.S. Government Accountability Office (GAO) reported that the project did not meet the agency's expectation and would not be replicated.
- In response to policymakers who want to see stepped up interior enforcement along with border enforcement, several DHS efforts have been expanded, including ICE raids (discussed below). The E-Verify program is an Internet-based employment-verification sys-

tem administered by U.S. Citizenship and Immigration Services (USCIS), which is also within the DHS, and supported by the Social Security Administration to enable employers to determine whether employees are authorized to work. As of April 2008, about 61,000 of the nation's 7.4 million employers have registered for E-Verify, a voluntary program.[2] The GAO estimates that a mandatory E-Verify program could cost $765 million from 2009 to 2012 if only newly hired employees are reviewed through the program and $838 million if both newly hired and current employees are reviewed. The USCIS would have to increase its staff from 250 to 340 full-time personnel by 2012 to operate a mandatory E-Verify system. An independent review of E-Verify funded by the DHS concluded that the program was not effective and generally did not detect identity fraud that occurs when an employee presents borrowed, stolen, or counterfeit documents. The program also was found to increase discrimination against foreign-born employees who are authorized to work.

Tom Barry of the Center for International Policy has conducted a similar analysis of the costs of enforcement. He found that the overall DHS budget has increased steadily since its creation in 2003—rising from $35 billion to $47 billion in 2008. But the funds dedicated to immigration control and border security have increased disproportionately, doubling in size, while total DHS funding increased by just a third. By way of comparison, the combined budgets of the CBP and the ICE in 2008 were 80 percent larger than the annual budget of the Environmental Protection Agency, and nearly $4 billion larger than the State Department's budget.

Barry also looked at the budgets of the Department of Justice and Department of Defense, which also have been expanded to cover the costs of the immigration crackdown. The Department of Justice does not provide a budget breakdown of what it spends for immigration enforcement, but immigration work is centered largely in its Executive Office for Immigration Review (EOIR), which houses immigration courts and the Board of Immigration Appeals (BIA), Civil Division, U.S. Attorneys, and U.S. Marshals Service. From 2001 to 2008, the EOIR budget increased 57 percent, to $249.2 million. New initiatives will allow the Department of Justice to hire forty federal marshals and nearly two hundred attorneys and judges to handle the flood of immigration cases as the DHS steps up its immigration enforcement. As part of a $100 million Southwest Border Enforcement initiative, the Department of Justice requested increases in the 2009 budgets of EIOR ($10 million), U.S. Attorneys ($8.4 million), and U.S. Marshals ($12.7 million). According to the Department of Justice, "Attorneys and paralegals are needed to respond to cross-border criminal activities and to the increases in immigration cases resulting from the substantial increases in Border Patrol agents and the U.S. government's overall effort to gain operational control of the border."[3]

The Department of Defense also takes part in immigration enforcement. Although the military is precluded by law from performing tasks of civilian law enforcement, the Pentagon plays a supportive role in counter-drug and immigration-control efforts. In 2006, President George Bush deployed six thousand National Guard in Operation Jump Start to support the Border Patrol in its surveillance operations. The National Guard's border mission has been covered by Department of Defense allocations ($708 million for 2006; $415 million for 2007; and $247 million for 2008) authorized by Congress.

Stepped-up immigration enforcement also imposes severe costs on the legal system, as immigration cases clog the courts. Consider the federal Court of Appeals in the western part of the country. Since 2002, the immigration caseload of the Ninth Circuit Court of Appeals has risen dramatically in response to the Department of Justice's directing what was then the Immigration and Naturalization Service (INS) to clear a backlog of appeals pending before the BIA. The BIA's rapid resolution of appeals, usually by denying relief, resulted in a staggering increase in appeals to the federal court. In 2001, the Ninth Circuit received more than 950 immigration appeals, amounting to 9 percent of its caseload. In 2007, there were more than 4,000 new immigration cases out of a total of 12,892 new filings in the court, which means that immigration cases represented more than 30 percent of the total filings in the court. In addition, the percentage of these immigration-appeals cases filed without counsel remains consistently in the 35–40 percent range. From 2000 to 2005, more than 50 percent of all circuit court immigration cases were in the Ninth Circuit.

These are not meritless cases that go to the federal courts. The enforcement-only approach to the immigration challenge has resulted in overzealous handling of cases that have made their way into the administrative hearings process. The prominent conservative Judge Richard Posner of the Seventh Circuit Court of Appeals has blasted the ineptitude of the BIA:

> This tension between judicial and administrative adjudicators is not due to judicial hostility to the nation's immigration policies or to a misconception of the proper standard of judicial review of administrative decisions. It is due to the fact that the adjudication of these cases at the administrative level has fallen below the minimum standards of legal justice. Whether this is due to resource constraints or to other circumstances beyond the Board's and the Immigration Court's

control, we do not know, though we note that the problem is not of recent origin. All that is clear is that it cannot be in the interest of the immigration authorities, the taxpayer, the federal judiciary, or citizens concerned with the effective enforcement of the nation's immigration laws for removal orders to be routinely nullified by the courts, and that the power of correction lies in the Department of Homeland Security, which prosecutes removal cases, and the Department of Justice, which adjudicates them in its Immigration Court and Board of Immigration Appeals.

Thus, in spite of intensive spending on enforcement, things have not improved. The undocumented population in the United States has roughly tripled, from an estimated 3.5 million in 1990 to more than 12 million today. In short, the United States is spending huge enforcement dollars that are not effective in reducing undocumented immigration, while resources are being diverted from other important government functions.

Employer Sanctions

Besides border enforcement, interior enforcement via enforcement of sanctions on employers has been stepped up. The Immigration Reform and Control Act (IRCA) of 1986 contained the first federal employer-sanctions law making the hiring of undocumented workers unlawful. In the past few years, an upsurge in enforcement of sanctions on employers has been evident. More than twelve hundred workers were arrested in highly publicized raids on Swift and Company in December 2006,[4] and about a year earlier, a complaint against Wal-Mart resulted in a multimillion-dollar fine.[5] The increase in enforcement was coordinated with President Bush's call for a guest-worker program, seemingly as a tradeoff for support from enforcement-minded legislators for the guest-worker proposal.

The efficacy of employer sanctions is debatable. In addition to the many social and economic phenomena that historically cause undocumented migration to the United States from Mexico, we now know that NAFTA and the effects of globalization create great migration pressures on Mexicans. The push–pull factors are strong. As the Mexican consul from Douglas, Arizona, once noted, the border could be "mined" and migrants would still attempt to cross. Consider Ismael Rojas, who left his family in Mexico many times over a twenty-five-year period to work in the United States as an undocumented worker. In his words, "You can either abandon your children to make money to take care of them, or you can stay with your children and watch them live in misery. Poverty makes us leave our families."[6] Using employer sanctions to address the phenomenon of Mexican migration in this context of poverty and globalization is doomed to fail. Arresting and deporting workers for working without authorization as a way to discourage them from coming here for a better life is doomed to fail in the face of such grave economic and social forces. We also need to think seriously about whether we can really justify punishing workers who are here because of the effects of many U.S. economic policies.

The other problem with employer sanctions is the discrimination that results. Long before the recent evaluation of the discriminatory effects of the E-Verify program, discrimination was rampant. In its final report to Congress on employer sanctions in 1990, the GAO estimated that of 4.6 million employers in the United States, 346,000 admitted applying IRCA's verification requirements only to job applicants who had a "foreign" accent or appearance. Another 430,000 employers hired only applicants born in the United States or did not hire applicants with temporary work documents in order to be cautious.[7]

Direct and indirect recruitment of Mexican workers has continued in spite of the implementation of employer-sanctions legislation in 1986. In 2001, researchers continued to identify organized groups of farm-labor contractors who travel to Mexican cities and towns, where they offer loans and work guarantees to convince potential farm workers to cross the border into the United States. The process involves well-organized networks of contractors and contractors' agents representing major U.S. agricultural companies. The headhunters are themselves often Mexicans who recruit in their own hometowns and farming communities, where earning the trust of eager farm hands is not difficult. One of the contractors' favorite tactics to attract workers is to offer them loans to help pay off debts, coupled with a pledge to find work for the person north of the border. Due to the lack of willing farm hands in the United States, many U.S. companies rely on these networks of recruiters.

The impulse to punish employers for hiring undocumented workers is derived, in part, from the theory that this will discourage such hiring, thus drying up jobs for the undocumented and discouraging them from migrating. The main problem with this theory is that employers really need more workers from abroad. The impending retirement of U.S. baby boomers and the increased employment opportunities in many sectors of the economy are clear. President Bush recognized the situation when he proposed a guestworker plan. While we should put pressure on employers to pay all of their workers a fair wage and provide proper work conditions, that is quite a different question from whether we should punish fair and well-meaning employers who treat their workers right but who are relying on an undocumented workforce. The empirical evidence supports their claim that they need these workers, but our immigration policies are not facilitating their efforts to hire workers so that they can stay in business. Employer sanctions are counter-productive in that regard.

Death Traps along the Border

Perhaps the most disturbing aspect of the immigration debate in Congress is the virtually unanimous support for more fencing and the build-up of the Border Patrol. This militarization of a border is troubling enough when we pause to remember that this is a border that we share with a friendly, peaceful neighbor and trading partner. However, the strategy becomes indefensible when we realize that the policies have led to unconscionable death traps along the Mexican–U.S. border.

A year after President Bill Clinton took office in January 1993, the Border Patrol embarked on a strategy of "control through deterrence" that has proved deadly. During the presidential campaign, Clinton was asked what he proposed to do about "illegal immigration." He had no plan, declaring that "immigration is the most complex issue facing the nation."[8] Early in 1993, his administration's Office of National Drug Control Policy commissioned a study of new methods to increase border security from Sandia National Laboratories, a government-supported federal facility devoted to research for the military. The study recommended that the Border Patrol focus on preventing illegal entries by deterring them rather than trying to apprehend the undocumented after they entered. The Sandia report recommended various measures to increase the difficulty of illegal entry, including the installation of multiple physical barriers, the use of advanced electronic surveillance equipment, and so forth.[9]

Around the same time, in El Paso, Texas, the regional Border Patrol supervisor Sylvestre Reyes (who is now a U.S. congressman) had his own ideas about what to do. He stationed his agents in closely spaced vehicles, right along the Rio Grande, and kept them there continuously, thereby intimidating would-be illegal entrants from even trying to cross. With only halfhearted approvals from his superiors in Washington, Reyes implemented his strategy, which was called Operation Blockade, and it had apparently dramatic short-term results; apprehensions of undocumented aliens plummeted within the El Paso sector, suggesting that migrants were being discouraged from entering.[10] This outcome was noticed by the media and Congress, and the INS soon found itself under great pressure to replicate what was immediately dubbed the "successful" El Paso experiment along other segments of the border, beginning with San Diego County. This set off a chain of policy decisions that led to the establishment of "concentrated enforcement" operations along other parts of the border. The deadliest was Operation Gatekeeper.

Operation Gatekeeper was one of several operations that resulted from the Clinton administration's commitment to a new, aggressive enforcement strategy for the Border Patrol. In August 1994, Commissioner Doris Meissner of the INS approved a new national strategy for the Border Patrol.[11] The plan relied on a vision of "prevention through deterrence," in which a "decisive number of enforcement resources [would be brought] to bear in each major entry corridor," and the Border Patrol would "increase the number of agents on the line and make effective use of technology, raising the risk of apprehension high enough to be an effective deterrent."[12] The specific regional enforcement operations that resulted included (1) Operation Blockade (later renamed Hold the Line), which commenced in September 1993 in the greater El Paso area; (2) Operation Gatekeeper, which commenced in October 1994 south of San Diego; (3) Operation Safeguard, which also commenced in October 1994 in Arizona; and (4) Operation Rio Grande, which commenced in August 1997 in Brownsville, Texas. The idea was to block traditional entry and smuggling routes with border-enforcement personnel and physical barriers.[13] By cutting off traditional crossing routes, the strategy sought to deter migrants—or, at least, to channel them into terrain less suited to crossing and more conducive to apprehension.[14] To carry out the strategy, the Border Patrol was to concentrate personnel and resources in areas with the highest number of crossings of undocumented aliens, increase the time agents spent on border-control activities, increase use of physical barriers, and carefully consider the mix of technology and personnel needed to control the border.[15]

In the San Diego sector, efforts would be concentrated on the popular fourteen-mile section of the border beginning at the Pacific Ocean (Imperial Beach) and stretching eastward.[16] That stretch was the focus of some resources before Gatekeeper. Steel fencing and bright lighting were already in place in sections of the corridor, erected in part with the assistance of the U.S. military.[17] Yet because of the persistent traffic of undocumented entrants along this corridor, phase one of Gatekeeper continued to concentrate on increased staffing and resources along the fourteen-mile area.[18]

In implementing its national strategy beginning in 1994, the INS made a key assumption about its "prevention through deterrence" approach: "Alien apprehensions will decrease as [the] Border Patrol increases control of the border."[19] In other words, the INS anticipated that as the show of force escalated through the increasing of agents, lighting, and fencing, migrants would be discouraged from entering without inspection, so the number of apprehensions naturally would decline. In fact, the Border Patrol predicted that within five years a substantial drop in apprehension rates border-wide would result.[20] The deterrence would be so great that "many will consider it futile to continue to attempt illegal entry."[21] These assumptions and predictions have not been borne out.

Apprehension data confirm that what Operation Gatekeeper actually achieved was to move the undocumented foot traffic out of the public eye. Empirical research demonstrates that undocumented Mexicans keep trying to enter until they are successful. In sending communities that have been restudied since Gatekeeper began, most prospective migrants "said that they would only consider changing their destination within the United States (avoiding California, for example) rather than forgoing migration altogether." Migrants have learned quickly to avoid the heavily fortified areas and now cross "in places where their probability of apprehension is no higher than it used to be."[22] Thus, border-enforcement strategies initiated in 1994 were "affecting migration patterns, but not preventing unauthorized entry."[23]

The ineffectiveness of the INS to "control the border" after several years of a new strategy would be easy enough to dismiss in a "So what else is new?" attitude were it not for a dark side of border enforcement that resulted from Operation Gatekeeper. Certainly, southwestern border control always had an evil, racist aspect with its targeting of Mexican migration during a thirty-year period in which Mexicans made up far less than half of the undocumented population in the United States.[24] However, the tragedy of Gatekeeper is the direct link of its prevention through deterrence strategy to a horrendous rise in the number of deaths of border crossers who were forced to attempt entry over terrain that even the INS knew presented "mortal danger" because of extreme weather conditions and rugged terrain.[25]

As Operation Gatekeeper was implemented to close the Imperial Beach corridor, the border-crossing traffic moved east. Frustrated crossers moved first to Brown Field and Chula Vista and subsequently to the eastern sections of the San Diego sector.[26] Before Gatekeeper began in 1994, crossers were just as likely to make a second try in the westernmost part of the sector, but that changed very quickly. By January 1995, only 14 percent were making a second try near Imperial Beach. The illicit border traffic had moved "into unfamiliar and unattractive territory."[27] Clearly, the increasing number of deaths from dehydration and exposure was the result of concentrated efforts to block the normal, easier crossing points, forcing migrants "to take greater risks in less populated areas" as migration was redirected rather than deterred by Gatekeeper.[28]

The death statistics are revealing. In 1994, 23 migrants died along the California–Mexico border. Of these, 2 died of hypothermia or heat stroke, and 9 died from drowning. By 1998, the annual total was 147 deaths: 71 from hypothermia or heat stroke and 52 from drowning. Figures for 1999 followed this unfortunate trend, and in 2000, 84 were heat-stroke or hypothermia casualties. The total death count along the entire border for the year 2000 was 499. Of these, 100 died crossing the desert along the Sonora–Arizona border.[29] Since 2000, the number of such deaths along the border has averaged 300–400 per year.[30] Nearly 500 border crossers died in 2005, and more than 450 bodies were found in 2009.[31]

Why the radical surge in deaths? The new routes are death traps. The correlation between increasing deaths and Gatekeeper's closure of the westernmost corridors is clear. The chief of the Border Patrol stressed that, although the distances migrants had to traverse in places like Texas were enormous, California had the "more difficult terrain." In fact, the San Diego and El Centro sectors encompass three of the four places considered by the Border Patrol "the most hazardous areas"—that is, East San Diego County, the Imperial Desert, and the All-American Canal. The fourth is Kennedy County in Texas.[32] The INS recognized the challenges of the new routes: rugged canyons and high desert; remote, desolate stretches; and risks of dehydration and exposure.[33] However, the fourteen-mile area from Imperial Beach to the base of the Otay Mountain, the less rigorous original route, is "easy terrain and [has] gentle climbs." A typical crossing there lasted only ten to fifteen minutes from point of crossing to pick up. The eastern mountain route crossings can last anywhere from twelve hours to four days.[34] The Otay Mountains are "extremely rugged, and include steep, often precipitous, canyon walls and hills reaching 4,000 feet." Extreme temperatures that range from freezing cold in the winter to searingly hot in the summer can kill the unprepared traveler.[35] The Tecate Mountains are full of steep-walled canyons and rocky peaks. Nighttime temperatures can drop into the twenties, and snow can fall to altitudes as low as eight hundred feet. From mid-October to mid-April, there is a greater than 50 percent probability of below-freezing temperatures.[36] The All-American Canal parallels the border for forty-four of its eight-five miles in Imperial County. It is unfenced and unlighted, twenty-one feet deep, and nearly as wide as a football field. It has strong currents and is one of the most polluted rivers in the United States.[37] Sadly, Border Patrol agents acknowledge that the number of bodies recovered is only an indication of a much larger death toll; many bodies simply have not been discovered in the rugged territory.[38]

Operation Gatekeeper has not stopped the flow of border crossers, but it has made border crossing more dangerous. Gatekeeper and the increased militarization of the border ironically have curtailed one thing: circularity. Mexican seasonal workers commonly traveled back and forth across the border because their families often remained in Mexico. But now the number of undocumented migrants who actually want to return to Mexico has been reduced. Given the difficulty in crossing into the United States, once many undocumented people arrive, they remain to work and may even look for family members to join them. This has contributed to the increase in the undocumented population in the United States.[39]

ICE Raids

As the backlash against undocumented immigrants has heightened, raids and other internal enforcement efforts have been stepped up by the ICE. The methods have included worksite operations, home invasions, and even monitoring of public schools. In the process, U.S. citizens and lawful permanent residents have been detained along with undocumented immigrants, resulting in a multitude of lawsuits against the DHS. And while several thousand deportable aliens have been arrested as a result of these efforts, the totals are a far cry from the estimated 12 million undocumented immigrants living in the country. We really have to wonder whether such tactics are worth the effort. Consider some of the operations that have taken place.

Stillmore, Georgia

I began the Introduction to this volume with a short description of the ICE raid in Stillmore, Georgia, the Friday before Labor Day weekend in 2006. The impact was evident, underscoring just how vital the undocumented immigrants were to the local economy. Trailer parks lie abandoned. The poultry plant scrambled to replace more than half of its workforce. Business dried up at stores where Mexican laborers once lined up to buy food, beer, and cigarettes. The community of about a thousand people became little more than a ghost town.

In May 2006, the ICE launched Operation Return to Sender, an aggressive effort to rapidly increase the deportation of undocumented immigrants who had violated removal orders. At this time, ICE officials also began discussing enforcement issues with the Stillmore-based Crider poultry plant. Stillmore is a quiet community with few small businesses, a gas station, and two convenience stores intended to service local employees of the Crider plant, the largest employer in a community with roughly a thousand inhabitants. The plant employed slightly over nine hundred people, about seven hundred of whom had work-documentation discrepancies when the ICE began discussions with Crider's senior management in mid-2006.

At the state level, the immigration debate in Georgia was intensifying. The state attracted attention after a federal report noted that Georgia had the fastest-growing population of undocumented immigrants in the country.[40] In early 2006, the state legislature passed what many considered to be some of the farthest-reaching immigration legislation in the nation: the Georgia Security and Immigration Compliance Act. The legislation has been likened to California's Proposition 187 and includes several strict requirements to curb immigration into the state and the hiring of undocumented workers. These provisions include requiring employers to use the E-Verify a federal database system to check employees' documentation; corrections officials to notify the state of undocumented people who were incarcerated; and recipients of many medical and welfare benefits to provide proof of citizenship.[41]

In the summer months preceding the raid, the Crider plant began firing employees and pressuring others to resign when it suspected improper work documentation. ICE officials swiftly cracked down at summer's end. The agency took the unusual approach of researching employees' home addresses and raided several homes shortly before midnight on Friday, September 1, the first day of the Labor Day weekend. The ICE's Labor Day weekend raid launched what became a series of raids lasting three weeks in the Stillmore area and the surrounding counties. The Stillmore raid focused mainly on male employees from the Crider plant, leaving many female and child family members stranded. Many remaining family members fled into the nearby woods in the hope of avoiding detection. There was one report of a family hiding in a tree for two nights to avoid capture.[42]

Local residents witnessed the events, as ICE officials raided local homes and trailer parks, forcing many members of the community out of Stillmore. Officials were seen stopping motorists and breaking into homes, and there were even reports of officials threatening people with tear gas.[43] Bystanders imagined "Nazi Germany" as the disturbing roundup was implemented.[44]

The Crider poultry plant was the primary employer in the town of a thousand. Other local businesses complained that they faced a severe drop in business in the weeks after the raids. One local caregiver in the community, a legal resident, took in a 2-year-old boy, a U.S. citizen born to undocumented Mexican parents, because his mother feared she could no longer sufficiently provide for him. The caregiver noted that all of her other customers had disappeared after the raid, having been forced to leave Stillmore.[45]

San Rafael, California

On March 6, 2007, ICE officials raided the small communities of San Rafael and Novato in Marin County, arresting roughly thirty undocumented immigrants. This raid was also part of ICE's Operation Return to Sender, the federal effort to crack down on immigrants who had stayed past their deportation orders. ICE officials parked several vans outside apartment complexes before dawn on the Tuesday morning of the raids. Armed with warrants, many bearing dated or incorrect information, the police stormed homes and began arresting violators, regardless of whether they were named in the original warrant. Many children were handcuffed along with their parents. The San Rafael raid drew criticism at the local and national level because of the nature and timing of the operation.

The San Rafael raid became a national symbol of the negative effects raids have on children. Juan Rodriguez, principal of Bahia Vista Elementary School, noted that on a typical day the school might have eight to ten children absent, but seventy-seven children were absent the day of the raid.[46] Another local principal, Kathryn Gibney of San Pedro Elementary, testified before a congressional committee on the effect of the ICE raids on her school's children and their families. Stressing the level of fear the ICE raids generated in the community, Gibney noted that families kept kids at home and in hiding, describing an increased level of paranoia in the community. Gibney recounted instructions from the wife of man who had just been arrested to her daughter to pack a backpack and leave it by the door. If the child came home and found no one present, she was to take the backpack to her aunt's house and stay with her in case her mother had also been arrested and deported.[47] Gibney further lamented the long-term effects of the raids, describing a frightened community with children asking teachers whether police would be coming to school, as well as "higher absenteeism, lower test scores and increased counseling for her students. . . . [ICE] left behind them a trail of fear."[48]

A young boy, Kebin Reyes, a U.S. citizen, symbolizes one of the ICE's more egregious actions. Kebin, who was six on the day of the raid, was seized along with his father, Noe Reyes, who did not have citizenship, and held at an ICE processing center in San Francisco. Kebin and his father were held for more than ten hours with only bread and water. Noe Reyes's requests to contact a family member to take Kebin home were repeatedly denied. Eventually, an uncle was able to pick up Kebin and remove him from the processing center. The American Civil Liberties Union filed a lawsuit on Kebin's behalf.[49]

Mayor Alberto Boro of San Rafael criticized the raid's effect on the entire community. Boro was particularly disturbed by the broken relationship between local law enforcement and San Rafael's immigrant community. He criticized federal officials for identifying themselves simply as police, noting that this caused confusion within the community that thought local law enforcement was responsible for the raids. He noted that the raid had resulted in a drop in calls to local law-enforcement agencies and signaled a heightened level of mistrust of police within the community.[50]

New Bedford, Massachusetts

In March 2007, nearly 500 ICE officials descended on the small southern New England community of New Bedford, Massachusetts. ICE officials targeted the local Michael Bianco plant, a leather-goods manufacturer that had made goods for Coach, Rockport, Timberland, and other brands.[51] Recently, however, the factory had contracted with the government to produce goods for military operations in Iraq. Officials arrested 361 factory employees during the raid.

As with other, larger raids, the event split families and underscored the negative effects the raids have on communities. Many of Bianco's employees were women, creating a crisis in caring for their children. Roughly a hundred children were stranded with babysitters and other caregivers when their mothers were seized during the raid.[52] The majority of those arrested were moved to detention centers halfway across the country, in Texas. Eventually, about sixty employees were released on humanitarian grounds, such as Rosa Herrara who was eight and a half months pregnant at the time of her arrest.[53] Representatives from the Massachusetts State Department of Social Services went to Texas to lobby for the release of twenty-one detainees who were parents of children who had been left behind in New Bedford. Additional pleas from Governor Deval Patrick and two U.S. senators had to be made before the ICE released a handful of detainees back to Massachusetts so they could care for their children.[54] A seven-month-old infant who had been nursing became dehydrated after her mother's arrest; the baby lacked milk and needed urgent medical care.[55]

In communities across the country where raids occurred, local churches often provided safe haven and advocacy for the affected families. The National Council of La Raza released a report in late 2007, *Paying the Price: The Impact of Immigration Raids on America's Children*, documenting the effects of ICE raids, including community response, and used the events in New Bedford as part of its case study. The report noted a common theme throughout towns where raids had occurred: the use of local churches as a resource for affected communities. In New Bedford, St. James and Our Lady of Guadalupe became gathering places and a refuge for those affected. The report pointed out that in the short term, the church provided a recognizable meeting point that was central to the lives of members within the Latino community and was able to provide quick, short-term relief without being slowed by bureaucratic gathering of information or fear of offending partner organizations. In the long term, however, the churches were ill equipped and limited by small staffs to meet the long-term needs of immigrant communities.[56]

The La Raza study also analyzed the emotional and mental side effects on children. While the long-term effects of the raids are still unraveling, psychologists have already observed and are concerned about long-term depression and other mental illness in family members. Psychologists have observed a level of fear among children resulting from separation from one or both parents. Children feared leaving the parent who was not seized and questioned their parents' feelings for them. The report found that because younger children do not think in conceptual terms of citizen versus non-citizen, they translated the temporary parental absence as abandonment. Parents also noticed changes in behavior, such as children becoming more fearful and sometimes even more aggressive. One parent repeated that her child had feared that her father "love[ed] money more than he loves me."[57]

Postville, Iowa

One of the largest immigration raids in U.S. history occurred in April 2008 in the small Midwestern town of Postville, Iowa. Postville represents the quintessential American melting pot in a community with a population of roughly twenty-six hundred people. The community houses a mix of Hasidic Jews, who originally moved to Postville to open a kosher meatpacking plant. They work alongside immigrant workers from Mexico and parts of Central American who staff the plant, along with other residents, including descendants of German Lutheran migrants. The raid occurred at the kosher meat plant Agriprocessors Inc., the largest employer in town, and one of the largest in northeastern Iowa. The ICE seized more than four hundred undocumented workers, including eighteen juveniles.[58]

Agriprocessors Inc. employed approximately 970 workers, 80 percent of whom were believed to have fraudulent identification.[59] After the raid, both Agriprocessors Inc. and the entire Postville community were in recovery mode. The company brought in a skeleton crew from New York to meet its staffing needs. Community residents observed the sudden drop in business and worried about the town's future. Postville is home to many Latino businesses, and in the days after the raids many storefronts posted signs in Spanish reading "closed."[60] Postville's Mayor Robert Penrod speculated on the effect of a possible closure of the Agriprocessors plant on the town, estimating that "two-thirds of the homes here will sit empty [and] 95% of downtown business . . . will dry up."[61] One witness to the effects of the ICE raid in Postville labeled the government strategy "criminal," as the women were made to wear restrictive, "humiliating [global positioning system] bracelets" while caring for their children, and hundreds of women and children were faced with the threat of being left "homeless and starving."[62]

As in other communities, the school system felt the immediate impact of the raids. The local school district estimated that 150–220 students from immigrant families were absent the day after the raid.[63] As in other communities, the Catholic church became a refuge for the local immigrant population. Sister Kathy Thrill, a nun in nearby Waterloo, where the detainees were being held at a local fairground, spoke out against the raids. She participated in an effort to collect donations for the affected families but noted the fear in the community. Many residents heard a story of someone who was stopped while shopping at a local Wal-Mart, and tales like these were scaring many families into hiding. Sister Thrill also spoke of her own apprehension as she got word of possible checkpoints set up by ICE officials while she was en route to deliver donated items to families.[64]

This huge raid also sparked criticism for the potential aftershocks on the American Jewish population who observes kosher dietary practice. Approximately a million American Jews follow kosher law. The Agriprocessors plant's slowdown likely affected the kosher meat industry; there were reports of increased meat prices and hoarding of food in the days following the raid.[65]

The May raid was not the first sign of trouble for Agriprocessors Inc. The company had been under scrutiny for numerous violations of environmental and labor laws and was on notice that there was an alleged methamphetamine lab being run from inside the plant.[66] By October 2008, Iowa Workforce Development had announced that it would levy nearly $10 million in fines against the company for alleged labor infractions. The next day, the former manager was arrested and charged with bank fraud, harboring undocumented immigrants for profit, and abetting document fraud and identity theft.[67]

Conclusion

Increased ICE raids, stepped-up border enforcement, and sanctions on employers have not reduced undocumented immigration to the United States. The failure of these harsh efforts must teach us something. The enforcement-only approach has resulted in human tragedy and the separation of families while undocumented workers continue to flow into the United States. This is a challenge that requires us to understand why workers come here and to address the challenge in a more sensible manner.

The inhumanity of the situation is apparent to many. As Tom Barry puts it, "We are wasting billions of dollars at home in what has become a war on immigrants. The collateral costs of this anti-immigrant crackdown—including labor shortages, families torn apart by deportations, overcrowded jails and detentions centers, deaths on the border, courts clogged with immigration cases, and divided communities—are also immense."[68] And after we get through this period of the "Great Immigration Panic," the *New York Times* mourns, "Someday, the country will recognize the true cost of its war on illegal immigration. We don't mean dollars, though those are being squandered by the billions. The true cost is to the national identity: the sense of who we are and what we value. It will hit us once the enforcement fever breaks, when we look at what has been done and no longer recognize the country that did it."[69]

Isn't it time that we come to our senses and realize that the enforcement-only approach has failed? Undocumented migration is the result of factors and phenomena way beyond the control of intimidation, guns, and militarization. The time to get smart has arrived; we must begin considering more creative approaches by understanding the forces at work.

7

Contemplating North American Integration and Other Alternatives

The failure of the current immigration enforcement strategy and the role that NAFTA has played in putting more pressure on Mexican migration demands that we look for alternative approaches to the challenge of undocumented Mexican migration. The enforcement-only approach to immigration that fails to address visa demands and a trade policy that has helped to dry up work for poor workers in Mexico are essentially working at cross-purposes. Understanding the effects of NAFTA and other aspects of the globalized economy provides us with the foundation to develop a better approach to the flow of Mexican workers to the United States and the challenges that industry and agriculture face in Mexico. The responses to date have failed to address the social and economic needs of migrants. They also fail to take notice of demographic changes in the U.S. workforce. Recognizing that the United States actually needs immigrant workers—even those who are low skilled and paid low wages—also is good reason to consider a European Union–style approach to labor migration, which has benefited nations of Europe.

One consideration would be to transform the United States, Mexico, and Canada into a North American Union. NAFTA can form the preliminary basis for this integration, but with modifications that advanced a true partnership among the three countries. The idea would be to promote the general welfare of the workers of each nation, as well as the welfare of the corporations that employ them.

In essence, North American countries need to develop a new vision of their relationships and of their borders. That vision must consider closely the forces of globalization on their borders. And the vision needs to be formed with an understanding of the social, economic, and political strategic needs of the region, as well as those of each nation.

Investing in Mexico

The United States and Canada need to make serious investments in the economy and infrastructure of Mexico. In the EU, wealthy nations invested heavily in poor regions to prevent mass migration; that worked. Economic development in Mexico is often cited as the real way to stop undocumented migration.[1] The idea is that economic development would create more jobs, and the availability of more jobs would provide fewer reasons for Mexicans to come to the United States to find work.[2]

Some may argue that my call for investment in Mexico already was attempted as part of NAFTA and that the attempt failed to reduce immigration pressures. But we need to be careful not to confuse what happened within the terms of NAFTA, which, as we saw, chose not to address migration, and what occurred during EU expansions where open labor migration was explicit. In fact, the terms of investment in Mexico under NAFTA were a far cry from the EU's investment in poor nations beyond the significant difference in scale.

Yes, the proponents of NAFTA argued that undocumented migration from Mexico would decrease because jobs would be created in Mexico under the agreement, reducing the need to leave. However, we know that did not happen. And yes, substantial U.S. investment did flow into Mexico, mostly to finance factories that manufacture automobiles, appliances, television sets, apparel, and the like. However, the Mexican government was then expected to invest billions in roads, schooling, sanitation, housing, and other needs to accommodate the new factories as they spread through the country. But that did not happen, so foreign factories congregated in the north, within three hundred miles of the American border, where some infrastructure already existed. Meanwhile, Mexican manufacturers, who once had been protected by tariffs on a host of products, were driven out of business as less expensive, higher-quality merchandise flowed into the country. Later, China, with its even cheaper labor, added to the pressure, luring away manufacturers and jobs. Mexican corn farmers suffered a similar fate because of U.S.-subsidized corn, and, of course, the financial crisis in Mexico of the 1990s did not help.[3]

In contrast, the EU assumes little about government spending on the part of economically weaker nations that join the union. The EU itself provided the huge subsidies for the improved services that entering countries such as Portugal, Spain, Greece, and Poland needed rather than leave financing to the relatively meager resources of those countries. The money is used not only for public investment but also to subsidize companies setting up operations in the entering countries and to support government budgets. For countries to converge economically, more than a trade agreement is required. NAFTA was a failed "shortcut to convergence" because it did not include the substance needed to succeed.[4]

Given the need to rethink the U.S.–Mexican border, U.S. investment in Mexico must be part of the strategy. The EU has been successful in integrating neighboring countries into its union by investing heavily in the candidate states. The EU investment policies that proved effective are instructive. To begin, the United States and Canada should consider comprehensive funding that covers all areas of Mexico's economy, as well as its social and political infrastructure. Such investments will ensure Mexican economic growth, as well as political and social stability and progress. Programs in Mexico should be funded that will employ people more efficiently within a given economic sector. When people are employed efficiently, the need for migration is reduced.

In Europe, the establishment of a European Social Fund moderated significant immigration from poor countries to wealthy nations. The fund boosted living standards in Spain, Portugal, and Ireland as those countries entered the EU.[5] The EU was able to reduce the volatility that would prey most heavily on weak economies. The key was to narrow the disparities in income between its rich and poor members.[6]

The United States and Canada can learn from the successes of EU investments in candidate countries. The two major policies that the United States and Canada should follow are (1) to invest in all areas of Mexico's economy and social and political infrastructure; and (2) to fund programs that help Mexico's economy and labor market become more efficient. Through such investments, the NAFTA countries all can benefit from an open border, an efficient labor force, and strong economic growth. But, as exemplified by the EU enlargements, an open-border policy works best when investments are focused on all areas of the economy and infrastructure. Such comprehensive investments are the best way to achieve economic growth and political and social stability and progress. Thus, to help candidate countries meet these goals most effectively, EU investments target all aspects of the economy and the country's infrastructure. PHARE (Poland and Hungary: Assistance for Restructuring Their Economies) covers administrative and political infrastructure, among other things; SAPARD (Special Accession Program for Agriculture and Rural Development) covers the agricultural sector; and ISPA (Instrument for Structural Policies for Pre-accession) funds environmental and transportation development. Such large-scale and all-inclusive funding ensures that no political, social, or economic sector of a country will lag behind and impede it from reaching EU standards.

Another aspect of EU investments that the United States and Canada should follow is the focus on funding programs that help promote an efficient labor force. In Romania, for example, the EU emphasized the need to restructure the agricultural sector. Romania has significant agricultural land that was historically farmed by families.[7] The EU felt that family farms lead to inefficient employment of people (whole families tending to one parcel).[8] The EU therefore attempted to change this aspect of Romanian agriculture and employ people more efficiently.[9] One of the main goals of SAPARD in Romania was to fund programs to develop and diversify economic activities within the agricultural sector to better employ people within the field.[10] Creating more diverse jobs in agriculture was intended to help better employ the rural population and curb migration to urban areas or other EU countries.[11] Investing in more efficient employment within certain economic sectors or regions therefore helps avoid unnecessary migration; it also creates a more efficient labor force and a stronger economy. Applied to Mexico, this approach would help the Mexican economy grow, likely reducing outmigration.

Consider Ireland's turnaround. As Chapter 5 shows, membership in the EU provided Ireland with the investments that bolstered its tourism, agriculture, and infrastructure. The average Irish person benefited greatly from the economic turnaround induced by EU-sponsored programs.

The EU approach has not gone unnoticed in North America. Former Mexican President Vicente Fox had urged all three NAFTA countries (especially the United States) to contribute to an analogous North American development fund, but fate rendered his timing bad, coming shortly before September 11, 2001.[12] Among other things, the funds would have been used for highways to bridge the three countries better, for development in rural parts of Mexico, and to improve the Mexican education system to expand opportunities for the next generation.[13] But after 9/11, Fox's proposals for investment and immigration reform were placed on the back burner.

Investment was part of the NAFTA debates. In fact, President Clinton favored the establishment of a North American Development Bank (NADBank). Resources were limited, however, and when the NADBank became operational, the mandate was limited to loans for environmental border projects.[14] Furthermore, NADBank's mandate is to lend at market rates of interest for "sustainable" projects. Most Mexican communities cannot afford to take on the kind of debt needed to fund projects; there simply is no revenue to repay such loans, and charging higher utility rates to residents to fund the projects is not possible.[15]

We now know that Mexico's infrastructure needs attention. A national plan for infrastructure and transportation has not been developed.[16] Yet clearly, reducing geographical disparities within Mexico would decrease pressures to emigrate; some believe that a first priority should be to improve the road system from the U.S. border to the central and southern parts of Mexico.[17] If that were done, investment could be attracted. The states of Oaxaca, Zacatecas, Michoacan, and Guanajuato, in central and southern Mexico, have the highest unemployment rates and are the primary sources of migrants to the border and to the United States.[18] Yet despite the growth in trade under NAFTA, significant investment in transportation and infrastructure has not been made. Before NAFTA under the Salinas administration (1988–1994), Mexico invested in poorly designed toll roads, and the roads charged hefty tolls that few were willing to pay. As Mexico's debt rose, investment in infrastructure was slashed from about 10 percent in the 1980s to less than 2 percent in 1998. So all transportation sectors—roads, rail, air, and ports—face serious challenges.[19] Investment in Mexico's infrastructure must become a priority again.

Taking a cue from the EU's European Social Fund, Robert Pastor, director of the Center for North American Studies, understands the need for investment in Mexico. He believes that the three NAFTA countries should establish a fund to invest in roads, telecommunications, and postsecondary education in Mexico.[20] As the EU invested huge sums in roads and education in new, poor member states and narrowed their income gap with the rest of Europe, workers decided to stay home.[21]

Mexico lacks the capital to build the infrastructure that is necessary to narrow the gap with Canada and the United States.[22] Pastor argues that if its northern neighbors contributed 10 percent of what the EU spends on aid, with wise investments in infrastructure and education, Mexico could experience growth at a rate twice that of Canada and the United States. "The psychology of North America would change quickly, and the problems of immigration, corruption, and drugs would look different," he says. "North America would have found the magic formula to lift developing countries to the industrial world, and that would be the twenty-first-century equivalent of the shot heard round the world."[23] Although Mexico and the United States have developed the border area, and NAFTA has helped to infuse new investment in there, the border region is burdened. Building up the central part of the country could relieve congestion at the border, and the whole system could be better managed.[24]

Focusing on the educational system in Mexico is another key. Mexican students fall near the bottom in cross-country comparisons on basic literacy, math, and science.[25] While the education level of adults in the United States is almost thirteen years, in Mexico, the level is about seven.[26] This low education level has severe implications for competitiveness and the standard of living of Mexicans, whether they remain in Mexico or migrate to the United States.[27]

Limited investment in education in Mexico has infused energy already. Mexico's Progresa, or Oportunidades, program provides incentives to poor families to keep their children in school by offering grants that are the equivalent of about two-thirds of what the children would earn working.[28] About 2.5 million rural families received $1 billion through the program in 2000. The percentage of students who go from elementary school to high school has increased by 20 percent under the program.[29]

Other data indicate that Mexico is taking its responsibility to support education seriously. The average education level of adults of seven years is up from an average level of three years twenty years ago.[30] School enrollment for children (age 6–14) reached 92.1 percent in 2000, compared with 85.8 percent in 1990 and 64.4 percent in 1970.[31] Students are required to complete nine years of school, and enrollment in general has increased more than 80 percent at the primary level.[32]

One thing that NAFTA has taught us is that if we expect employment growth in Mexico to materialize as a result of trade agreements, investments have to be targeted. We should determine how to help Mexico's domestic industries—for example, by using domestic parts and supplies in production exports.[33] Local industries must be strengthened.[34]

The rural areas of Mexico really suffered under NAFTA. Unlike the Irish experience, subsistence farmers in Mexico were not given assistance or time to make adjustments. Nothing was done to help protect their income as trade conditions changed. And rural workers forced to leave agriculture had little help in moving into other sectors.[35]

For a significant effect on migration from Mexico to take place, serious investment in new technologies in small and medium-size industries is necessary.[36] Some of this can be achieved through tax incentives to spur economic growth in the country's interior. The development of fruit and vegetable production can absorb some of the rural workers who have been displaced.[37]

Businesses in Mexico also need access to financing. Koos Mexico, a maquiladora with twelve hundred workers that makes jeans, had access to U.S. investment capital because its Los Angeles-based parent company helped secure the capital needed to invest in new machinery. But even then, international competition cannot be ignored. In 2003, Koos lost its contract when the Gap moved most of its orders to China.[38]

Mexico has not been ignored by the World Bank. Since the bank's formation, Mexico has ranked third (after India and China) in terms of loans. In 1999, for example, the World Bank lent $5.2 billion to Mexico for two years to improve social conditions for the poor, strengthen public-sector reforms, and reinforce macroeconomic stability. Mexico has received more loans from the Inter-American Development Bank than any other country.[39] And central bankers provided major support to Mexico in 1982 in the midst of its debt crisis.

Mexican migrants are among the country's ablest workers who leave for better wages—and not necessarily because they are unemployed. They make more money in the United States than they did in Mexico, but what remains unclear is whether the productivity—measured in part by their remittances—is higher than it would have been had they remained in Mexico. But by concentrating on investing in Mexico to create more jobs, even if labor movement is opened up, fewer Mexicans will migrate than expected because incentives for able Mexican workers to remain home will have been created.

There is another good reason for the United States and Canada to contribute financially in grand ways vis-à-vis Mexico: China. China's role in the world economy is affecting Mexico and, in turn, Mexican migration. After Canada, China is now the second-biggest U.S. trading partner, having moved ahead of Mexico in 2004. China's manufacturing sector can produce many products cheaply, and this has forced some Mexican manufacturing plants to close. Over the past several years, a serious trade imbalance has developed between the United States and China, and that trade deficit affects the ability of the United States to trade with Mexico. This impact on Mexico's manufacturing and trading ability in turn has affected jobs, creating pressure on Mexican workers to look north for work opportunities. These results should challenge us to think about how a more meaningful partnership between North American countries could be one way to help all of North America.

The United States–China trade imbalance has resulted from a trade relationship between the two countries where the number of exports from China to the United States dramatically exceeds the number of imports from the United States to China. In other words, U.S. consumers are buying substantially more Chinese goods than U.S. companies are able to sell to China. Why? Chinese goods are cheap, and U.S. consumers are always looking for bargains. This resulted in a $268 billion deficit in 2008.

Here is the opportunity. The United States and other nations have increased pressure on China to relax the exchange rate, and ultimately, China

must decide whether to relax do so. If Mexico could reform its economy, perhaps with the assistance of the United States, to provide cheaper exports
than China and other places to outsource production, this could decrease the
U.S. dependence on China; Mexico's export manufacturing could increase;
and more jobs could be developed for Mexicans who want to stay home.

More controversially, due to low input and labor costs, U.S. businesses
now outsource production facilities to China to capitalize on exchange-rate
and investment opportunities. China promises high returns to U.S. firms that
have invested there.[40] For some of these firms, China acts as an assembly
center, importing raw materials for production. The U.S. net international
investment position with China was -25 percent in 2004, yet due to the high
returns U.S. firms earned on foreign investments, U.S. net investment returns
totaled $24.1 billion that year.[41] This positive number, despite a largely nega-
tive net investment, reveals how U.S. investments abroad return high rates,
probably on investments in factories and foreign companies. Meanwhile, of
the foreign-owned investments in the United States, the majority are in low-
yield, short-term government debt.[42]

At the end of the day, China must decide whether or not to float its currency, the yuan, in order to appreciate it and subsequently depreciate the
dollar. However, Mexico may be able to help the United States in some way.
If Mexico could provide exports that are competitive in price with those from
China, it could reduce the desire in the United States to purchase China's
exports. But the mainly agricultural economy in Mexico has been damaged
by NAFTA and is inefficient. Thus, Mexico is exporting much less than it
is importing in part because its exported products are more expensive than
those the United States can produce for itself at home. The instability of
the peso is also a problem. But these are challenges that, with the support
of the United States and Canada, Mexico could begin to address and that in
the long run would be beneficial to all of North America. These challenges
strongly suggest a development approach in Mexico that would assist in its
manufacturing sector. Instead of the current situation, in which the enforcement-only approach to immigration does not address demands and trade
policy dries up jobs for poor workers, thus working at cross-purposes, the
investment approach in Mexico would have the multiple positive purposes of
helping Mexico develop jobs for Mexicans, reducing pressures to migrate, and
lessening U.S. dependence on manufactured goods from China.

Essentially, Mexico needs to reform its economy to be more efficient and
to provide more jobs. After some economic reform, Mexico might be able
to provide cheaper exports to the United States or places where the United
States can outsource production facilities to capitalize on exchange-rate and
investment opportunities. Currently, though, China's economic policies are

allowing it to dominate the export market and trade relations with the United States.

The Chinese government dramatically transformed the country from an independent, government-controlled economy to a largely market-driven, rapidly growing economy that is among the ten largest in the world. The U.S. economy depends on China's demand for dollars, but this relationship is reciprocal because China is now dependent on the value of the dollar. Today, China's government must deal with increased pressure to allow its currency to appreciate and to increase its peoples' standard of living, along with domestic concerns about increased prices and reduced imports and an internal need to receive a higher return on their reserves. Mexico can assist the United States in becoming less dependent on China, but that would require a true North American partnership.

Economic investment in Mexico will not—and probably should not—be done without close monitoring. The EU enlargement policy sets standards, known as the Copenhagen Criteria, for candidate countries. These criteria require a country that wishes to join the EU to meet certain political, social, and economic standards. The image of Mexico as corrupt—or, at least, as a political gamble, especially in light of its recent rocky presidential transition— is strong. For example, Vice President Joe Biden has warned, "Mexico is a country that is an erstwhile democracy where they have the greatest of wealth. . . . It is one of the wealthiest countries in the hemisphere and because of a corrupt system that exists in Mexico, there is the 1 percent of the population at the top, a very small middle class, and the rest is abject poverty."[43] Even with meaningful economic investment in Mexico, the Mexican economy is not going to turn around overnight. That type of change may take generations.[44]

However, if done correctly, comprehensive investment in Mexico's economy and its political and social infrastructure will ensure that its economy will grow and that the region will remain politically and economically stable. EU investments are concerned with not only a country's economic growth but also its political and social stability. This idea of inclusive investment is to ensure that no political, economic, or social sector will lag behind.

EU-Style Labor Movement

In contrast to the failure of NAFTA to incorporate labor migration into its provisions, the development of the EU proceeded with the movement of workers clearly in mind. For that reason, looking to the European experience for guidance or even as a model is appealing, especially since the EU permits open labor and engages in development assistance to poor nations to reduce migration pressures, yet maintains border control.[45] The EU experience teaches that if one of the goals of a new approach to the border is to reduce Mexican migration to the United States, then the United States should not limit the number of migrant workers from Mexico. This may sound counterintuitive. However, if investments in Mexico are made without an open migration policy, the U.S.–Mexican labor market will not function properly.

Central Spain and other agricultural areas of the EU-15 that have not adopted a fully open border policy have had problems, and reports about Romanian migrants in Castilla La Mancha, Spain, make it clear that an open, cross-border labor market is best for the economy. Romanian migrants working in vineyards there who had obtained work permits were earning a living wage, had adequate housing, and, most important, had enough money to return to their families in their home country after the harvest season.[46] Being part of a legal seasonal workforce allowed these migrants to earn a good income and boost the economy in Spain (through their labor and the time they spend there), as well as in Romania (through the additional income they brought home). However, since the Spanish government issued only a limited number of work permits to Romanians, some agricultural employers felt that they needed to hire undocumented workers.[47] The undocumented workers lived in slums, were not protected in the workplace, and had unpredictable income flows.[48] Moreover, because the undocumented Romanians were not earning a living wage, they could not afford to pay their way home.[49] They also were not able to take part in the seasonal migration patterns that followed job demands. Instead of becoming part of a flow of labor that most efficiently helped build the economies of both the host country and the home country, these workers were stranded in Spain without necessary protection or means of income.

The problem with limiting the number of seasonal and other workers is presented in other parts of Europe, as well. In Germany, the number of work permits granted to agricultural laborers from other countries does not meet actual demand for such workers.[50] Foreign workers who are following job demands therefore end up working as undocumented migrants, much the way that undocumented Romanians do in Spain.[51]

Within the EU, a central component of economic integration is the mobility of people. This is done with a commitment to "harmonizing" labor standards in terms of wages, work weeks, and other labor-cost factors.[52] The idea is that to really integrate the member nations' economies, the free movement of workers is necessary, and they should have the right to accept employment in any member nation.[53] The workers' families have the right to follow and establish new residence with the workers.[54]

The EU approach to labor migration has been thoughtful and deliberate. At the outset, leaders and planners knew that, as open migration was contemplated, a necessary underpinning was the reduction of economic difference among various regions of Europe. The adhesion-fund approach worked. The gap between the poor and rich nations narrowed. By the beginning of the new millennium, Ireland's economy had been transformed, and the country's per capita GDP was above the EU average. Incredibly, Ireland—a nation that for years had been a constant source of emigrants—began attracting immigrants. The feared "mass migration of the unemployed" fizzled. People stayed in their own countries because work opportunities were created. Only 2 percent of EU citizens looked for work in other EU countries.[55]

The lesson of the EU is that with open trade, limiting the number of migrant workers is a mistake. Open migration of workers creates the most efficient labor market, allowing the flow of workers to follow job demand. In this way, workers remain above ground, earning a protected wage and helping the local economy and the economies of their home countries. Such an open border policy helps to guarantee workers' rights and ensure that migrant workers are not doomed to substandard living conditions.

Considering Open Borders or Migration without Borders

Even without the EU model for guidance, many scholars have seriously raised the idea of open borders, especially with regard to the United States and Mexico. For example, Kevin Johnson has made the case for open borders, given the era of globalization in which we live and the range of related questions, such as the special relationship between the United States and Mexico, the civil rights of Mexican migrants, and the culture of migration that has evolved among Mexicans.[56] And in Gerald López's seminal work on the migration of undocumented Mexicans, an ethics-driven notion of an open border with Mexico is implicit in his description of the cultural, sociological, and economic history between the United States and Mexico.[57]

Others advocate for a more open border system from a range of theoretical and practical perspectives. For example, after his landslide victory in the Mexican presidential elections in 2000, Vicente Fox, acknowledging that Mexico could not offer its workers the same salaries or living standards found in the United States, argued for a more open border because Mexican workers were able to fill the great needs of U.S. employers.[58] In fact, as governor of his home state of Guanajuato, Fox had instituted job training for residents in landscaping, construction, factory work, and domestic work to help fill job demands in the United States.[59] Political philosophers such as Mark Tushnet, Joseph Carens, and R. George Wright have argued that restricting law-abiding immigrants is antithetical to the notion of an open society.[60]

In the theoretical realm, Antoine Pécoud sets forth arguments for the concept of open borders, or what he terms "migration without borders." He begins by noting that Article 13–2 of the Universal Declaration of Human Rights states: "Everyone has the right to leave any country, including his own, and to return to his country." This recognition of emigration as a fundamental right, in his view, necessarily has no meaning without the ability to immigrate and a right to mobility.[61] Mobility is a resource to which everyone should have access.[62]

As if speaking about the U.S.–Mexican border specifically, Pécoud recognizes that migration has become part and parcel of the economy and social life of countries, and that sending and receiving countries often become dependent on migration that is difficult to stop. In spite of that, the conventional wisdom is that an open border is not feasible because massive migration would result. But Pécoud argues that such fear is not grounded on any empirical understanding.[63] We actually do not know what would happen if borders were opened, but we do know that the results of immigration policies are hard to predict.[64] As the UN High Commissioner for Refugees has stated, "It may be assumed that, unless he seeks adventure or just wishes to see the world, a person would not normally abandon his home and country without some compelling reason."[65] As we know from the EU's experience, massive migration from poor countries did not occur.[66] Furthermore, this continued immigration flow and the apparent inability of a government to control it can lead to lack of confidence on the part of the public and even anti-immigrant sentiment. More walls and fences are essentially an admission that the system is not working.[67] And curiously, restrictions on mobility curtail circularity, which can lead to undocumented migrants' residing more permanently in the host country. Open borders enable migrants to return home, as well.[68]

To Pécoud, border controls raise questions about our values:

> The human costs of border controls raise the issue of compatibility with the core values of the international community. To what extent can tough measures of border controls coexist with the harmonious functioning of democracies? The liberal values and human rights principles that guide societies cannot stop at their borders; they must guide countries' behavior toward outsiders arriving at their gates. The way society handles the fate of foreigners ultimately reflects the values upon which it is based, and the issue regards the price—in terms of dignity and human rights—developed countries are prepared to

pay to control their borders. In other words, the evolution of migration controls towards greater harshness might eventually back-fire
and threaten the liberal principles and freedoms that lie at the core of
democratic societies.[69]

Class has its privileges when it comes to migration. Pécoud reminds us
that the ability to travel and settle in different parts of the world is certainly
more available to those who have money and those who live in developed
countries than to those who do not. Those from less developed countries
simply do not have the same mobility.[70] Migration controls actually distort
the world economically. Free migration would lead to more equality; the
movement of labor from poor to rich countries would increase world GDP
and, ironically, would reduce the pressure to migrate as wages converge.[71]
Inequalities would then be addressed through market forces.[72]

Thus, to Pécoud the lot of undocumented migrants would improve in an
open border scenario; underground economies would decrease, and workers
would become contributors to the social-safety-net system.[73] And to give such
a system the best chance to succeed, migrants should be extended a welcome
into our communities. A more welcoming approach would reduce levels of
resentment and feelings of ostracism that many migrants experience.[74]

Migration without borders is consistent with globalization and free trade,
in Pécoud's view. Borders were once used to stop capital, goods, and people,
but after free-trade movements, borders now just to stop people. Migration
becomes the exception to globalization.[75] The EU appears to be the only
region with open migration; even Mercosur in the South American Cone,
the Association of South East Asian States, and the Asian Pacific Economic
Cooperation Forum do not allow free movement.[76]

While his arguments are idealistic and morally driven, Pécoud recognizes
that open borders would affect a multitude of issues, such as wages, welfare,
and race. Thus, cooperation between nations and affected communities must
take place. This must not be about one country taking advantage of another
country's goodwill.[77] While not perfect, the EU is a good example of the
type of cooperation that is needed, where workers tend to stay in their native
countries despite open borders.[78] The consequences of migration without
borders may be difficult to anticipate, but at least to Pécoud, the notion is
ethically defensible.[79]

Robert Flanagan provides another perspective that supports the liberal
movement of labor migration across borders. In reviewing the long history
of the waves of workers around the globe, he concludes that as trade and
migration expand, wage differences among nations narrow. In essence, international inequality in work conditions is reduced.[80] World output increases,

because migrants get higher wages in the receiving country, and the value of their work product exceeds the output lost in the country they left.[81] Open migration has the other extremely important added benefit of reducing human trafficking in forced labor.[82]

When it comes to labor migration, the concern often focuses on the effect on receiving countries. Flanagan encourages us to look at the effect on the sending countries, as well. By doing so, he finds that workers who stay in the sending country benefit in terms of more work, higher wages, and even better working conditions because of less competition. Also, with fewer people unemployed, the sending country saves on social expenditures.[83] Flanagan argues that even "modest relaxation of migration barriers" would result in important improvement in working conditions around the world.[84]

Of course, Flanagan also reminds us that remittances sent back from abroad are beneficial to the sending country. In fact, he argues that remittances help to offset any concern one might have about the "drain" of educated people from the poor country. While I am skeptical of his claim about stability, Flanagan believes that remittances are increasingly used for investment in developing countries and provide a stable source of foreign exchange. He also argues—though not convincingly, from my perspective—that emigration of the educated from a poor country puts pressure on that country to invest more in education and other human capital.[85] He posits that more people in the poor country, lured by job prospects abroad, will want to become educated, but not every educated person will in fact leave, and that increases the country's pool of skilled workers.[86]

In his influential article on open borders, Kevin Johnson outlines the most salient points in support of a new way of looking at immigration.[87] Under liberal theory, closed borders are antithetical to the rights of noncitizens; liberals ought to support "relatively unrestricted immigration."[88] The moral grounds to exclude "ordinary, peaceful people, seeking only the opportunity to build decent secure lives" are simply hard to locate.[89] Our Judeo-Christian foundation also provides a "moral imperative" to treat immigrants in a humanitarian way.[90]

In Johnson's view, the special relationship between the United States and Mexico suggests a greater moral obligation to Mexican migrants.[91] That relationship has led to a culture of migration from Mexico (built on economics and family reunification); as such, broad immigration restrictions are impossible to enforce because they run counter to migration pressures.[92] Those restrictions have led to policies such as the institution of Operation Gatekeeper and other militarization at the U.S.–Mexican border that has resulted in an untenable death toll among border crossers.[93] Johnson observes that today's immigration laws contribute to racism in the United States, and their enforcement leads to civil-rights harms.[94] By contributing to an environment conducive to discriminatory sentiment, the current regime has helped to generate a large pool of undocumented workers who are subject to exploitation by U.S. employers.[95]

Advocating open borders is not a challenge to a nation's sovereign authority to restrict immigration. Johnson notes that a nation can "affirmatively choose open borders in its exercise of sovereign power."[96] One advantage to a more open system in the post-9/11 era is that resources would be freed up and more attention could be paid to true dangers to public safety and national security.[97] Another is that a more open immigration system that promotes labor mobility would be economically beneficial to the United States in this period of globalization.[98]

Johnson challenges us to take a broad worldview:

[We need] a far-reaching immigration response to the changing world. Open borders would mark a true revolution in current U.S. immigration law, and would create an admissions system in which migration effectively approximated demand. The fundamental premise of the U.S. immigration laws is that exclusion of immigrants is the norm and admission of noncitizens is the exception to the rule. This need not be. [We must] shift the debate over immigration to consider the possibility of making the U.S. borders more permeable to people, as well as to goods, services, and capital.

No coherent intellectual justification for immigration restrictions like those enforced by the United States has emerged. More importantly, the U.S. elimination of border controls would offer many benefits. Elimination of border controls would end the brutality inherent in enforcement of the current immigration controls, which result in physical abuse, promote racial discrimination, and relegate certain groups of U.S. citizens and lawful immigrants to second-class status. Rampant civil rights deprivations have resulted. Such consequences render U.S. immigration enforcement immoral.

Moreover, the nation stands to reap economic benefits from free labor migration in a globalizing world economy. As a matter of economic theory, international trade with Mexico and much of the world, which the United States has eagerly embraced, differs little from labor migration. A utilitarian argument would allow for labor migration and add the benefits of a low-wage labor force to the national economy.

Last but not least, strong policy arguments exist for the abolition of border controls. Experience demonstrates that, at least within modern sensibilities, border controls cannot be enforced.

Undocumented immigration is not viewed as criminal by most law-abiding Americans, nor is the employment of undocumented immigrants. Abolition of border controls would recognize the economic and social reality of immigration, including the fact that millions of undocumented immigrants make valuable contributions to the U.S. economy but are forced to live on the margins of society and, subject to exploitation because of their uncertain immigration status, work in poor conditions for substandard wages. Foreign policy benefits also would accrue from a system in which the nationals of other societies were in fact welcomed rather than labeled a public menace, barred from entry, and treated as pariahs in our midst.[99]

Gerald López paints a clear picture of the historical relationship between Mexican migration that provides a moral understanding for Mexican workers in the United States. Long before NAFTA and terms such as "globalization" and "transnationalism" were in vogue, Mexicans were living the reality of interconnected economies and societies. Today, the effects of that reality remain.

López points out that in entering into the Treaty of Guadalupe Hidalgo in February 1848, the United States gained California and New Mexico (including present-day Nevada, Utah, and Arizona) and recognition of the Río Grande as the southern boundary of Texas. This represented 55 percent of Mexico's territory. Although some Mexicans moved to Mexico, most remained in what became U.S. territory. In the years immediately following the treaty, many Mexicans, especially those migrating from the annexed territories, thought of the territories as Mexico's. Mexicans and Americans paid little heed to the newly created international border, which was unmarked and wholly unreal to most. In essence, the boundary was at first an artificial one and did not effectively separate the new U.S. possessions from those south of the border.

We learn from López that promotion of Mexican migration is part of a larger pattern of labor recruitment that began to emerge in the United States in the late nineteenth century. When the Chinese were excluded, widespread and long-distance Mexican migration began. The expansion of agriculture, particularly in the Río Grande valley of Texas and the central valley of California, created the demand.

What emerges from this brief account is American involvement in a pattern of recruitment designed to serve the self-perceived needs of American employers for cheap temporary labor. The most vital aspect of the process, at least for later analysis, is Mexican workers' growing dependence on wages earned in the United States.

From 1910 to 1920, approximately two hundred thousand Mexicans were admitted into the United States. During World War I, others were actively recruited to fill severe manpower shortages resulting from Americans' involvement in military service and the curtailment of the migration of cheap European labor. Events in the decade after World War I provide evidence that American recognition of Mexican labor's value matured from appreciation into economic attachment. During the 1919–1920 and 1920–1921 seasons, the Arizona Cotton Growers Association spent approximately $425,000 recruiting and transporting Mexican workers. According to one official, the association's recruitment of Mexican workers saved the growers $2.8 million in picking costs by maintaining "as perfectly an elastic supply of labor as the world has ever seen."[100]

In the face of a post–World War I recession, an increasingly powerful domestic labor movement, and mobilized restrictionist sentiment, the success of Southwestern employers during the 1920s was remarkable. Employers argued that domestic workers, despite the recession, would not fill available jobs at any wage. Some jobs were seasonal or casual, at best. Judging from numbers and from the cooperation of the federal government, the employers' strategy worked. The best evidence available indicates that nearly half a million Mexican workers crossed the border during the 1920s.

In 1942, the United States negotiated a treaty with Mexico in the form of the Labor Importation Program—more commonly referred to as the Bracero Program—providing for the use of Mexicans as temporary workers in U.S. agriculture. Unlike previous measures, the treaty purported to regulate the employment of Mexicans as temporary agricultural workers through qualitative and quantitative provisions. In terms of serving American economic interests, however, the program was without historical peer. Even with huge organizations such as the American Federation of Labor–Congress of Industrial Organizations (AFL-CIO) in opposition to the exploitation of migrant labor that was inherent in the Bracero Program, it was renewed consecutively throughout the administrations of five U.S. presidents. *Braceros* constituted a quarter of the farm labor force in California, Arizona, New Mexico, and Texas, contributing not only to the vital food production of the period but also to increasing U.S. dominance in agriculture.

López points out that the U.S. role in undocumented entry cannot be depicted as unintentional, naïve, or innocent. Policymakers in the United States must have been aware that recruitment activities designed to promote the Bracero Program would encourage poor Mexicans to believe the United States was a land of opportunity, thereby encouraging those who could not be admitted legally to enter without inspection. The relative attractiveness of undocumented entry was increased by the failure to enforce the promises that had been made in connection with the adoption of the Bracero Program.

In 1954, more than a million undocumented Mexicans were deported as part of an Immigration and Naturalization Service initiative dubbed Operation Wetback. Employers in the Southwest, who probably saw the operation as little more than a temporary setback, responded by making more extensive use of workers under the Bracero Program. Despite continuing assault on the Bracero Program's legitimacy, the "emergency wartime measure" survived twenty-two years, through 1964, and employed nearly 5 million Mexican workers.

With immunity intact, employers had little to do after 1964 but reap the benefits of a century of promotion. Direct and indirect recruitment, though still undertaken, was most likely unnecessary. Tradition alone provided an adequate pool of potential workers. In addition, immigrant labor's traditional reliance on access to American wages was magnified by population growth and patterns of development in Mexico. Finally, to the extent that the border served as a barrier, employers learned to rely on the wily skills and self-interest of *coyotes* (commercial smugglers) and on the undocumented workers' knowledge of evasive tactics that had become an integral part of the migratory culture.

Many commentators, including Kevin Johnson and myself, have also argued that there are national security reasons for being more flexible in our approach to the border.[101] More liberal admissions policies across our southern border would enhance our country's security because we would know the identities of those who cross; resources currently wasted on border militarization could be spent on really ferreting out those who may be attempting to enter to do harm to the nation. Robert Pastor also argues that NAFTA had a national security purpose that should not be neglected. The hope was to lessen migration pressures by supporting a stable Mexico. Thus, he submits that we should act to prevent a "serious internal crisis" in Mexico that could lead to massive migration; thus, we should help Mexico, for example, to develop its natural gas and oil industries for economic development as well as for security.[102]

No one knows for sure what would happen if the borders with Mexico and Canada were opened. If this is done with an EU-style investment approach, an inundation of immigrants will not occur. As Johnson notes, we should not forget that the life-altering decision to immigrate is not made easily, and an open floodgate should not be the assumed response.[103] Douglas Massey has found that most undocumented workers from Mexico want to work in the United States temporarily to finance projects back home, such as building a house, purchasing land, or buying consumer goods. If given the opportunity, they would work on temporary trips to the United States and retire home to "enjoy the fruits of their labors in the United States."[104] Demographic changes also suggest some slowing of migration to the United States from Mexico over time. The Mexican birthrate is dropping; the population growth rate is lower; and fewer youngsters are approaching working age.[105]

Beyond North American Integration

Strong and meaningful North American integration, along the lines of the EU model, is necessary for a permanent, long-term solution to undocumented Mexican migration. However, other measures can be taken in the interim to ameliorate the challenge of undocumented migration.

The Need for Immigrant Workers

Anti-immigrant advocates are in a state of denial. Their complaints continue to stand on a rocky foundation—namely, that immigrants, especially undocumented immigrants, take jobs from native workers. In fact, for the past couple of decades economists have concluded that immigrants fill jobs that are hard to fill, and, perhaps more important, the presence of immigrants helps to create jobs. Immigrants are consumers; in economic terms, their demand for services and products are met by the need for more workers to provide those services and produce the goods. Time and again, studies demonstrate that areas of the country with the most immigrants actually have the lowest unemployment rates, and those regions with the fewest immigrants have the highest unemployment rates.[106]

The United States is now reaching a new demographic reality that provides a new response to the immigration naysayers: the retirement of the baby-boom generation. Fully aware of the situation, Ben Bernanke, chairman of the Federal Reserve, has concluded that the U.S. economy will need 3.5 million additional laborers each year to replace the 78 million baby boomers who began to retire in 2008.

Without an adequate visa system to accommodate the need for immigrant workers, market forces have made adjustments through the employment of undocumented workers. Undocumented immigrants account for about 4.3 percent of the civilian labor force—approximately 6.3 million workers in a labor force of 146 million.[107] Although they can be found in many different sectors of the economy, undocumented workers tend to be overrepresented in certain occupations and industries. They are much more likely to be in broad occupation groups that require little education or do not have licensing requirements.[108] Three times as many undocumented immigrants work in agriculture, construction, and resource extraction as do U.S. citizens.[109] In contrast, undocumented immigrants are conspicuously underrepresented in white-collar occupations. While management, business, professions, sales, and administrative support account for half of native citizen workers (52 percent), less than one-quarter of the undocumented workers are in these areas (23 percent).[110]

The list below shows the proportion of workers in "detailed occupation groups" who are undocumented. The list includes only those occupations in which undocumented workers are overrepresented—that is, the percentage of undocumented workers in the particular occupation is greater than the proportion of undocumented workers in the entire workforce (4.3 percent).[111]

Drywall/ceiling tile installers	27 percent
Grounds maintenance workers	26 percent
Butchers/meat, poultry workers	25 percent
Dishwashers	24 percent
Miscellaneous agricultural workers	23 percent
Cement masons and finishers	22 percent
Graders and sorters, agricultural products	22 percent
Hand packers and packagers	22 percent
Maids and housekeepers	22 percent
Roofers	21 percent
Cleaning/washing equipment operators	20 percent
Construction laborers	20 percent
Painters, construction, etc.	20 percent
Brick/block/stone masons	19 percent
Cooks	18 percent
Sewing machine operators	18 percent
Packaging/filling machine operators	17 percent
Dining and cafeteria attendants	14 percent
Food preparation workers	13 percent
Metal/plastic workers, other	13 percent
Carpenters	12 percent
Janitors and building cleaners	12 percent[112]

Close to 60 percent of the undocumented population in the United States is from Mexico, with another 24 percent from other Latin American countries.[113] Although most undocumented immigrants in the United States today entered the country without inspection, about 40 percent entered lawfully as non-immigrants—for example, as students or tourists—and overstayed their visas.[114]

The U.S. Bureau of Labor Statistics (BLS) provides data that support

Bernanke's observations and explain why the market for undocumented workers has responded as it has. The BLS estimates that the number of people in the labor force age 25–34 is projected to increase by only 3 million between 2002 and 2012, while the number of those 55 and older will increase by 18 million. By 2012, those who are 45 and older will have the fastest growth rate and will constitute a little more than 50 percent of the labor force. According to estimates by the United Nations, the fertility rate in the United States is projected to fall below replacement level by 2015–2020, declining to 1.91 children per woman (lower than the 2.1 children per woman rate needed to replace the population). By 2010, 77 million baby boomers will have retired, and by 2030, according to projections, one in every five Americans will be a senior citizen.

While the U.S. population is aging and retiring, the country will continue to experience job growth, according to the U.S. Chamber of Commerce, including in lower-skilled occupations. Most jobs in our economy do not require a college degree. Close to 40 percent of all jobs require only short-term on-the-job training. In fact, of the top ten largest-job-growth occupations between 2002 and 2012, all but two require less than a bachelor's degree. At the same time, six of the top ten occupations require only short-term on-the-job training, including retail sales personnel, nursing aides, janitors and cleaners, waiters and waitresses, and combined food-preparation and serving workers.[115]

However, shortages of essential workers are not limited to the largest-growth occupations. In fact, the need for essential workers cuts across industry sectors. In February 2004, Emily Stover DeRocco, assistant secretary of labor for employment training, projected in a speech to the National Roofing Contractors Association an increase of more than thirty thousand jobs for roofers between 2002 and 2012 and, at the same time, attrition in this occupation of about forty thousand jobs—a net deficit of seventy thousand. The Construction Labor Research Council projects that the industry will need 185,000 new workers annually for the next ten years.

The National Restaurant Association foresees the addition of more than 1.8 million jobs in the restaurant industry between 2005 and 2015, an increase of 15 percent. However, the U.S. labor force is projected to increase only 12 percent during the next ten years, which will make it more challenging than ever for restaurants to find the workers they need. A study by the National Restaurant Association notes that the age 16–24 labor force—the demographic group that makes up more than half of the restaurant industry's workforce—is projected to increase only 9 percent during the next ten years.[116]

A U.S. Chamber of Commerce study concludes that employers have a real problem finding the workers they need. The chamber surveyed local chambers of commerce, businesses, and associations representing a wide range of industries, including arts, entertainment and recreation, professional science, technical services, social assistance, and nonprofit organizations. Difficulties in finding both entry-level and skilled workers, and developing solutions for this problem, ranked extremely high in importance to those surveyed.[117]

Importantly, the Cato Institute, a libererian public-policy research foundation based in Washington, D.C., has found that, of the thirty job categories with the largest expected growth, more than half fall into the least-skilled categories, such as combined food preparation and serving workers, including fast food; waiters and waitresses; retail sales personnel; cashiers; security guards; nursing aides, orderlies, and attendants; janitors and cleaners; home-health aides; manual laborers and freight, stock, and material movers; landscaping and groundskeeping workers; and manual packers and packagers. But with the supply of American workers suitable for such work continuing to fall because of an aging workforce and rising education levels, Cato concludes, Mexican migrants provide a ready and willing source of labor to fill the growing gap between demand and supply on the lower rungs of the labor ladder.[118]

Without a doubt, we need immigrant workers of all stripes. Immigrants who enter in family immigration categories fill many of the needs, but many of those categories are backlogged. Employment-based immigration categories are very limited in number and scope. So expanding the family immigration and employment-based numerical limitations would be wise.

Immigrant Enterprise Zones

In spite of tensions over immigration that have arisen in some communities, certain areas of the country already recognize immigration as an answer to economic problems. They understand how immigrants have benefited so many parts of the country. Thus, efforts are under way in many regions to recruit more immigrants.

Iowa is one example. As in states and cities in other regions of the country, a considerable part of Iowa's population has disappeared over the past two decades. A large number of its high school graduates leave the state each year shortly after graduation. But even if Iowa were able to retain every high school senior after graduation, it would still face a 3 percent decline in its adult work force within five years. Iowa also ranks third in the nation for elderly citizens; an average Iowa farmer is 58 years old, and the average assembly-line worker at the Maytag Company in Newton, Iowa, is 57 years old. Iowa's loss of its young homegrown population comes at a time when the state has enjoyed a vibrant and growing economy for a decade, with annual unemployment of only 2 percent. Iowa's farms employ fewer workers than ever; the state's population is aging at a time when it needs young workers and the state wants to attract high-technology industries.

As Iowa is losing people, it wants immigrants to replace them. When he was governor, Tom Vilsack (the current U.S. secretary of agriculture) established a bipartisan state commission known as the "2010 Commission." It was composed of prominent Iowans, and its mandate was to devise a plan to improve the state's economy by the year 2010. Having set their economic goals, the commission's members realized the state did not have the population to meet them. The commission concluded that Iowa's population needed to increase by about 10 percent by 2010. Some of its recommendations included (1) making Iowa technologically competitive by developing nonagricultural industries; (2) establishing "Diversity Welcome Centers" to help immigrants locate housing, learn English, and find health care; (3) designating Iowa an "immigrant enterprise zone" and seeking a federal exemption from immigration quotas; and (4) assisting Iowa companies in recruiting prospective employees from abroad.

The City of Philadelphia faces similar challenges. During the past decade, the city has lost more than sixty-eight thousand residents—about 4 percent of its population. This has continued a downward trend in the population that began in the late 1950s. As more and more residents depart—primarily middle-income residents looking for better schools and safe neighborhoods—Philadelphia faces a further erosion of its already shrinking tax base and potential reductions in its federal-dollar allocation. Many of the city's leaders believe that Philadelphia must act to maintain its residential base and explore ways to attract residents from other regions of the country and from around the world. They believe that this is critical for revitalizing many neighborhoods and for increasing local tax revenues and have instituted programs to attract more immigrants to their city and convince foreign students who attend local colleges to consider remaining in the city after graduation.

Not to be outdone, Pittsburgh, across the state, is also embracing new strategies to attract immigrants. While Philadelphia lost 4 percent of its population in the 1990s, Pittsburgh's population fell by 9.5 percent. Local organizations have received foundation grants to help attract immigrants with jobs, encourage foreign students to stay after graduation, and teach the community about diversity. The city hopes to remake its outdated "smoky" image to attract immigrants to thousands of jobs at new health-care, biotechnology, and computer-software companies.

Kentucky is a state whose reliance on immigrants appears to be understood in similar terms. Farmers have come to depend on immigrants when native sources of labor find other jobs or remain in school. Initially, migrant workers arrived in Kentucky to cut tobacco on their swing through the nation before heading home for the winter. They became invaluable when other workers could not be found. Kentucky's chief demographer put it a little differently, as he recognized immigrant labor as a hedge against the graying of the state: "I don't think we're going to have an indigenous labor force. Boomers are done having kids. The boomlet is over."[119] Officials from the city of Louisville also want to attract immigrants. The city's population fell 5 percent in the 1990s and would have dropped more had it not been for the arrival of approximately twenty thousand immigrants and refugees from places such as Cuba, Somalia, and Vietnam. The city's Office of International and Cultural Affairs provides a list of interpreters for community-service providers to use. Efforts to help immigrants establish their own businesses are also under way.

Recently, many residents of places such as Pittsburgh; Cleveland; Erie, Pennsylvania; Youngstown, Ohio; Detroit and Ann Arbor, Michigan; and Buffalo, New York have come together to rally around a proposal that would create an immigrant enterprise zone in this "Rustbelt," or former manufacturing, region. The idea is to infuse these areas with new immigrant talent matched with incentives for companies to locate there by convincing Congress to loosen immigration restrictions in parts of the country that are lagging economically. Proponents advocate a lobbying strategy to create immigration incentives that would attract companies to co-locate, remain, and grow within the zone. If successful, the companies would be free of many of the immigration restrictions that severely limit their ability to hire foreign-born talent within U.S. borders.[120]

Broaden the Permanent Visa System

America's immigration system requires comprehensive reform that serves everyone who lives and works in America. Our country's outdated immigration policy is incapable of dealing with twenty-first-century immigration patterns and economic realities. In effect, it undermines the very ideals and values on which our country was built and serves neither business nor workers.

Each year, perhaps five hundred thousand undocumented immigrants are absorbed into the U.S. labor force. These numbers likely will increase until U.S. immigration laws are reformed to adequately address the global economic realities of the twenty-first century. We now have a better understanding of why these individuals and their families take such risks to migrate and the roles they play in the U.S. workforce.

Instead of short-term "guest-worker" visas similar to those proposed for several years by President Bush, labor shortages should be filled with workers with full rights, a path to permanent residence, and, if they choose, citizenship. Congress has arbitrarily set the number of employment-based admissions for permanent visas at 140,000 annually. This number falls far short of satisfying the actual need for visas based on the U.S. demand for labor and family reunification.

The number of visas available should respond to actual, demonstrated labor shortages. The new visa program must ensure that U.S. workers are considered first for available jobs and that the economic incentives are in place for U.S. employers to hire U.S. workers first. Businesses should be required to search widely for workers already in the United States, and wage-rate requirements should be high enough to make jobs attractive to U.S. workers. Access to the program should be frozen in areas with high unemployment, and application fees paid by employers that hire new foreign workers under the program should be significant. But once those assurances have been established, visas to accommodate the legitimate needs of employers acting in good faith should be granted generously.

This approach would satisfy employers' needs for workers. More important, it would prevent the creation of an underclass of workers, because immigrants would have full employment rights and access to a permanent future in the American community, economy, and democracy. A visa program that also assures permanent rights to the workers would also minimize their exploitation and make their choice to remain in the United States or return to their native country volitional.

In addition, under the current visa program, families often have to wait five to twenty years to be reunited with their family members. These unreasonable waiting periods contribute to undocumented migration. The visa limits and structural delays must be revamped to end the separation of families and reduce the number of undocumented immigrants entering the country. Family reunification categories must remain a benchmark of our immigration system because we know that family immigrants contribute greatly to U.S. society socially and emotionally, as well as economically.

Revise Harmful Policies on Trade, and Craft Meaningful Labor Standards

We now know the roles that economic globalization and harmful U.S. trade policies have played our failed immigration system. U.S. trade policies have consequences for workers around the world. Thirteen years of NAFTA have resulted in the loss of millions of jobs on both sides of the border. In Mexico, real wages have declined by 20 percent; millions of farmers have been dislocated; and millions more have been consigned to poverty, fueling the flight of labor into the United States.

Our lawmakers must choose to revise harmful policies on trade; to craft meaningful international labor standards; and to work with unions, corporations, and community organizations around the globe to promote better jobs, living standards, and stable communities everywhere. Otherwise, the pressure for undocumented immigration will persist. We can craft trade policies in an era of globalization while respecting the rights and dignity of working people and their families throughout the world.

Too often, when companies cannot export jobs in search of cheap wages and weak labor laws, they import workers to create a domestic pool of exploitable labor, effectively importing the labor standards of developing nations into the United States. Immigration reform must provide meaningful and enforceable penalties for companies that violate health, safety, and labor laws, regardless of the status of their workers. The resources and investigative authority of the U.S. Department of Labor and the Occupational Safety and Health Administration should be expanded to allow the consistent, coordinated, and adequate enforcement of health, safety, and labor laws.

Conclusion

The debate over trade and migration needs to be reframed. Acknowledging and understanding how NAFTA and similar agreements have influenced migration from Mexico is a start. Understanding Mexico's infrastructure and its needs for economic assistance is important, as is understanding the labor needs of U.S. employers. In short, we need to stand back and take a very real look at these issues and craft solutions that will be beneficial to Mexico, as well as to the United States and Canada.

Transforming the United States, Mexico, and Canada into a more integrated North America should be put on the table. Modifying NAFTA is a start, as long as workers and not just corporations benefit. True integration can benefit all three NAFTA countries, as they attempt to meet the tremendous economic challenges presented by the EU and Asia. Workers actually could have benefited under NAFTA if a single internal market had been created—that is, a customs union like that of the EU. In that vision, a protected, internal market would emerge. Businesses from all three countries could benefit from economies of scale; access to raw materials and technology; and shared research and development, training, and business subsidies.[121] But what emerged was far different. Instead, NAFTA was crafted to enhance profitmaking for big business, not for everyday workers. Each country maintained its own markets, but multinationals could trade freely across borders, taking advantage of whatever each country had to offer.

Short of a North American Union, portions of NAFTA, such as the agricultural chapter, should be renegotiated. For example, Mexico should be permitted to regulate its own basic food production and supply. Poor Mexican farmers should not be forced to compete with subsidized agribusinesses in their own markets. Corn and beans should be withdrawn from the free-trade agreement, and compensation funds should be provided to rural parts of Mexico.[122] Viewing international markets as a tool of economic policy is fine, but workers' rights deserve protection, and development should be promoted with certain safeguards and exemptions.[123] We also need to revamp our current visa system and get smart about U.S. businesses' needs for workers, as well as about the social and psychological needs of our immigrant families.

However, if we are to solve the challenge of undocumented Mexican immigration, heavy investment in Mexico's infrastructure and economy must be made. The EU did this successfully in bringing in poor nations, avoiding huge migration from poor to wealthy nations and creating more jobs at home. All three NAFTA countries have much to gain from this approach.

Epilogue

The Ethical Border:
Thinking Outside the (Big) Box

The U.S. immigration system is broken, and enforcing that dysfunctional system has led to troubling results. Hundreds of border crossers have died each year for many years now as a result of Operation Gatekeeper, which pushes migrants to attempt to enter at the most treacherous parts of the deserts and mountains. Anti-immigrant ordinances and laws fomented by resentment over undocumented workers have been proposed and enacted in states and towns across the country, causing great division in those communities. Gestapo-style U.S. Immigration and Customs Enforcement (ICE) raids have disrupted workplaces and surrounding communities, leaving witnesses (and, in some cases, victims) who are U.S. citizens outraged and protesting the treatment of victims "like animals."[1]

Of course, there is another side to immigration enforcement—the Wal-Mart side. After several years of investigation by immigration-enforcement agents and federal prosecutors in Pennsylvania and the arrest of 245 undocumented workers hired as janitors, the big-box retail giant Wal-Mart agreed to pay $11 million in March 2005 to settle claims that it had violated employer-sanctions laws. Federal investigators focused on sixty Wal-Mart stores in twenty-one states, questioning whether the company knew that its janitorial contractors were using undocumented workers. The settlement quelled accusations that Wal-Mart executives or associates (employees) were aware that their contractors used undocumented workers.

While an actual judgment was never made, evidence surfaced that Wal-Mart officials were aware of the workers' status. The arrests stemmed from a probe in Pennsylvania in 1998 and an investigation in 2001 that expanded to New York, Ohio, and Missouri. Both investigations targeted contractors and subcontractors used by Wal-Mart to clean stores. The subcontractors were from more than a hundred third-party contractors who employed individuals to clean stores in nearly one-third of Wal-Mart's more than three thousand stores across the United States. Following the arrests, a grand jury convened, charging Wal-Mart executives with labor-racketeering crimes for knowingly hiring undocumented workers to work in their stores. Although Wal-Mart executives attempted to place the blame on the third-party subcontractors, wiretapped phone conversations revealed that Wal-Mart executives were aware of the subcontractors' illegal activities.

While Wal-Mart is certainly the biggest target, other large U.S. companies have run afoul of employer-sanctions laws against the hiring of undocumented workers. Tyson Foods, Swift and Company, and Golden State Fence Company, which (ironically) helped to build part of the southern border fence designed to prevent undocumented aliens from entering the United States, are just a handful of other examples. Even small companies, including a Wichita painting company, have been caught and punished for recruiting undocumented workers. In every one of these cases, the undocumented workers generally were Mexican, and the jobs paid low wages.

The hiring of substantial numbers of undocumented Mexican workers by large U.S. companies raises a number of questions. Why do these companies rely on such workers? Is it strictly for higher profits? Should we be upset about this phenomenon, and if so, what should we be upset about? Why are undocumented Mexican workers so willing to take these low-paying jobs? What we have learned about the effect of NAFTA and globalization on Mexico at the very least gives us a start on trying to answer the last question.

Given the pressure under which the managers of Wal-Mart stores work, it should come as no surprise that many would turn to janitorial contractors who hire undocumented workers to keep costs down. Despite the fact that Wal-Mart executives attempted to push the blame onto the third-party subcontractors, the presence of recorded phone conversations suggested that Wal-Mart executives were aware of their illegal activities. In a separate lawsuit, some of the janitors claimed that Wal-Mart had violated labor regulations regarding wages and hours. The janitors asserted that Wal-Mart had cheated them out of $200,000 in overtime pay. One plaintiff contended that he had worked seven days a week for eight months and received only $325 for each sixty-hour workweek.

We now know that current immigration-enforcement strategies have gotten us nowhere. More and more undocumented workers are crossing into the United States each year. Industries are demanding more workers from abroad. Many immigrants remain separated from their families. All the while, anti-immigrant forces dominate the airwaves, despite public polling that reveals sentiment in favor of a comprehensive approach to immigration reform.

To break out of the current quagmire, we need to think outside the box, and we need leadership to push for new ideas.

Avoiding Exploitation

To consider solutions, the first task is determining the problem. What part of the story of big-box Wal-Mart hiring undocumented workers is troubling? For years, much public and political reaction to such stories has been expressed in terms of outrage that the workers are taking jobs away from native workers. I am convinced by the data that demonstrate that undocumented immigrants fill jobs that do not interest native workers; that the immigrants are complementary workers; and that as consumers, immigrants tend to help create jobs from which native workers benefit. But stories of companies like Wal-Mart and Tyson Foods hiring undocumented workers are disturbing because of the exploitation of the workers through low wages and poor working conditions. To me, any solution must involve enabling these workers to come out of the shadows so that they will not be so vulnerable to exploitation and work conditions can improve. If available native workers become interested in such jobs after better work conditions and pay are instituted, that's great. The problem with stopping there, however, is that in the case of Wal-Mart, even native U.S. workers continue to be exploited. The solution to the general problem of the abuse of workers at Wal-Mart is a wholly separate challenge that needs to be addressed through labor laws.[2]

So how could undocumented workers come out of the shadows so they would not be so vulnerable to exploitation? How could these workers achieve a status that would enable them to bargain for better working conditions? The obvious answer is that, minimally, they must obtain some type of legal status.

The hiring of substantial numbers of undocumented Mexican workers by large U.S. companies raises a number of questions. Why do these companies rely on such workers? Many companies and, apparently, President Bush (see below), supported by Bureau of Labor Statistics data, believe that there is a great need for low-wage workers in our economy. Is it strictly for better profits? In the case of Wal-Mart, profitmaking is likely a big motivation for hiring undocumented workers. Why are undocumented Mexican workers so willing to take these low-paying jobs? As we have seen, they take these jobs because of the economic disparity between Mexico and the United States (i.e., they need the jobs) and because they are recruited. Should we be upset about this phenomenon, and if so, what should we be upset about? More to the point, should we blame undocumented workers? The blame-the-immigrant game simply does not measure up to what we now know about the impact NAFTA and globalization have had on Mexican workers and growing labor needs in the United States. If we are upset with the Wal-Mart picture, then our outrage is better expressed at the exploitative situation in which the workers are placed.

An Avenue for Workers

Whatever the cause for concern, real solutions to the undocumented immigration situation have to be considered. The standard, well-rehearsed solutions have revolved around border enforcement—for example, in the form of more fencing and agents—and greater enforcement of penalties against employers who hire undocumented workers. But we have seen that those standard solutions have had little impact on the flow of undocumented migrants. The real solution is to develop a system that regularizes a flow of workers to the United States as we help Mexico with its infrastructure and economy so that Mexico can retain many of its workers, as well.

Among the most prominent proposals is the guest-worker program President George W. Bush offered at the halfway point in his administration. Under the plan, first presented on January 7, 2004, undocumented immigrants and workers from abroad would "be able to apply for a three-year work permit, which would be renewable at least once. . . . Workers would be allowed to switch jobs and to move from one type of work to another. . . . Those coming from abroad would be able to bring family members."[3]

The Bush proposal was shrewd; the fact that it did not include an automatic path toward citizenship for the workers addressed the concerns of some anti-immigrant groups. But by providing an opportunity to work for up to six years, many undocumented workers would step forward and reveal themselves, while a large pool of low-wage workers would make the business community extremely happy. In fact, providing a perpetual pool of low-wage workers would revolutionize the labor market.

Legalization (or amnesty) proposals for the estimated 12 million undocumented immigrants in the United States have gone through several iterations during the past few years. In 2005 and 2006, Senator John McCain (R-Ariz.), Senator Edward Kennedy (D-Mass.), Representative James Kolbe (R-Ariz.),

Representative Jeff Flake (R-Ariz.), and Representative Luis Gutierrez (D-Ill.) introduced sweeping immigration reforms that included major guest-worker components. Under the proposed reforms, a new temporary worker visa (H-5A) would be created for jobs that do not require special skills. To qualify, the person would have to have a job offer. For the first year, at least four hundred thousand visas would be made available, with permission for more, depending on demand. After four years of work, H-5A visa holders would be able to apply for lawful permanent resident status through an employer or through self-petition.

The legalization component of the McCain–Kennedy bill (the H-5B program) would have allowed aliens (including undocumented aliens) to obtain a lawful status. The person's spouse and children could also apply. The applicant would pay a $1,000 fine, as well. The person would have to establish that he or she had worked in the United States before the date of introduction and since that date. The initial period of authorized stay would be for six years. After a period of time, the person would be eligible to apply for a green card. Much of the McCain–Kennedy bill was incorporated into a package that received strong bipartisan support in the U.S. Senate in the spring of 2006, but the legislation never passed.

A similar approach for resolving the labor needs of employers and addressing the migration pressures from Mexico has been offered by an independent task force assembled by the Migration Policy Institute. The task force has recommended establishing a "new provisional visa" that begins with an approach similar to that proposed by President Bush: a three-year work visa that is renewable once. Provisional visa holders would include workers with special skills, as well as those who would hold "low- and semi-skilled jobs." The visas would be "suitable for large numbers of workers who are not in temporary or seasonal jobs across the occupational spectrum."[4] Provisional workers could then obtain permanent status by graduating to immigrant status later. Essentially, the task force and other commentators have advocated creating larger programs for temporary workers, as well as expanding permanent opportunities for immigration. Douglas Massey goes a step further, arguing that the number of permanent immigration visas for Mexicans should be increased fivefold to a hundred thousand visas each year, given the special relationship the United States has with Mexico.

Ethical Dimensions

Whether we adopt a provisional worker approach, a fivefold increase in permanent visas to Mexicans, or an approach to open labor migration like that of the European Union, what we now know about the effect of NAFTA and glo-

balization on the Mexican workforce compels us to consider new approaches
to the border. At the very least, the facts demand that we soften the rhetoric
on the so-called immigration problem. Recognizing that we very well may
need immigrant workers—even low-skilled, low-wage workers—may also
encourage us to tone down the anti-immigrant bluster. What we now know
challenges the ethics of our immigration policies and enforcement approach,
given the forces that place pressure on Mexican laborers to migrate north and
the fact that those global forces are far beyond the control of individual laborers. What we now know provides the ethical response to the anti-immigrant
contingent, which claims the high moral ground in opposing legalization on
the grounds that granting amnesty would reward illegal activity. The "illegal
activity" is the result of pressures that our own policies (e.g., subsidies for our
corn farmers) and other forces, such as our thirst for Chinese-made products,
have induced. Thus, the case can be made that legalization and a broader visa
regime not only are the right things to do; they are the least we can do.

Understanding the effects of NAFTA and other aspects of the globalized economy provides us with the foundation to develop a better approach
to the flow of Mexican workers to the United States. The failure of current
militarized and racialized enforcement strategies to stem that flow further
challenges us to step back and address the issue more thoughtfully. In the
United States, we tend to hear about the job losses suffered by U.S. workers
because of NAFTA, but we hear little about job losses for Mexican workers
and fail to consider the fact that the United States very well may need immigrant workers of all sorts.

When we consider the devastating impact on Mexico that NAFTA and
other international monetary and trade agreements supported by the United
States have had, the responsibility for exploring creative answers to help
Mexico out of its current quagmire is placed at our doorstep. Any serious
conversations about Mexican migrants must start with an understanding that
border crossers from Mexico are not simply migrant workers; they are in fact
"economic refugees."[5] Yet in considering the U.S. relationship with Mexico
and migration, economic concerns should not be our strict guide. After all,
"Migration policies have important implications in terms of ethics, human
rights or global justice."[6]

The values that underlie a more expansive view of migration are far different from those that some regard as the populist views of the Minutemen
or Lou Dobbs. However, the ethics or values of a more expansive view of
migration are not elitist. Most people have convictions about what is right
and wrong based on religious beliefs, cultural roots, family background,
personal experiences, laws, organizational values, professional norms, and
political habits. These may not be the best values by which to make ethi-

cal decisions—not because they are unimportant, but because they are not universal.[7]

In contrast to consensual ethical values—such basics as trustworthiness, respect, responsibility, fairness, caring, and citizenship—personal and professional beliefs vary over time, among cultures, and among members of the same society. They are a source of continuous historical disagreement, even wars. There is nothing wrong with having strong personal and professional moral convictions about right and wrong, but unfortunately some people are "moral imperialists" who seek to impose their personal moral judgments on others. The universal ethical value of respect for others dictates honoring the dignity and autonomy of each person and cautions against self-righteousness in areas of legitimate controversy.[8] The universal ethical values of fairness and respect for others are the ones to which I would appeal.

Our current border policy is not an ethical one. It fails to respect the dignity of workers and families who cross the border. It fails to recognize how NAFTA and other global phenomena have helped to exacerbate the economic imbalance between the United States and Mexico. It fails to seriously consider the implications of U.S. trade and agricultural subsidies on developing nations and future migration flows. Yes, failed leadership in Mexico has been a problem, but the United States helped to set the stage for many of those failures. The militarization of the border and stepped-up emphasis on raids in residential neighborhoods, as well as at workplaces, are difficult to justify in that light.

Those who oppose my position may argue that undocumented immigrants have broken the law and that, to respect the law, we should not assist law breakers. That criticism is leveled principally at any proposal (including elements of mine) that advocate legalization for the undocumented. My major proposals for investment in Mexico and visa liberalization are about methods of reducing undocumented migration. But even when contemplating what to do about the undocumented population, the effects of NAFTA, globalization, the recruitment of Mexican workers, and the contributions of those workers to the U.S. economy should be reason enough to support legalization. Legalization is the right response for other reasons, as well.

Even a cursory review of the ICE raids in the past few years reveals an obvious disparity in the targeting of undocumented workers over the employers who hire them. Anyone who sympathizes with the undocumented worker's position but feels that "the law is the law" must hold employers to the same standard. As I argue in Chapter 6, I do not support the employer sanctions laws of 1986 because they lead to discrimination and address the wrong problem. However, I do support the enforcement of labor laws against unscrupulous employers who take advantage of low-income workers—documented or undocumented. Labor-law fines imposed against Agriprocessors Inc. were an exception that proves the rule. All too often, the undocumented workers who are paid less than minimum wage and work in conditions that violate health and safety standards are hauled away, and the employer receives no punishment. Instead of deporting the workers, we should be permitting them to place pressure on the employers to improve wages and working conditions. In the process, the jobs may in fact become more attractive to native workers— something that, ironically, anti-immigrant forces want.

Ken Georgetti, president of the Canadian Labour Congress, and John Sweeney, president of the AFL-CIO, wrote to President Barack Obama and Canadian Prime Minister Stephen Harper, reminding them that "the failure of neoliberal policies to create decent jobs in the Mexican economy under NAFTA has meant that many displaced workers and new entrants have been forced into a desperate search to find employment elsewhere. . . . We believe that all workers, regardless of immigration status, should enjoy equal labor rights. . . . We also support an inclusive, practical and swift adjustment of status program, which we believe would have the effect of raising labor standards for all workers."[9] Although employer sanctions have little effect on migration, they have made workers more vulnerable to pressure by employers. Because working is illegal for them, undocumented workers fear protesting low wages and bad conditions.

Employer sanctions bar the workers from receiving unemployment and disability benefits, although they make payments for them. If they are fired for complaining or organizing, it is much harder to find another job. Despite these obstacles, immigrant workers, including the undocumented, have asserted their labor rights, organized unions, and won better conditions. But employer sanctions have made this harder and riskier. Using Social Security numbers to verify immigration status has led to firing and blacklisting many union activists. Even citizens and permanent residents have felt this impact, because in our diverse U.S. workplaces, immigrant and native-born workers work together. Making it a crime for one group to enforce the law or use its rights has simply created obstacles for everyone else.

Unions now have greater difficulty defending the rights of their own members and organizing new ones. The exploitation of the undocumented workforce will end only if workers are free to make complaints and organize. Eliminating the undocumented workforce without providing an avenue for its labor to be used in the United States also would have devastating economic consequences. Earlier, I cited data on the many U.S. job categories that rely on undocumented workers.[10] Also, we should not lose sight of the fact that immigrants are consumers. Their consumption creates demand for certain goods and services, which in turn creates jobs. Gordon Hanson's findings for the Council on Foreign Relations support these arguments. He notes that between 1960 and 2000, the number of U.S. residents with fewer than twelve years of schooling fell from 50 percent to 12 percent.[11]

The undocumented have filled a void many Americans feel overqualified to fill. In turn, the staffing of these industries stimulates the economy. Low-skilled workers help agricultural, textile, industrial, and food-service companies thrive and then benefit the local economies where those businesses are located. Arizona stands to see the negative effects of massive exclusion of an undocumented workforce. Before the state enacted the Legal Workers Arizona Act, it experienced decades of growth, boosted by its estimated 12 percent undocumented labor force. The new law caused many headaches and loss of production for Arizona employers who need workers.[12]

Those who believe that the law should be abided by at any cost are unfamiliar with the details of immigration law. Legal avenues for obtaining status under current immigration law are quite complicated. Considering the irrationality of certain immigration provisions may help the naysayer understand why many would-be immigrants do not or cannot pursue legal means of obtaining status. Backlogs in family immigration categories can range up to twenty years. Visas for those who want to work or be with family members for part of the year are highly difficult to obtain. The H-2A visa is a good illustration of other problems.

The H-2A visa allows foreigners to enter to perform temporary agricultural labor or services.[13] When foreign workers obtain H-2A visas, they have permission to enter the United States to work only for the petitioning employer and only in the job for which the labor certification was granted.[14] Working at other jobs or for other employers may be grounds for revocation of a foreign worker's H-2A visa.[15] In other words, the H-2A visas bond the workers to a single employer; the worker cannot work for anyone else. Being tied to one employer undermines the enforcement of regulations. The U.S. General Accounting Office has explained that H-2A workers are less aware of their rights than U.S. workers and that they are "unlikely to complain about worker protection violations . . . fearing they will lose their jobs and not be hired in the future."[16] These fears are not imaginary. To illustrate, Florida sugarcane growers operated a "no return list" to weed out complainers and other undesirable workers. Compounding the problem, the U.S. Department of Labor lacks the staff and resources "to adequately police the program."[17] The Department of Labor rarely imposes penalties on growers for violating regulations. Being undocumented allows workers at least to switch jobs if they are being mistreated, whereas obtaining H-2A status carries the danger that workers can be mistreated by their employer. So it does not make sense for many workers to take part in such a program and follow these procedures.

Over the course of history, the U.S. government has made terrible mistakes in its treatment of certain groups of people and has, at times, turned bad policies into laws. Most notably, the U.S. Constitution as it was originally adopted included Article IV, Section 2, which states: "No person held to service or labor in one state, under the laws thereof, escaping into another, shall, in consequence of any law or regulation therein, be discharged from such service or labor, but shall be delivered up on claim of the party to whom such service or labor may be due." It was unconstitutional for a slave to seek freedom in a different state, and fugitive slaves had to be extradited upon the claims of their enslavers. Comparing the history of oppression of the undocumented with that of slaves may not seem fair to many, but there is a clear lesson: The U.S. government can have policies and laws in place that seriously undermine the individual liberties of people living within its borders. When the time comes for these laws to be amended (i.e., the Thirteenth Amendment, which abolished Article IV, Section 2), those who have been the victims of the laws should not be punished for having disobeyed them.

We can be innovative in creating an ethical border. Under the circumstances, one approach to the ethical border is to consider a pure open border. Another might be something along the lines of more flexible, innovative visas. Still another—which is my preference and will be more beneficial to Mexico in the long term—is helping Mexico keep committed, able workers in Mexico by helping to improve economic and social opportunities there. An EU-style approach of serious investment would diminish incentives to migrate. Vicente Fox's pre-9/11 call for a common market in North America with the free movement of labor as well as goods, services, and capital was on the right track.[18]

When the worldwide economic crisis hit, the Group of Twenty Finance Ministers and Central Bank Governors, from nineteen of the world's largest national economies plus the EU, met November in 2008 and again in April 2009 to discuss strategies. President Obama attended the gathering in 2009. The United States, Canada, and Mexico are all members, but so are Great Britain, France, and Germany. To work in this international economic setting, the three NAFTA countries should do all they can to establish heightened "leverage and credibility" and influence on the international stage.[19] This collaboration is important, given the economic challenges presented by the power of the EU and the omnipresence of China. In the fall of 2009, former Mexican President Fox urged the United States to invest 2 percent of its GDP in Mexico to narrow the wage gap while helping the economies of both countries to compete with China.[20]

What we have now learned about the effect of NAFTA on Mexican corn production, for example, provides further impetus for U.S. investment in Mexico. Mexico's ten thousand–year heritage of corn production was destroyed under the NAFTA rules. Mexican corn prices spiraled down in competition from heavily subsidized U.S. imports. Local farm incomes were slashed, resulting in rural suffering and misery from which millions of workers sought escape. Oxfam goes so far as to call the arrangement "rigged," as U.S. corn was dumped into Mexico at artificially low prices—essentially between $105 million and $145 million a year less than the cost of production.[21]

The Mexican government should be criticized for liberalizing the corn market with little regard for the 3 million Mexican farmers who suffered as a result. However, the United States shares much of the blame for so heavily subsidizing its corn industry and for dumping its corn in Mexico without considering the consequences. As Oxfam summarized: "If the benefits of world trade are to be shared fairly—as everyone says they want to see happen—developing countries like Mexico must be allowed to protect their weaker industries. And rich countries like the U.S. must stop subsidizing their agricultural exports."[22] There is a good argument that the United States has a historical debt to pay for what it has done to the agricultural sector in Mexico.

Environmental and health values also provide a strong incentive to change U.S. border policy and invest in the development of Mexico. Sharing more than two thousand miles of border provides an automatic reason for the United States to be concerned about environmental and health issues in Mexico. Data indicate that U.S. economic and border policies have led to environmental degradation in Mexico that is dangerous for both nations. For example, the U.S.–Mexican border includes large deserts, numerous mountain ranges, rivers, wetlands, large estuaries, and shared aquifers. Air, water, and other natural resources flow back and forth in this area, regardless of the border. In recent years, the border region has experienced explosive growth. Currently, 90 percent of the border population resides in fourteen paired, interdependent sister cities. Rapid population growth in urban areas has led to unplanned development, greater demand for land and energy, increased traffic congestion and waste generation, overburdened or unavailable waste-treatment and waste-disposal facilities, and more frequent chemical emergencies. Residents in rural areas suffer from exposure to airborne dust and pesticides, as well as inadequate water supply and waste-treatment facilities. Border residents suffer disproportionately from many environmental health problems, including waterborne diseases and respiratory problems. Projected population growth rates in the border region exceed anticipated U.S. average growth rates (in some cases by more than 40 percent) for each country. By 2020, the population is expected to reach 19.4 million.[23]

The United States already has recognized the need to invest to protect the environment and public health in this cross-border region. In 2001, the U.S. Environmental Protection Agency, together with Mexican agencies, explored ways to improve environmental planning in the region.[24] As a result, these binational agencies created the Border 2012 program, which aims to reduce water and land contamination and air pollution and address other cross-border environmental concerns.[25] In addition, as part of the Border 2012 program, the Centers for Disease Control's Environmental Hazards and Health Effects Program has been and continues to be active in environmental-health activities along the U.S.–Mexican border.[26]

The United States is aware of the need to invest in Mexico to reduce pollution and other environmental hazards that affect a region regardless of jurisdictional or legal boundaries.[27] However, increasing border controls undermine the binational efforts to protect the environment and the public health. The United States needs to augment its efforts of investing in and regulating the development of the Mexican border region in the interest of protecting its own environment and public health.

The United States also needs to acknowledge that public health and environmental interconnectedness is not limited to the border region. Mexico faces a variety of serious environmental problems ranging from extensive damage to the waters and fisheries because of inadequately regulated petroleum exploitation in the Gulf of Mexico, to deforestation, and soil destruction.[28] Irrigation and farming are seriously affected by the pollution problem and lack of environmental regulation in Mexico. For example, wastewater from Mexico City that flows north and is used for irrigation in the state of Hidalgo has been linked to congenital birth defects and high levels of gastrointestinal diseases in that state.[29]

These environmental disasters not only affect our common natural resources, like the air and oceans, but they also affect the agricultural goods entering into the United States, which could undermine U.S. public health. Recall the summer of 2008, when U.S. officials asked Mexican growers to stop importing tomatoes because of a salmonella scare. Although Mexico was not found to be the source of these tainted tomatoes,[30] the investigation ended "in questions."[31] Ultimately, the outbreak and the cross-border investigation demonstrated the interconnection of the United States and Mexico in terms of the environment, agricultural and food industry, and public health. U.S. investment in Mexico's agricultural and environmental development would be prudent, given the relation to U.S. natural resources and public health.

Public-safety concerns are also relevant. Drug trafficking between the United States and Mexico is widespread, and the drug trade and the war on drugs is becoming increasingly violent on both sides of the border.[32] The

United States is "ready" to increase military assistance in Mexico to fight the war on drugs.[33] It would be wiser, however, to improve its economic and border policies if it wants to weaken the drug trade and improve public safety. Economic policies that increase poverty in Mexico also fuel the drug trade.[34] In a report on the Latin American Drug problem, the International Crisis Group (ICG) emphasized the need to increase economic opportunity and infrastructure to reduce the supply of drugs fueling the international drug trade. The ICG stated that, to reduce supply, "much greater recognition is also needed of the pressures produced by extreme poverty, lack of economic opportunities and basic infrastructure, and government abandonment of indigenous populations in the Andean countryside."[35] If the United States wants to be realistic about the war on drugs and improve public safety, it has to seriously invest in developing the Mexican economy to protect the rights and minimize suffering of poor Mexicans.

Calming Fears about a North American Union

The prospect of a North American Union is a panacea to some and a threat to U.S. sovereignty to others. Congressmen Duncan Hunter (R-Calif.), Ron Paul (R-Tex.), and Tom Tancredo (R-Colo.) bristle at the mention of anything resembling a North American Union. The former Cable News Network show-man Lou Dobbs warns that the 2005 Security and Prosperity Partnership of North America among the three nations was a step toward giving up U.S. sovereignty, even though the accord focused on trade regulations and bor-der congestion without touching on migration. The questions raised by these opponents are similar to concerns raised by various members of the EU over the years. In the end, however, through negotiation, planning, and careful implementation, EU members have recognized the overwhelming benefits of their partnership while maintaining sovereignty over their own matters. Skeptics need only consider the ability of EU members to block the adoption of a uniform European Constitution and the Lisbon Treaty if they are con-cerned with loss of sovereignty.[36]

A North American partnership that incorporates serious investment in Mexico to boost its economy would be good for Mexico as well as for the United States. A system in which Mexico loses large numbers of its able-bodied workers cannot be good for Mexico. Consider the Mexican state of Zacatecas, a major source of labor migration to the United States. About a million dollars in remittances flow into the state each day. Yet local assembly plants had to close because of a lack of workers.[37] An open border without economic opportunity in Mexico could hurt Mexico psychologically, as well. Workers could focus more on their plan to leave Mexico than on how to use their talents in Mexico.[38] Thus, the type of sequencing used by the EU, in which substantial investments were made in the poor country prior to opening the border to all labor migrants, should be followed. In the meantime, however, we should expand labor and family migration categories to begin resolving tensions that have led to undocumented migration. A balance is necessary, but as in the EU's experience with poor members after investments are made, we would eventually see fewer Mexicans migrants than expected, because incentives for able Mexican workers to remain home would be felt. In other words, the undocumented immigration challenge would be solved.

The Politics of Reform

Enacting immigration legislation that includes a large investment component for Mexico or coming up with a separate Mexico investment piece on its own or as part of NAFTA reform with Canada is, of course, a political challenge. However, I believe that our nation is up to that challenge and that a proposal for massive investment in Mexico coupled with EU-style labor migration can find support from what are regarded as pro- and anti-immigrant quarters. Pro-immigrant groups want Mexican workers and their families treated fairly and humanely. Anti-immigrant groups want Mexican workers and their families to stay in Mexico and stop entering the United States illegally. The violent approach to immigration enforcement has not accomplished anything for either group. Smart-thinking anti-immigrant forces should be able to see how invest-in-Mexico and open-labor-migration approaches will actually help move them closer to achieving their goals.

Stranger political coalitions have come together in the past. In the 1920s, long after the enactment of the Chinese exclusion laws and the curtailment of Japanese labor migration to the United States, a wave of anti-Filipino sentiment arose along the West Coast. The large number of Filipino workers coming in stirred up economic and social complaints among white workers, and calls for the exclusion of Filipinos ensued. At the time, however, the Philippines were a possession of the United States, and Filipinos were considered U.S. nationals not subject to immigration laws. Ultimately, a coalition of anti-Filipino advocates and Filipino nationalists seeking Philippine independence was able to convince Congress to enact the Philippine Independence Act of 1934. The law, which would take effect in 1946, granted the Philippines its independence and reduced Filipino immigration to the United States to an annual quota of 50 visas.[39]

From my perspective, stories of victims of ICE raids; the senseless prosecution of human-rights workers who provide water and medical aid to border

crossers facing death in the desert; accounts of contributions that undocumented migrants continue to make to the United States; and the existence
of Development, Relief and Education for Alien Minors (DREAM) Act students who are at the threshold of greatness are reason enough for policymakers to realize that we need a new, nonviolent approach to the U.S.–Mexican
border. When you add the information on the effect of NAFTA on the
Mexican economy and the example of the EU approach to poor nations who
have been welcomed into that union, I would hope that little doubt would
be left in the minds of the thoughtful public and clear-headed policymakers
that the solution to the so-called problem of undocumented immigration lies
in the realm of a generous approach to the border and assisting Mexico with
its economy.

After more than thirty-five years of advocacy on behalf of immigrants,
I know that getting policymakers to do the right thing will require political
will, power, and jockeying. Political forces have come together to drive dramatic changes in immigration policy in my lifetime. In 1952, Harry Truman
vetoed legislation because it failed to correct the inherent racism embedded
in the national-origins quota-selection system. "The time to shake off this
dead weight of past mistakes is now," he said. "The time to develop a decent
policy of immigration—a fitting instrument for our foreign policy and a true
reflection of the ideals we stand for, at home and abroad—is now."[40] Then
in 1958—two years before he was elected president—John F. Kennedy set
out his broad philosophy on immigration policy in the book *A Nation of
Immigrants*. He wrote: "Immigration policy should be generous; it should
be fair; it should be flexible. With such a policy we can turn to the world,
and to our own past, with clean hands and a clear conscience."[41] Truman's
and Kennedy's hopes finally were embodied in the 1965 amendments that
opened up immigration to the United States to migrants from all over the
world.

The legalization program contained in the Immigration Reform and
Control Act (IRCA) of 1986, albeit limited and a narrow political victory,
gave a second chance to 3 million undocumented immigrants. Ronald Reagan
supported the legalization provision. When he signed IRCA, he stated: "We
have consistently supported a legalization program which is both generous to
the alien and fair to the countless thousands of people throughout the world
who seek legally to come to America. The legalization provisions in this act
will go far to improve the lives of a class of individuals who now must hide
in the shadows, without access to many of the benefits of a free and open
society." Even before he became president, Reagan wondered about what he
called "the illegal alien fuss. Are great numbers of our unemployed really
victims of the illegal alien invasion, or are those illegal tourists actually doing

work our own people won't do? One thing is certain in this hungry world: No regulation or law should be allowed if it results in crops rotting in the fields for lack of harvesters."[42] Political leadership was necessary in both the 1960s and the 1980s, and the leadership emerged.

Today, the debate over what is termed "comprehensive immigration reform" does not even contain the investment elements of my proposals. It is hard enough to get legalization seriously considered, I am told. How could I ask for billions to be invested in Mexico? My answer is relatively simple: Major resistance to legalization today is couched in terms of "If you reward these law breakers, then more will come" or "We have to get control of the border first." My proposal to invest in Mexico and create an EU-style border for labor migration are major building blocks to the long-term reduction of undocumented migration. The violent, intrusive enforcement approach has failed because it does not address the root causes of migration or the need that many U.S. employers have for low-wage workers.

I believe that there is political interest in the approach I advocate. After meeting with the Congressional Hispanic Caucus in March 2009, President Obama confirmed his strong support for comprehensive immigration reform and explained why a piecemeal approach will not work:

> I think the American people . . . appreciate and believe in immigra-
> tion. But they can't have a situation where you just have half a mil-
> lion people pouring over the border without any kind of mechanism
> to control it. So we've got to deal with that at the same time as we
> deal in a humane fashion with folks who are putting down roots here,
> have become our neighbors, have become our friends, they may have
> children who are U.S. citizens. That's the kind of comprehensive
> approach that we have to take.[43]

While he campaigned for the presidency, Obama recognized the strategic link between investment in Mexico and the reduction of undocumented migration:

> At a national level, our diplomacy with Mexico must aim to amend
> NAFTA. I will seek enforceable labor and environment standards—
> not unenforceable side agreements that have done little to curb
> NAFTA's failures. *To reduce illegal immigration, we also have to help
> Mexico develop its own economy, so that more Mexicans can live their
> dreams south of the border.* That's why I'll increase foreign assistance,
> including expanded micro-financing for businesses in Mexico.[44]

And soon after inauguration day, the White House posted this on the "Agenda" section of its Web site under immigration that invoked similar sentiment:

> For too long, politicians in Washington have exploited the immigration issue to divide the nation rather than find real solutions. Our broken immigration system can only be fixed by putting politics aside and offering a complete solution that secures our border, enforces our laws, and reaffirms our heritage as a nation of immigrants.
>
> Create Secure Borders: Protect the integrity of our borders. Support additional personnel, infrastructure and technology on the border and at our ports of entry.
>
> Improve Our Immigration System: Fix the dysfunctional immigration bureaucracy and increase the number of legal immigrants to keep families together and meet the demand for jobs that employers cannot fill.
>
> Remove Incentives to Enter Illegally: Remove incentives to enter the country illegally by cracking down on employers who hire undocumented immigrants.
>
> Bring People Out of the Shadows: Support a system that allows undocumented immigrants who are in good standing to pay a fine, learn English, and go to the back of the line for the opportunity to become citizens.
>
> *Work with Mexico: Promote economic development in Mexico to decrease illegal immigration.*[45]

An influential immigrant-rights organization, America's Voice, describes its reform agenda this way:

> Our prescription for reform is to deal with the byproducts of our broken immigration system—the 12 million undocumented immigrants living and working in this country—while simultaneously updating our immigration laws to prevent a future build-up of undocumented immigrants. Our reform agenda combines the following:
>
> - Smart and professional border enforcement
> - A crackdown on employers who hire undocumented workers to exploit them
> - A controlled increase in legal visas for the future flow of needed workers and close family members
> - An earned citizenship program that requires those here ille-

gally to get on the right side of the law by passing background checks, studying English, paying taxes, and getting
to the back of the citizenship line
- *Efforts to reduce migration pressures in sending countries over time*

Once implemented, a workable reform law would dramatically reduce current and future unauthorized immigration, restore the benefits of legal immigration, secure the border, and level the playing field for law-abiding employers and all workers in the United States. It would replace a chaotic black market with a properly regulated legal immigration system and a significant reduction in illegal immigration.[46]

Observers such as Robert Pastor have called for substantial EU-style investments in Mexico.[47] Laura Carlsen, director of the Americas Policy Program in Mexico City, advocates a renegotiation of NAFTA that "should include a view toward job generation and retention in Mexico, and a compensation fund similar to the European Union's transition funds for less-developed countries." Why? In part because when Mexican real wages drop by 10 percent, apprehensions at the border rise by about 8 percent. Real wages in Mexico fell by 24 percent from December 2006 to August 2008 and are plummeting now with the economic crisis.[48]

The sooner the anti-immigrant forces recognize these connections, the better. It is in their interests, as well as the interests of all residents of the NAFTA countries, to make the connections between real investment and development in Mexico. The investment strategy is the sensible way to relieve the pressures for undocumented migration.

The most influential immigrant-rights advocates in Washington, D.C., have adopted an interesting rule-of-law political strategy in the past few years to push for comprehensive immigration reform. Tom Barry offers a stinging rebuke of what he regards as the prevailing beltway strategy:

Leading up to the adoption of the [Democratic] party's [2008] platform, a coalition of immigrant-rights, ethnic, and policy groups came together around a strategy intended to co-opt the law-and-order rhetoric of immigration restrictionists. With great success, they advocated that the Democratic Party and all CIR [comprehensive immigration reform] proponents rally around a "get right with the law" framework for immigration reform. . . . [T]he platform propagated the language advanced by the Center for American Progress, America's Voice, [the National Council of La Raza], and others in the CIR coalition, stating:

"We must require them to come out of the shadows and get right with the law."

The "rule of law" and "get right with the law" now reverberates among the circle of Washington organizations that are leading the charge for a new CIR bill in the Obama administration. As if to declare their law-and-order credentials, the National Immigration Forum, America's Voice, Center for Community Change, NDN [New Democrat Network], and others routinely insert rule of law language in all their communications.

In their new strategy for liberal immigration reform, these immigrant-rights advocates haven't been entirely clear about their priorities. While advancing the tough "rule of law" enforcement and "get right with the law" language, they haven't explicitly rejected the "enforcement-first" approach.

Rather than forthrightly saying that it is impossible to restore the "rule of law" or promote "smart law enforcement" when the laws are inadequate and unjust, they have incorporated the law-and-order language to widen their political reach.

With the hope of winning center-right support for liberal immigration reform, [these advocates] have retooled their own messaging. But in the process they have lent moral support to the law-and-order regimen while burying their message.

Nor did they outline a logic for immigration reform that was more holistic than the simplistic rule of law framework they embraced as a central argument for comprehensive immigration reform. They presented no vision of a future immigration policy that would ensure that immigration flows are sustainable socially and economically.

It shouldn't be surprising, then, that the Democratic Party leadership, like the Republicans, have interpreted the apparent political consensus around a "rule of law" immigration and border policy as a political mandate to continue along the "enforcement first" path set by the Bush administration. [Secretary of Homeland Security Janet] Napolitano is doing just that, and it may be time for liberal immigration reform advocates to revisit their opportunistic "rule of law" messaging and center-right framing of the immigration crisis.[49]

From what I know of the advocacy groups upbraided by Barry, they have appeared to adopt a rule-of-law theme probably, in their view, to gain credibility with the public and the media while co-opting the law-and-order rhetoric of restrictionists. Like Barry, I fear that this theme can be interpreted as an endorsement of the "enforcement-first" methods of the Bush administration, with all of its ugly trappings. However, when a Bush administration–style ICE raid took place in Washington State in February 2009 after Napolitano took the reins at the Department of Homeland Security, she appeared surprised and ordered an investigation. No other such raids have occurred since then, and Napolitano has indicated that enforcement should focus on employers who hire undocumented workers, not on the workers themselves. America's Voice consistently has been super-critical of ICE raids. Also, a review of the immigration advocacy positions of the organizations identified by Barry do in fact include what might be labeled an "outline" for immigration reform that is "holistic."

The National Council of La Raza (NCLR) states its position this way:

> NCLR supports comprehensive immigration reform that includes the following principles: 1) restoring order by getting the 12 million undocumented people in our country to come forward, obtain legal status, learn English, and assume the rights and responsibilities of citizenship while creating smart enforcement policies that uphold national security and the Constitution; 2) cracking down on unscrupulous employers whose practices undermine conditions for all workers; 3) unclogging legal channels to reunite families and allow future workers to come in with the essential rights and protections that safeguard our workforce; and 4) enacting proactive measures to advance the successful integration of new immigrants into our communities.[50]

Still, there is danger that the right can take the requirement that undocumented immigrants "get on the right side of the law" or "restoring order" themes and call it an endorsement of raids and an agreement that the border must be secure before legalization can be considered.

So while I do not like the rule-of-law political strategy, especially if it is interpreted to mean that the border must be secure before anything else can be legislated, the advocacy of my positions for investment in Mexico and a new vision of the border for labor migration can be part of any strategy that seeks progressive immigration reform. My real concern is that the debate over whether millions of undocumented workers in the United States should be granted legalization distracts us from the more important questions about how we can structure the relationship among Mexico, the United States, and Canada in a manner that is good for all three countries. In my view, the debate actually has to be recast to focus on the causes of undocumented migration from Mexico and address those causes. The cause is not the recruitment of undocumented workers by U.S. employers;

it is the economic problems in Mexico in which the United States has had a hand. My investment proposal is more about addressing push factors than pull factors of migration.

Long-Range Solutions

My advocacy for legalization of undocumented immigrants often generates the question: What about those who enter illegally after the first 12 million are granted amnesty? The question assumes that undocumented migration would continue. The question also assumes that legalization would be legislated without anything else. That is the key: Without comprehensive reform, legalization alone will solve nothing but the status for those who benefit from the program. Minimally, legalization must be complemented with liberalization of the labor and family immigration categories. However, as I have argued, in addition to visa liberalization, a better approach would be to include EU-type investment in the Mexican economy and infrastructure and adjust the agricultural chapter of NAFTA. What we do know for sure is that the current enforcement-only approach is not working. The EU evidence is clear: A visa expansion and investment approach is much more likely to have a real, long-term impact on Mexican migration.

Those looking for a permanent, overnight solution to the challenge of undocumented migration will not find it. We certainly have not found it in the enforcement-only strategy in which our nation is currently engaged. And, truth be told, many of the policies I advocate will take years to fully take effect. Certainly, legalization for the undocumented, an expansion of the labor and family visa categories, and allowing Mexico to regain control of its own food production will have significant, immediate effect. However, the long-range task of building Mexico's infrastructure and economy to significantly reduce emigration will take time. That process took time in Ireland, Spain, and Portugal in the EU experience, as well. However, the longer we wait to embark on that task of providing effective assistance to Mexico, the longer we delay making progress along those lines.

Some may find my position contradictory. In addition to legalization for the undocumented, I advocate open labor migration for nationals of NAFTA countries the same way that EU nationals have it within the EU. That position is grounded in the rights that I believe workers should hold inherently, as well as in the fact that U.S. businesses need workers. However, my call for deep investment in Mexico, if heeded, will result in more employment opportunities in Mexico, encouraging Mexicans to stay home. This is important for Mexico: The country's loss of able-bodied workers is not a good idea.

Mexico will need workers to build its economy and infrastructure with the investment funds. Is this really a contradiction? I think not. First of all, since there are millions of workers involved, both outcomes can co-exist; it will be a matter of balance. But in the long run, I believe that more Mexican workers will stay at home rather than travel to work.

Some U.S. core industries thrive because there is an immigrant labor base willing to do the work necessary to keep them going. Consider agriculture and the broader hospitality and food and restaurant industry. In many parts of the country, there are not enough willing U.S. workers to fill these jobs. The migrant labor force meets this need and thus helps these industries grow and stimulate the economy, thereby helping the business owners and businesses remain viable.

We should not lose sight, however, of the different reasons that workers migrate. Many come because they want to join family here. However, others come simply for the work; they really do not want to uproot their homes, their lives. Coming to the United States is not an easy, or always a desirable, path for many. They would stay home if real employment opportunities existed for them. The current economic imbalance does not allow fully voluntary decisions to be made.

I realize the need for bold leadership if a North American Union or critical aspects of such integration (such as serious investment in Mexico and expanding the visa system) are to be implemented. Our nation has experienced that bold leadership in the immigration context: when, as noted earlier, Harry Truman vetoed major legislation in 1952 and chastised Congress for not overhauling the visa system; when Dwight Eisenhower called for an end to the racist national-origins quota system; when John Kennedy and Lyndon Johnson led the country to finally reform the vision of the immigration-selection system in the 1960s; and when Ronald Reagan spoke out in support of granting legalization to undocumented workers in the 1980s. Investment in Mexico will take serious money—billions. However, we have wasted billions on an enforcement-only approach, and the money would be better spent encouraging Mexicans to stay home through investment. Following World War II, the United States demonstrated leadership and made massive investments in the futures of the nation and the world in efforts such as the Marshall Plan to help rebuild Europe and the GI Bill to repay and invest in our soldiers.[51] These efforts were publicly financed, but they helped the United States experience an impressive period of economic growth; they were investments that paid off.[52] Call it a bailout of Mexico, if you must, but my proposal concerns a broader vision of North America that will help to stabilize the region as well as that country. In the process, undocumented Mexican migration will come under control.

Closing

Many recent calls for immigration reform that would benefit Mexican migration tend to fall into the trap of viewing such migration purely in terms of filling the employment needs of U.S. businesses or emphasizing the economic boon that immigrants represent to the United States. The Nobel laureate Gary Becker argues that we should give priority to immigrants from our NAFTA partners, recognizing them as human capital, resembling the movement of goods, services, and financial capital.[53] Similarly, after she left office in 2009, Secretary of State Condoleezza Rice lamented the Bush administration's failure to achieve immigration reform. "We need immigration reform. I don't care if it's for the person who crawls across the desert to earn $5 an hour, or for Sergey Brin, who came here from Russia and founded Google," she said. "As a country, we can't have people living in the shadows. It's just wrong. It's not only ineffective, it's wrong." She also said that immigrants were critical to the country's financial health and that reform was needed to fuel the next round of economic growth.[54] This is an alluring approach that caters to economic concerns that apparently matter a great deal in the public's attitude toward immigration.

However, when we focus purely on the economic well-being of the country in judging immigration, we miss an opportunity to make a bold statement on immigration and to reframe the debate in a manner that can demonstrate our humanity.[55] I believe that the vast majority of Americans, if given the choice, would not endorse the mistreatment of immigrants—documented or undocumented. Currently, Americans see no immediate way to intervene in uncivil immigration-enforcement methods such as Operation Gatekeeper and Gestapo-type ICE raids. If Americans understood the impact of NAFTA and globalization on Mexico, they would recognize the need to work with Mexico as regional partners with much to gain. But a vocal minority represented by the Federation for American Immigration Reform (FAIR) and Lou Dobbs have hijacked the issue. As with many other policy debates, in the area of immigration policy and enforcement, the "fervor and activism of [a] small minority greatly magnify their influence, especially within the U.S. Congress."[56]

When it comes to the treatment of fellow human beings who have crossed into our territory, we should consider what has driven or attracted them to travel before we become overly judgmental. As American culture, economic influence, political power, and military presence affect the far reaches of the globe, we cannot be too surprised about the attraction that the United States holds throughout the world. Coupled with the ubiquity of American culture, the United States appeals to would-be immigrants and refugees who seek the

American dream of freedom, prosperity, and consumerism. Migrant workers, refugees, high-tech workers, multinational executives, and familial relatives (both professionals and those from the working class) all respond to this attraction. Thus, America itself is responsible for luring countless migrants to our shores each year as the phenomenon reinvigorates the Statue of Liberty's call to those "yearning to breathe free."

In many respects, the problem with NAFTA was not what the treaty included, but what it did not include: a "unified approach" that recognized the need for the three countries to come together across social and economic lines.[57] At the same time, we must balance the fact that open borders could actually harm Mexico through the continued loss of workers that the country needs to thrive. Thus, as part of the North American community, the United States, along with Canada, must help Mexico in its economic development. We must finally address the missing parts of NAFTA as we all recognize our responsibility for the entire region.

The debate over trade and migration needs to be reframed. NAFTA and similar agreements have had tremendous influence on migration pressures from Mexico. Mexico needs infrastructure and economic assistance. We need a new vision of the border and labor migration. In short, we need to stand back and reexamine these issues to craft solutions to benefit both the United States and Mexico.

The anti-immigrant lobby has used the politics of fear to generate much of the hysteria over immigration today. It advances the image of hordes of immigrants coming to take our jobs and commit crimes, all the while not wanting to speak English. Of course, all of the empirical data contravene those myths. Yet fear and intimidation have stalled comprehensive immigration reform. Fear makes us lose our conscience. It paralyzes us, and we lose our sense of analysis and reflection.[58]

Fear and lack of analysis have led us to our current state. It is rather ironic that we militarize the border that we share with a "friendly, peaceful nation" that is an "ally and a large trading partner."[59] We treat workers from Mexico as the enemy because they have pierced the national border surreptitiously. Without reflection, we demonize them.

We should know better.[60] The evidence on NAFTA and other factors of globalization are clear. As long as the economic imbalance between Mexico and the United States persists, Mexican migration will persist. The market forces are simply too strong to be overcome by standard enforcement-only responses through more fencing, ICE raids, and renewing efforts to place sanctions on employers. Instead, seriously working with the Mexican economy should be viewed as serving the social, economic, and political strategic needs of North America, as well as those of the United States.[61]

The time has come to think beyond enforcement-only approaches—to think creatively. The movement of labor is part and parcel of the regional and global economy in which we are engaged. NAFTA is riddled with oversights and mistakes. But the EU has taught us that investment in Mexico's economy and infrastructure can have an impact on migration and benefit the entire region. The smart thing to do—and the right thing to do—is to recognize that a brighter economic and social future will come with an open-minded, integrated, ethical partnership with our neighbors.

Notes

ACKNOWLEDGMENTS

1. Thomas More, *Utopia Book* 1 (1516), available at http://www.quotationspage.com/quote/33910.html.

INTRODUCTION

1. The Pew Hispanic Center estimates that 12 million undocumented immigrants resided in the United States in 2007, but the number declined in 2008, in part because of the slowdown in U.S. economic growth. About 57 percent of the undocumented population is from Mexico: see Jeffrey Passel and D'Vera Cohn, *Trends in Unauthorized Immigration: Undocumented Inflow Now Trails Legal Inflow* (Washington, D.C.: Pew Hispanic Center, 2008).

2. Dahleen Glanton and Tribune National Correspondent, *For Immigrants, Raid Dims Hope for a Better Life*, CHICAGO TRIBUNE, December 11, 2006.

3. Id.

4. Id.

5. Russ Bynum, *Immigration Raid Cripples Georgia Town*, ASSOCIATED PRESS, September 15, 2006.

6. *SPLC Files Federal Lawsuit Challenging Constitutionality of Immigration Raids That Terrorized Latino Residents of Southeast Georgia Towns*, P.R. NEWSWIRE, PUBLIC INTEREST SERVICES, November 1, 2006.

7. Id.; Patrick Jonsson, *Crackdown on Immigrants Empties a Town and Hardens Views*, CHRISTIAN SCIENCE MONITOR, October 3, 2006.

8. Russ Bynum, *Immigration Raids Leave Georgia Town Bereft, Stunned*, SEATTLE TIMES, September 16, 2006.

9. *Immigration Raid Still Hurting Pork Producer*, ASSOCIATED PRESS, December 28, 2006 (quoting Brad Freking, owner and managing partner of New Fashion Pork).

10. See Lydia Saad, *Most Americans Favor Giving Illegal Immigrants a Chance*, GALLUP NEWS SERVICE, 2007 (a Gallup Poll in April 2007 found that more than 80 percent of Americans favor a path to citizenship for undocumented immigrants). The article discusses polling data: "A USA Today/Gallup poll conducted April 13–15, 2007, finds the American public in broad agreement with Bush's desire to give illegal immigrants a path to citizenship. Forty-two percent of Americans say their preferred approach to dealing with illegal immigrants is to require them to leave the United States but then allow them to return and become U.S. citizens if they meet certain requirements. Another 36% would prefer a more liberal system that allows illegal immigrants to remain in the United States while they work toward meeting requirements needed to gain citizenship."

11. Letter from Edward Tuffy II, president, Local 2544, National Border Patrol Council, to the Hon. Jon Kyl, U.S. Senator, May 24, 2007, available at http://www.nbpc2554.0rg/docs/kyl_letter_amnesty.pdf.

12. Tom Tancredo, *Join Tom's Army against Amnesty and Together Let's Defeat Amnesty and Amnesty Politicians*, press release, available at http://web.archive.org/web/20070710151006/http://www.teamtancredo.com/save_america_index.asp.

13. 153 CONGRESSIONAL RECORD S8641–07, June 28, 2007, at S8645 (statement of Senator Corker).

14. Pamela Constable, *"No Amnesty" Is Cry at D.C. Immigration Protest*, WASHINGTON POST, April 23, 2007, at B1.

15. Nathan Thornburgh, *The Case for Amnesty*, TIME, June 18, 2007, at 38.

16. Barbara Ehrenreich, *What America Owes Its "Illegals,"* NATION, June 13, 2007.

17. Bill Ong Hing, *Deporting Our Souls: Values, Morality and Immigration Policy* (Cambridge: Cambridge University Press, 2006); Bill Ong Hing, *To Be an American: Cultural Pluralism and the Rhetoric of Assimilation* (New York: New York University Press, 1997).

18. Cliff Olin, *Masses of Immigrants Demand Amnesty*, LOS ANGELES INDEPENDENT MEDIA CENTER, April 9, 2007.

19. Mike Allen, *Bush Proposes Legal Status for Immigrant Labor: Workers Could Stay Six Years or More*, WASHINGTON POST, January 8, 2004, at A1.

CHAPTER 1

1. Kevin R. Johnson, *Free Trade and Closed Borders: NAFTA and Mexican Immigration to the United States*, 27 UC DAVIS LAW REVIEW 937, 940–42 (1994).

2. Id. at 59–60 (citing Congressman Robert Matsui, a key NAFTA supporter in the House of Representatives).

3. Bill Ong Hing, *Defining America through Immigration Policy* 188–190 (Philadelphia: Temple University Press, 2004).

4. Bill Ong Hing, *Deporting Our Souls: Values, Morality and Immigration Policy* 12–13 (Cambridge: Cambridge University Press, 2006). The low wage labor sector is not the only migration from Mexico that has accelerated since the country initiated new economic reforms. Business visas for Mexicans have tripled to about 438,000

annually, while the number of intra-company transferees (for corporate executives and key managers) and investors also has grown dramatically. The number of Mexican tourists has increased by six times (to over 3.6 million each year), while the number of foreign students doubled. Douglas S. Massey, *Backfire at the Border: Why Enforcement without Legalization Cannot Stop Illegal Immigration*, Trade Policy Analysis no. 9, Cato Institute, June 13, 2005, at 3.

5. Massey writes, "Despite the fact that politicians sold NAFTA as a way for Mexico 'to export goods and not people,' everything that occurs in the course of integrating the North American market makes the cross-border movement of people—including workers—more rather than less likely in the short and medium run. The expanding binational network of transportation and communication that evolves to facilitate trade also makes the movement of people easier and cheaper. The interpersonal connections formed between Mexicans and Americans in the course of daily business transactions create a social infrastructure of friendship and kinship that encourage migration and facilitate further movement": id. at 5.

6. Jason Ackleson, *Achieving "Security and Prosperity": Migration and North American Economic Integration*, 5 IMMIGRATION POLICY IN FOCUS, no. 2 (February 2006) at 1.

7. See Deborah White, *Pros and Cons of Free Trade Agreements*, available at http://usliberals.about.com/od/theeconomyjobs/i/FreeTradeAgmts.htm.

8. Id.

9. Id.

10. Id.

11. Id.

12. Id.

13. Massey, *Backfire at the Border* at 3.

14. Id.; see Chapter 2.

15. Christopher J. Cassise, *The European Union v. the United States under the NAFTA: A Comparative Analysis of the Free Movement of Persons within the Regions*, 46 SYRACUSE LAW REVIEW 1343, 1348 (1996).

16. Johnson, *Free Trade and Closed Borders* at 940–941.

17. Robert A. Pastor, *Toward a North American Community: Lessons from the Old Word for the New* 6 (Washington, D.C.: Institute for International Economics, 2001).

18. Johnson, *Free Trade and Closed Borders* at 938–939.

19. Id. at 951.

20. Johnson, *Free Trade and Closed Borders* at 939.

21. Id. at 940.

22. Id. at 941.

23. Id. at 960.

24. Cassise, *The European Union v. the United States under the NAFTA* at 1372.

25. Johnson, *Free Trade and Closed Borders* at 941.

26. Massey, *Backfire at the Border* at 1.

27. Ackleson, *Achieving "Security and Prosperity"* at 3–4.

28. Jennifer E. Harman, *Mexican President Vicente Fox's Proposal for Expanding NAFTA into a European Union–Style Common Market—Obstacles and Outlook*, 7 LAW

AND BUSINESS REVIEW OF THE AMERICAS 207, 212 (2001). Mexico supplies $200 billion a year in goods and services to the United States now, compared to $60 billion before NAFTA: id.

29. Robert J. Flanagan, *Globalization and Labor Conditions* 14 (Oxford: Oxford University Press, 2006).

30. Bradly J. Condon and J. Brad McBride, *Do You Know the Way to San Jose? Resolving the Problem of Illegal Mexican Migration to the United States*, 17 GEORGETOWN IMMIGRATION LAW JOURNAL 251, 261 (2003).

31. Pastor, *Toward a North American Community* at 79.

32. Jeff Faux, *The Global Class War: How America's Bipartisan Elite Lost Our Future—and What It Will Take to Win It Back* 134 (Hoboken, N.J.: John Wiley and Sons, 2006).

33. Condon and McBride, *Do You Know the Way to San Jose?* at 293.

34. Monica L. Heppel and Luis R. Torres, *Mexican Immigration to the United States after NAFTA*, 20 FLETCHER FORUM OF WORLD AFFAIRS 51, 58 (Fall 1996).

35. Id.

36. Ackleson, *Achieving "Security and Prosperity,"* at 3–4.

37. Pastor, *Toward a North American Community* at 108–109.

38. Michael Pollan, *The Omnivore's Dilemma—a Natural History of Four Meals* 54 (New York: Penguin, 2007).

39. Id. at 61.

40. Sandra Polaski, *Twelve Years of the North American Free Trade Agreement: Hearing before the Subcommittee on International Trade of the S. Comm. on Finance*, CQ Congressional Testimony, 109th Cong. (September 11, 2006).

41. Id.

42. Faux, *The Global Class War* at 134.

43. Id.

44. Polaski, *Twelve Years of the North American Free Trade Agreement*.

45. Id.

46. Laura Carlsen, *NAFTA and Immigration: Toward a Workable and Humane Integration*, unpublished ms., March 2008 at 6.

47. Id.

48. Polaski *Twelve Years of the North American Free Trade Agreement*.

49. Id.

50. Louis Uchitelle, *NAFTA Should Have Stopped Illegal Immigration, Right?* NEW YORK TIMES, February 18, 2007.

51. Faux, *The Global Class War* at 136.

52. Polaski, *Twelve Years of the North American Free Trade Agreement*.

53. Uchitelle, *NAFTA Should Have Stopped Illegal Immigration, Right?*

54. Nina Bernstein, *Most Mexican Immigrants in New Study Gave Up Jobs to Take Their Chances in U.S.*, NEW YORK TIMES, December 7, 2005, at A30 (citing Kathleen Newland, director, Migration Policy Institute).

55. Celia W. Dugger, *Report Finds Few Benefits for Mexico in NAFTA*, NEW YORK TIMES, November 19, 2003 (citing study by Carnegie Endowment for International Peace).

56. Rakesh Kochhar, *Survey of Mexican Migrants, Part Three: The Economic Transition to America*, Pew Hispanic Center, Washington, D.C., December 6, 2005, at 1.

57. Douglas S. Massey, *An Exercise in Self-Deception*, NEWSWEEK, January 19, 2004, at 41.

58. Faux, *The Global Class War* at 136.

59. Polaski, *Twelve Years of the North American Free Trade Agreement*.

60. Id.

61. Pastor, *Toward a North American Community* at 69.

62. Id. at 79.

63. See http://www.state.gov/r/pa/ei/bgn/35749.htm.

64. Pastor, *Toward a North American Community* at 79.

65. Polaski, *Twelve Years of the North American Free Trade Agreement*.

66. Carlsen, *NAFTA and Immigration* at 9.

67. David M. Neipert, *NAFTA Section 303, a Difficult Choice for Mexico*, 10 CURRENTS: INTERNATIONAL TRADE LAW JOURNAL 25 (2001) at 25.

68. Id.

69. Id.

70. Id.

71. Id. at 26.

72. Id.

73. Alejandro Alvarez-Bejar, *Industrial Restructuring and the Role of Mexican Labor in NAFTA*, 27 U.C. DAVIS LAW REVIEW 897, 907 (1994).

74. Id.

75. Id.

76. Neipert, *NAFTA Section 303, a Difficult Choice for Mexico* at 26.

77. Id.

78. Id. at 26–27.

79. Id.

80. Polaski, *Twelve Years of the North American Free Trade Agreement*.

81. Eliza Barclay, *An Unraveling Industry: Apparel Manufacturing Jobs Are in a Steep Decline*, HOUSTON CHRONICLE, April 23, 2006.

82. Id.

83. Id.

84. Faux, *The Global Class War* at 136. Only about 10 percent of the parts for maquiladora products come from Mexico: id.

85. Id.

86. Id. at 137.

87. Polaski, *Twelve Years of the North American Free Trade Agreement*.

88. Id.

89. Id.

90. Id.

91. Id.

92. Pastor, *Toward a North American Community* at 69.

93. Polaski, *Twelve Years of the North American Free Trade Agreement*.

94. Id.

95. Faux, *The Global Class War* at 12.

96. Id. at 16.

97. Id. at 31.

98. Carlsen, *NAFTA and Immigration* at 3.

99. Id. at 2.

100. Faux, *The Global Class War* at 32–33.

101. Id. at 37.

102. Id. at 35–36.

103. Id. at 45.

104. Id.

105. Id. at 46.

106. Id. at 46–47.

107. Id. at 109.

108. Id. at 138.

109. Id. at 139.

110. Carlsen, *NAFTA and Immigration* at 8.

111. Susan Ferris, *Twenty Years Later, 50% Still Poor: NAFTA, Global Competition Have Left Millions Behind*, AUSTIN AMERICAN-STATESMAN, August 10, 2003.

112. Carlsen, *NAFTA and Immigration* at 11.

113. Biography of Vicente Fox, available at http://www.answers.com/topic/vicente-fox.

114. Faux, *The Global Class War* at 212.

115. Id. at 213.

116. Id. at 153.

117. Id. at 157–158.

118. Id. (citing a retired U.S. State Department official).

119. Id. at 205.

120. Id. at 158.

121. Id. at 159.

122. Id. at 160.

123. Id. at 161.

124. Id. at 220–221.

125. Id. at 224

126. Id. at 221.

127. Carlsen, *NAFTA and Immigration* at 9.

128. Id.

129. Carlsen, *NAFTA and Immigration* at 10.

130. Faux, *The Global Class War* at 205.

131. Id. at 207

132. Id. at 209

133. See notes 95–107, infra, and accompanying text.

134. Faux, *The Global Class War* at 195–196.

135. Id. at 201.

136. *Andrew Batson*, China's Central Bank Welcomes U.S. Bailout Plan, WALL STREET JOURNAL, *October 6, 2008*.

137. Faux, *The Global Class War* at 197, 202.

138. Id. at 198–199.

139. Id. at 215–216.

140. Id. at 216–217.

141. Id. at 217.

CHAPTER 2

1. Marla Dickerson, *Economic Data Show Mexico Still Struggling for Growth*, Los Angeles Times, February 16, 2006.

2. Central Intelligence Agency, *The World Factbook—Mexico*.

3. Dickerson, *Economic Data Show Mexico Still Struggling for Growth*.

4. Sandra Polaski, *Twelve Years of the North American Free Trade Agreement: Hearing before the Subcommittee on International Trade of the S. Comm. on Finance*, CQ Congressional Testimony, 109th Cong. (September 11, 2006).

5. Dickerson, *Economic Data Show Mexico Still Struggling for Growth* (citing Suhas Ketkar, economist and Latin American specialist, RBS Greenwich Capital Markets, Greenwich, Conn., and Christian Stracke, market analyst, CreditSights, New York).

6. Bill Ong Hing, *Defining America through Immigration Policy* 120–122 (Philadelphia: Temple University Press, 2004).

7. See Gerald P. López, *Undocumented Mexican Migration: In Search of a Just. Immigration Law and Policy*, 28 UCLA Law Review 615 (1981).

8. Id.; Hing, *Defining America through Immigration Policy* at 127–129.

9. Financial institutions around the world were worried. They feared that Mexico would default on $80 billion in foreign loans, creating a financial crisis; about $30 billion was owed to U.S. banks alone. If Mexico defaulted, U.S. banks could lose half their total capital. The central banks of the world and the IMF were forced to provide bridge loans and loan-forgiveness packages to avoid the collapse of the world system: see Steven Solomon, *The Confidence Game: How Unelected Central Bankers are Governing the Changed Global Economy* 160, 199–210 (New York: Simon and Schuster, 1995).

10. Jeff Faux, *The Global Class War: How America's Bipartisan Elite Lost Our Future, and What It Will Take to Win it Back* 39 (Hoboken, N.J.: John Wiley and Sons, 2006).

11. Id. at 39.

12. Id. at 44.

13. Carlos Salinas, available at http://www.nndb.com/people/439/000096151.

14. Faux, *The Global Class War* at 110. See also Riordan Roett, *Mexico: Political Update*, memorandum, Emerging Markets Group, Chase Manhattan, January 13, 1995.

15. Timothy A. Canova, *Closing the Border and Opening the Door: Mobility, Adjustment, and the Sequencing of Reform*, 5 Georgetown Journal of Law and Public Policy 36, 43 (2007).

16. Faux, *The Global Class War* at 110–111.

17. Id.

18. Id. at 111–112.

19. Id. at 112.

20. Id. at 114.

21. Id. at 113.

22. Id. at 114.

23. Id. at 123.

24. Id.

25. Id. at 125.

26. *Mexican Telecom Magnate Slim May Be World's Richest*, SAN FRANCISCO CHRONICLE, July 4, 2007, at C2.

27. Faux, *The Global Class War* at 135.

28. Id. at 133.

29. Id. at 129.

30. Id. at 138–141.

31. Id. at 143.

32. Id. at 144.

33. Id. at 142.

34. Id. at 211.

35. Id. at 42.

36. Interview with Curtis Hill, Sheriff, San Benito County, January 9, 2008, Sacramento, Calif.

37. See Chapter 1 (discussion of maquiladoras).

38. Alejandro Alvarez-Bejar, *Industrial Restructuring and the Role of Mexican Labor in NAFTA*, 27 UC DAVIS LAW REVIEW 897, 907 (1994).

39. Id. at 909.

40. Id. at 907–908.

41. Id. at 911.

42. Manuel Pastor and Carol Wise, *The Origins and Sustainability of Mexico's Free Trade Policy*, 48 INTERNATIONAL ORGANIZATION 459, 462 (1994).

43. Id. at 466.

44. Id. at 469.

45. Id. at 478.

46. *The Chinese Dragon Threatens Mexico's Textile Industry, Again*, POLITICA Y GOBIERNO (February 9, 2005).

47. Id.

48. David Seth, *Responding to Striking Farmers, Mexico's Calderón Pimps NAFTA*, DOCUDHARMA BLOG, January 8, 2008.

49. Martin Jacinto, *Calderón, NAFTA and Mexico's Campesinos in 2008*, COUNCIL ON HEMISPHERIC AFFAIRS, April 1, 2008.

50. Seth, *Responding to Striking Farmers*.

51. Jacinto, *Calderón, NAFTA and Mexico's Campesinos in 2008*.

52. *Calderón Vows to Look U.S. in the Eye*, SAN ANTONIO EXPRESS-NEWS, April 1, 2008.

53. Vincente Fox, *Mexican Foreign Policy in the 21st Century*, speech delivered in Madrid, Spain, May 16, 2002.

54. Jacinto, *Calderón, NAFTA, and Mexico's Campesinos in 2008*.

55. Id.

56. Lourdes Garcia-Navaroo, *Economy, Politics Collide in a Divided Mexico*, NATIONAL PUBLIC RADIO, September 16, 2006.

57. Id.

58. Id.

59. *Mex[ican] President Calderón Supports NAFTA*, ONCE NOTICIAS, January 8, 2008, available at http://www.youtube.com/watch?v=WtJSSzITWfc.

60. Id.

61. Id.
62. Id.
63. Id.
64. Richard D. Vogel, *Calderón's Nightmare: Renegotiating NAFTA*, MONTHLY REVIEW, November 28, 2008.
65. Id.
66. Id.
67. *Slowdown Hits Mexico Remittances*, BBC NEWS, January 27, 2009.
68. Id.
69. According to *Extending NAFTA's Reach*, WORLDPRESS.ORG, August 26, 2007:

The Security and Prosperity Partnership (S.P.P.) was launched in Waco, Texas, in March 2005. The heads of state of the three NAFTA countries, other government officials, and business groups have met periodically to hammer out agreements to speed up integration and increase security. This has been done with almost no public input or Congressional oversight.

Since the S.P.P. is not a law or a treaty or even a signed agreement, no formal mechanisms of accountability are built in. It is essentially a "gentleman's agreement" between the executive branches and major corporations in the three nations.

This is what has people worried. Largely unknown to the public, the S.P.P. has spawned numerous working groups, reports, and recommendations. In 2006, the private sector was brought in with the formation of the North American Competitiveness Council (N.A.C.C.). This body is made up of business representatives from industries involved in intercontinental trade and investment, including Wal-Mart, Lockheed Martin, the Mexican Foreign Trade Council, Canada's Suncor Energy, and others. The council does not include representatives of labor, environmental or civil society organizations.

Government officials have justified the secrecy by stating that the S.P.P. is merely a forum for refining rules and standards for transborder transactions. However, the little that is known about it reveals that some major issues are on the table.

Many of those go way beyond what was passed by North American legislatures under NAFTA. They include extraterritorial rights over natural resources, extension of the Bush administration's vastly unpopular counter-terrorism agenda to Canada and Mexico, liberalization of financial services, and most likely a billion-dollar counternarcotics aid package to Mexico.

Although rarely identified as such, some S.P.P. recommendations have already popped up in policies and regulation reforms. These include accelerating environmentally damaging oil production in Mexico and Canada, and "harmonizing" national standards so they sing to the tune of corporate profits rather than consumer protection.

For example, . . . Mexico has adopted a counterterrorism law that contradicts its own foreign policy principles. . . .

Many of the recommendations of the S.P.P. will have a long-term impact on citizens' lives. While opposition has focused on resource use, consumer norms, and infrastructure, the security component of the partnership may prove to be the most far-reaching of all.

The Security and Prosperity Partnership was born in the post-9/11 era, when President Bush sought to extend U.S. counterterrorism strategies to Mexico and Canada, and Homeland Security became a major player in the trilateral relationship. The counternarcotics proposal falls under the rubric of this new area. The package would include the delivery of American arms and surveillance equipment, sophisticated espionage programs, and training for Mexico's police and army.

Although negotiations on security issues have been among the most tightly guarded, immigration crackdowns on Mexico's southern border and Canada's "no-fly" list of people banned from air travel were most likely negotiated in the context of the S.P.P.

70. Id.

71. Id.

72. Id.

73. Id.

74. Felipe Calderón, *Dropping NAFTA Would Damage the Economy,* WORLDNET DAILY, April 22, 2008.

75. Id.

76. Todd Gillman, *Obama Tells Calderón He Wants to "Upgrade" NAFTA,* DALLAS MORNING NEWS, January 12, 2009.

77. Id.

78. Id.

79. Laura Carlsen, *Obama Reaffirms Promise to Renegotiate NAFTA,* HUFFINGTON POST, February 11, 2009.

80. Id.

81. Barack Obama, *I Will Repair Our Relationship with Mexico,* DALLAS MORNING NEWS, February 20, 2008.

82. Les Whittington and Robert Benzie, *Harper, Calderón Agree to Oppose U.S. Trade Threat,* TORONTO STAR, February 6, 2009.

83. Id.

84. Id.; *That "Buy American" Provision* (editorial), NEW YORK TIMES, February 11, 2009.

85. Elizabeth Malkin and Marc Lacey, *Mexican President Proposes Decriminalizing Some Drugs,* NEW YORK TIMES, October 2, 2008.

86. Marc Lacey, *Mexico Accepts Anti-narcotics Aid from U.S.,* NEW YORK TIMES, June 28, 2008.

87. *Calderón Vows to Look U.S. in the Eye.*

88. Malkin and Lacey, *Mexican President Proposes Decriminalizing Some Drugs.*

89. Id.

90. Id.

91. Id.

92. Lacey, *Mexico Accepts Anti-narcotics Aid from U.S.*

93. Id.

94. Id.

95. Id.

96. See Malkin and Lacey, *Mexican President Proposes Decriminalizing Some Drugs.*

97. Id.

98. Id.

99. Id.

100. Gillman, *Obama Tells Calderón He Wants to "Upgrade" NAFTA.*

101. Richard Marosi, *Less Cocaine on U.S. Streets, Report Says,* Los Angeles Times, December 16, 2008.

102. Josh Meyer, *White House Unveils Plan to Fight Drug Cartels at Border,* Los Angeles Times, March 25, 2009.

103. Information for this section is from Manuel Roig-Franzia, *Mexico Revises Its Justice System,* Washington Post, June 18, 2008; Associated Press, *Mexico: New Legal System Set,* New York Times, June 18, 2008.

104. Adam Thomson, *Calderón Pleads for Energy Reform,* Financial Times, May 27, 2008.

105. Id.

106. Id.

107. Id.

108. Id.

109. *Mexico's Calderón Talked Energy Reform with Oil Co[mpanie]s at Davos,* Morningstar, January 30, 2009.

110. Id.

111. Id.

112. Id.

113. Elizabeth Malkin, *Mexico Enacts Tax Overhaul Bill,* New York Times, September 15, 2007.

114. *Mexico: Taxes, Pemex, and Calderón's Reforms,* Stratfor Global Intelligence, July 5, 2007.

115. Id.

116. Malkin, *Mexico Enacts Tax Overhaul Bill.*

117. *Mexico: Taxes, Pemex, and Calderón's Reforms.*

118. Adriana Arai and Patrick Harrington, *After Six Months, Mexican Leader Tries to Build Economic Momentum,* International Herald Tribune, June 25, 2007.

119. *Exige Calderón a EU frenar ley migratoria,* El Universal, March 25, 2006; James McKinley, *Mexican President Assails U.S. Measures on Migrants,* New York Times, September 3, 2007.

120. McKinley, *Mexican President Assails U.S. Measures on Migrants.*

121. *Calderón Vows to Look U.S. in the Eye.*

122. Sergio Javier Jiménez, *Ofrece Calderón pagar pension a mexicanos en EU,* El Universal, March 30, 2006.

123. Sergio Javier Jiménez, *Obama planea reunir a familias de migrantes,* El Universal, January 14, 2009.

124. McKinley, *Mexican President Assails U.S. Measures on Migrants.*

125. *Slowdown Hits Mexico Remittances,* BBC News, January 27, 2009.

126. *Testing Teachers,* ECONOMIST, June 21, 2008.

127. Elizabeth Malkin, *Mexico's Fiscal Prudence Fails to Avert a Slowdown,* NEW YORK TIMES, December 29, 2008.

128. Id.

129. Stephen Fidier, *Going South,* FINANCIAL TIMES, January 8, 2009.

130. Richard Basas, *Mexico 2009: Stimulus, Security and Neighbourly Assistance,* FOREIGN POLICY ASSOCIATION, January 8, 2009.

131. *Mexico's Peso Gains on U.S. Aid Hopes, Stocks Edge Up,* REUTERS, January 16, 2009.

132. Jeremy Schwartz, *Looming Economic Disaster in Mexico?* AUSTIN AMERICAN-STATESMAN, September 30, 2008.

133. Id.

CHAPTER 3

1. Economist Intelligence Unit, *Country Profile Canada* 14 (2006).

2. See id. at 13.

3. So named after the Progressive Conservative Party and the Canadian Alliance merged in 2003.

4. Essentially, this was a 7 percent national sales tax imposed at the retail consumer level.

5. Paul Martin's term in office (2003–2006) preceded Stephen Harper's and succeeded Jean Chrétien's. The Sponsorship Program was a media campaign by the Canadian government to counter the Quebec separatist movement. Later investigation revealed misdirection of government funds.

6. Department of Finance, Government of Canada, *Advantage Canada: Building a Strong Economy for Canadians,* Ottawa, November 23, 2006, at 18.

7. Economist Intelligence Unit, *Canada Economy: "Advantage Canada" Strategy Launched,* EIU VIEWSWIRE CANADA 3, February 12, 2007.

8. Economist Intelligence Unit, *Canada: Country Fact Sheet,* EIU VIEWSWIRE CANADA 54, March 13, 2007.

9. See Ian Fergusson, *United States–Canada Trade and Economic Relationship: Prospects and Challenges,* Congressional Research Service report no. RL33087, U.S. Library of Congress, October 13, 2006, at 1 (stating that the national economy of the United States is much larger than that of Canada. In terms of GDP, the United States was over 11 times greater than Canada in 2005).

10. The Group of Seven countries are the United States, the United Kingdom, Canada, France, Germany, Japan, and Italy. See Department of Finance, Government of Canada, *The Economic and Fiscal Update,* Ottawa, November 23, 2006, at 64.

11. See Central Intelligence Agency, *The World Factbook–Canada.*

12. See id.

13. See Economist Intelligence Unit, *Country Profile Canada* at 29.

14. Industry Canada, *Report on Canada's Industrial Performance* 18 (first half of 2006).

15. Economist Intelligence Unit, *Country Profile Canada* at 39.

16. See Industry Canada, *Report on Canada's Industrial Performance* at 18.

17. Economist Intelligence Unit, *Canada Economy: Jobs Growth Driven by Oil and Mining*, EIU VIEWSWIRE CANADA 4, February 12, 2007.

18. Industry Canada, *Report on Canada's Industrial Performance* at 16.

19. The Canadian dollar has increased in value against the American dollar by 40 percent between 2002 and 2006: Industry Canada, *Report on Canada's Industrial Performance* at 16–17; Department of Finance, Government of Canada, *Advantage Canada* at 21.

20. Industry Canada, *Report on Canada's Industrial Performance* at 15.

21. Economist Intelligence Unit, *Country Profile Canada* at 39.

22. The Canada–United States Automotive Agreement (Auto Pact) has since been phased out, after the WTO's finding that it constituted a trade barrier. The significance of this decision, however, is minimal in light of the favorable market access provided by NAFTA: see Industry Canada, *Overview: Competitiveness Factors for Attracting and Maintaining Automotive Investment: Comparison between Canada and Mexico*, November 21, 2003.

23. Industry Canada, *Report on Canada's Industrial Performance* at 15; see also Sadam Uddin, *Impact of Higher Commodity Prices on Canada's Trade Balance*, Foreign Affairs and International Trade no. 3, Government of Canada, 2006.

24. Economist Intelligence Unit, *Country Profile Canada* at 29.

25. Canadian Services Coalition and Canadian Chamber of Commerce, *Canadian Services Sector: A New Success Story* 3 (2006).

26. Id. at 2.

27. Id. at 5.

28. Id. at 3–4. All dollar figures are in U.S. dollars, unless noted otherwise.

29. Department of Finance, Government of Canada, *The Canadian Financial Services Sector*, Ottawa, June 2005.

30. Id.

31. World Trade Organization, *Trade Policy Review: Canada*, WTO doc. no. WT/TPR/S/112/Rev.1, March 19, 2003, at 14.

32. Id. at 12.

33. Department of Finance, Government of Canada, *The Canadian Financial Services Sector*.

34. These limits are 265 million Canadian dollars for WTO members and 5 million Canadian dollars for non-WTO members, and the standard of review is "net benefit to Canada": Economist Intelligence Unit, *Country Commerce Canada* 16 (2006).

35. See Canadian Services Coalition, *Canadian Services Sector* at 5.

36. Id. at 8.

37. See Economist Intelligence Unit, *Country Profile Canada* at 36.

38. Industry Canada, *Report on Canada's Industrial Performance* at 35.

39. See Keith Head and John Ries, *Regionalism within Multilateralism: The WTO Trade Policy Review of Canada*, 27 WORLD ECONOMY 1377, 1383 (2004).

40. See NAFTA Arts. 309, 703(2), Annex 703.2.

41. See Economist Intelligence Unit, *Country Profile Canada* at 36.

42. Department of Finance, Government of Canada, *The Economic and Fiscal Update* at 14.

43. Natural Resources, Government of Canada, *Statistics and Facts on Energy*, June 7, 2006, Ottawa.

44. Economist Intelligence Unit, *Country Profile Canada* at 27.

45. In 2005, natural gas was the top national export (valued at C$32.3 billion), crude oil was fourth (valued at C$8.0 billion), and light oils were ninth (valued at C$2.82 billion): Uddin, *Impact of Higher Commodity Prices on Canada's Trade Balance.*

46. Natural Resources, *Statistics and Facts on Energy.*

47. Embassy of the United States, Ottawa, *Canada–United States Relations,* January 2007.

48. *Canadian Encyclopedia,* available at http://www.thecanadianencyclopedia. com/ (defining recession as "two or more successive quarters of declines in real Gross Domestic Product, calculated by adjusting for price changes").

49. See generally Thomas Wilson et al., *The Sources of the Recession in Canada: 1989–1992,* CANADIAN BUSINESS ECONOMICS (Winter 1994) at 3.

50. Id. at 8.

51. See generally T. A. Wilson, *Lessons of the Recession,* 18 CANADIAN JOURNAL OF ECONOMICS 693 (1985).

52. Economist Intelligence Unit, *Country Profile Canada* at 33.

53. Id. at 44.

54. Jean-Philippe Cotis, *Benchmarking Canada's Economic Performance,* 13 INTERNATIONAL PRODUCTIVITY MONITOR 3, 4–5 (Fall 2006).

55. *The Impact of the Financial Crisis in Canada, Economic Viewpoint,* DESJARDINS ECONOMIC STUDIES, October 14, 2008.

56. Id.

57. Keith B. Richburg, *Worldwide Financial Crisis Largely Bypasses Canada,* WASHINGTON POST, October 16, 2008.

58. *Yet Another Huge Bank Failure in the USA,* VIRTUAL NONSENSE, January 13, 2009.

59. Richburg, *Worldwide Financial Crisis Largely Bypasses Canada.*

60. Roger Annis, *Economic Crisis Slams Canada,* GLOBAL RESEARCH, March 29, 2009. The Group of Twenty (G-20) Finance Ministers and Central Bank Governors was established in 1999 to bring together industrialized and developing economies to discuss key issues in the global economy. The inaugural meeting of the G-20 took place in Berlin on December 15–16, 1999, hosted by German and Canadian finance ministers. The G-20 is an informal forum that promotes open and constructive discussion between industrial and emerging-market countries on key issues related to global economic stability; it was created as a response both to the financial crises of the late 1990s and to a growing recognition that key emerging-market countries were not adequately included in the core of global economic discussion and governance. The G-20 is made up of the finance ministers and central bank governors of nineteen countries: Argentina, Australia, Brazil, Canada, China, France, Germany, India, Indonesia, Italy, Japan, Mexico, Russia, Saudi Arabia, South Africa, South Korea, Turkey, the United Kingdom, and the United States. The European Union, which is represented by the rotating council presidency and the European Central Bank, is the twentieth member of the G-20.

61. Compare this with the same statistic for the United States at just 20.7 percent of GDP: Fergusson, *United States–Canada Trade and Economic Relationship* at 3.

62. Head and Ries, *Regionalism within Multilateralism* at 1378.

63. Id. at 1383.

64. Except for Libya, Iraq, and North Korea, which are subject to a blanket 35 percent tariff on all imports: see id.

65. U.S.–Canada Free-Trade Agreement Implementation Act of 1988, Pub. L. No. 100–449, 102 Stat. 1851 (1988) (hereafter, CUFTA).

66. CUFTA, art. 401.

67. North American Free Trade Agreement (NAFTA), December 17, 1992, U.S.-Can.-Mex., 107 Stat. 2057 (1994), 32 I.L.M. 605 (1993).

68. North American Agreement on Environmental Cooperation, September 9, 1993, Can.-Mex.-U.S., 32 I.L.M. 1480 (1993) (Environmental Cooperation); North American Agreement on Labor Cooperation, September 13, 1993, Can.- Mex.-U.S., 32 I.L.M. 1502 (1993) (Labor Cooperation).

69. William J. Andrews, *An Environmental Perspective on the "Effective Enforcement" Provisions of the North American Agreement on Environmental Cooperation,* Winnipeg 95 National Legal Symposium, Canadian Bar Association, August 23, 1995.

70. This has been termed the "investor-state mechanism": see id.

71. Chapters 19 and 20 refer to Antidumping and Countervailing Duty Institutional Arrangements and Dispute Settlement Procedures, respectively.

72. *Free Trade Agreement between the Government of Canada and the Government of the Republic of Chile,* December 5, 1996, 36 I.L.M. 1079; *Agreement on Environmental Cooperation between the Governments of Canada and the Republic of Chile,* February 6, 1997, 36 I.L.M. 1196; see also *Canada–Chile Free Trade Agreement Implementation Act,* S.C., c. 14 (1997); *Canada–Israel Free Trade Agreement,* June 1, 1996, available at http://www.dfait-maeci.gc.ca/tna-nac/cifta-en.asp; see also *Canada Israel Free Trade Implementation Act,* S.C. 1996, c. 33 (Can.); *Canada–Costa Rica Free Trade Agreement,* November 1, 2002, available at http://www.dfait-maeci.gc.ca/tna-nac/costa_rica-en. asp; see also *Canada–Costa Rica Free Trade Agreement Implementation Act,* S.C. 2001, c.28 (Can.).

73. Head and Ries, *Regionalism within Multilateralism* at 1383.

74. Foreign Affairs and International Trade, Government of Canada, *Regional and Bilateral Initiatives: Canada–European Free Trade Association (EFTA) Free Trade Agreement Negotiations,* January 11, 2007 (stating, "In 2005, two-way merchandise trade was valued at C$11 billion [Canadian exports: C$2.7 billion; imports: C$8.2 billion]").

75. Foreign Affairs and International Trade, Government of Canada, *Regional and Bilateral Initiatives: Canada–Central America Four (CA4),* November 7, 2006.

76. See Foreign Affairs and International Trade, Government of Canada, *Canada to Hold Public Consultations on Proposed Free Trade Agreements with Andean Countries and Dominican Republic,* press release no. 139, November 4, 2002.

77. Foreign Affairs and International Trade, Government of Canada, *Regional and Bilateral Initiatives: Canada–Dominican Republic Free Trade Discussions,* February 6, 2007.

78. Notably, this excludes Cuba.

79. See Jeffrey J. Schott, *The Free Trade Area of the Americas: Current Status and Prospects,* 5 JEAN MONNET/ROBERT SCHUMAN PAPER SERIES 15, July 2005.

80. See *Free Trade Deals: What You Don't See May Be What You Get,* GLOBAL ECONOMIC JUSTICE REPORT 5 (February 2003) (referring to these bilateral trade agreements as "an insurance policy against the potential failure of the CUFTAA").

81. See Schott, *The Free Trade Area of the Americas.*

82. Privy Counsel Office, Government of Canada, *Canada and South Korea Explore Possible Free Trade Agreement*, press release, November 19, 2004.

83. Foreign Affairs and International Trade, Government of Canada, *Regional and Bilateral Initiatives: Canada–Korea Free Trade Agreement Negotiations*, February 27, 2007.

84. Total trading volume is composed of export plus import activity. In 2006, export activity was reported at C$439.5 billion and import activity was reported at C$396.4 billion: see Foreign Affairs and International Trade, Government of Canada, *Trade and Investment Reports Pocket Facts Canada (Annual)*, February 13, 2007.

85. *Free Trade Deals: What You Don't See May Be What You Get*, GLOBAL ECONOMIC JUSTICE REPORT, February 2003.

86. World Trade Organization, *Trade Policy Review: Canada* at 22.

87. Foreign Affairs and International Trade, Government of Canada, *Trade and Investment Reports Pocket Facts Canada (Annual)*.

88. World Trade Organization, *Trade Policy Review: Canada* at 23.

89. Foreign Affairs and International Trade, Government of Canada, *Seventh Annual Report on Canada's State of Trade* 25 (2006).

90. See Denis Poulin and Attah K. Boame, *Mad Cow Disease and Beef Trade*, Statistics Canada no. 11–621-MIE2003005, May 20, 2003, at 4 (stating that 90 percent of beef exports went to the United States in 2002); Carson Walker, *U.S. Ban on Canadian Beef Putting Farmers out of Business*, HIGH PLAINS/MIDWEST AGRICULTURAL JOURNAL, July 29, 2004.

91. USDA Foreign Agricultural Service, *Canada Agricultural Situation*, THIS WEEK IN CANADIAN AGRICULTURE, GAIN Report no. CA3049, August 12, 2003, at 2.

92. See *Notice of Amended Final Determination of Sales at Less than Fair Value and Antidumping Duty Order: Certain Softwood Lumber Products from Canada*, 67 FEDERAL REGISTER 36068 (May 22, 2002).

93. As of 2004, Canada has been the largest user of the WTO anti-dumping investigation process: see Head and Ries, *Regionalism within Multilateralism* at 1391. See NAFTA Panel Review, *In the Matter of Certain Softwood Lumber Products from Canada: Final Affirmative Antidumping Determination*, USA-CDA-2002–1904–02, March 5, 2004, available at 2004 CUFTAPD LEXIS 2; WTO Dispute Settlement Panel, *Final Dumping Determination on Softwood Lumber from Canada*, WT/DS264/R, April 13, 2004, available at 2004 WTO DS LEXIS 15; WTO Dispute Settlement Panel, *Final Dumping Determination on Softwood Lumber from Canada*, WT/DS264/AB/R, August 11, 2004, available at 2004 WTO DS LEXIS 18.

94. *Softwood Lumber Agreement between the Government of Canada and the Government of the United States of America*, September 12, 2006, available at 2006 WTO DS LEXIS 257; see also *Notice of Rescission of Antidumping Duty Reviews and Revocation of Antidumping Duty Order: Certain Softwood Lumber Products from Canada*, 71 FEDERAL REGISTER 61714 (October 19, 2006).

95. *Softwood Lumber Agreement between the Government of Canada and the Government of the United States of America*.

96. *Notice of Antidumping Duty Order: Hard Red Spring Wheat from Canada*, 68 FED. REG. 60641, October 23, 2003.

97. Canadian Wheat Board, *CWB Wins NAFTA Appeal on Tariff*, June 2005.

98. See NAFTA; Industry Canada, Government of Canada, *An Overview of Canada's Trade with Mexico*, available at http://www.ic.gc.ca/eic/site/ibi-iai.nsf/eng/bi18721.html.

99. Foreign Affairs and International Trade, Government of Canada, *Canada Trade Mission to Mexico,* available at http://www.tcm-mec.gc.ca/mexico/agri-en.asp (stating with reference to NAFTA members, "The majority of agricultural products will trade without duties between the two countries with the exception of dairy, poultry and egg products, which will continue to be subject to the Most Favoured Nation tariff rate provided to WTO members").

100. Foreign Affairs and International Trade, Government of Canada,, *Regional and Bilateral Initiatives, Canada-Korea—Free Trade Agreement Negotiations.*

101. Foreign Affairs and International Trade, Government of Canada, *Regional and Bilateral Initiatives, Canada-Korea—Free Trade Agreement Negotiations.*

102. Taken alone, the United Kingdom absorbs 2.29 percent of Canadian exports and provided 2.73 percent of Canadian imports, as of 2006. See Foreign Affairs and International Trade, Government of Canada, *Trade and Investment Reports Pocket Facts Canada (Annual).*

103. Head and Ries, *Regionalism within Multilateralism* at 1379.

104. Foreign Affairs and International Trade, Government of Canada, *Trade and Investment Reports Pocket Facts Canada (Annual).*

105. This deficit was valued by the Canadian government at C\$45.6 billion in 2005 and C\$42 billion in 2004. See Foreign Affairs and International Trade, Government of Canada, *Regional and Bilateral Initiatives, Canada-Korea—Free Trade Agreement Negotiations, .*

106. See id. at 25–26 (in the preceding year stones and metals comprised 16.4 percent of exports and mechanical machinery comprised 12.1 percent).

107. WTO, *Trade Policy Review: Canada* at 26.

108. Foreign Affairs and International Trade, Government of Canada, *Opening Doors to the World, Canada's International Market Access Priorities 2006.* This statistic treats the European Union as a single entity. If the constituent nations of the European Union are viewed individually, China's importance increases to second-largest source of imports.

109. This was down from C\$29.5 billion in 2005: see id.

110. Foreign Affairs and International Trade, Government of Canada, *Opening Doors to the World, Canada's International Market Access Priorities 2006,* June 5, 2006.

111. Foreign Affairs and International Trade, Government of Canada, *Opening Doors to the World, Canada's International Market Access Priorities 2006.*

112. Foreign Affairs and International Trade, Government of Canada, *Regional and Bilateral Initiatives, Canada-Korea—Free Trade Agreement Negotiations.*

113. Foreign Affairs and International Trade, Government of Canada, *Regional and Bilateral Initiatives: Introduction to the Canada–Japan Economic Framework and Joint Study,* 2008.

114. *How Rich Countries Are Predicted to Grow This Year,* THE ECONOMIST, September 3, 2009.

115. Economist Intelligent Unit, *Canada Economy: Quick View—GDP Growth Eases,* EIU VIEWSWIRE CAN. 2, March 5, 2007, available at 2007 WLNR 4197007.

116. *Biz: Natural Resources Outlook,* BROADCAST NEWS, January 23, 2007, available at 2007 WLNR 1299182.

117. Department of Finance, Government of Canada, *Advantage Canada* at 68.

118. Stephen S. Poloz, *Exports More Diversified in 2006,* EXPORT DEVELOPMENT CANADA, March 7, 2007.

119. Id. (exports to the EU grew by more than 15 percent).

120. Id.

121. Department of Finance, Government of Canada, *Canada's New Government Cuts Wasteful Programs, Refocuses Spending on Priorities, Achieves Major Debt Reduction as Promised*, press release, September 25, 2006.

122. Department of Finance, Government of Canada, *Advantage Canada* at 29.

123. Department of Finance, Government of Canada, *Fiscal Results for March 2007*, FISCAL MONITOR, March 2007, available at http://www.fin.gc.ca/fiscmon-revfin/2007–03-eng.asp.

124. Department of Finance, Government of Canada, *The Economic and Fiscal Update* at 38.

125. The tax-fairness plan will reduce corporate taxation by .5 percent, reduce the GST to 5 percent, and increase the age-credit amount: Department of Finance, Government of Canada, *Canada's New Government Announces Tax Fairness Plan*, press release, October 31, 2006.

126. Department of Finance, Government of Canada, *Advantage Canada* at 18.

127. *Mexican Workers in Canada on the Increase*, CAMPBELL COHEN IMMIGRATION LAWYERS WEB SITE, August 19, 2007.

128. *Canada Becoming the More Attractive North American Immigration Destination*, CANADIAN IMMIGRATION NEWSLETTER, August 2007.

129. Danna Harman, *Mexicans Head North for a Better Life—Way North*, CHRISTIAN SCIENCE MONITOR, October 28, 2005.

130. *Canada Attracting More Mexican Immigrants*, WORKPERMIT.COM, May 5, 2005.

131. Harman, *Mexicans Head North for a Better Life—Way North*.

132. Id.

CHAPTER 4

1. Jason Ackleson, *Achieving "Security and Prosperity": Migration and North American Economic Integration*, 5 IMMIGRATION POLICY IN FOCUS 1 (February 2006).

2. Jennifer E. Harman, *Mexican President Vicente Fox's Proposal for Expanding NAFTA into a European Union–Style Common Market—Obstacles and Outlook*, 7 LAW AND BUSINESS REVIEW OF THE AMERICAS 207, 214 (2001).

3. Ackleson, *Achieving "Security and Prosperity"* at 4–5.

4. Id. at 4–5; Harman, *Mexican President Vicente Fox's Proposal for Expanding NAFTA* at 214.

5. Id. at 216.

6. Ackleson, *Achieving "Security and Prosperity"* at 4–5.

7. Bradly J. Condon and J. Brad McBride, *Do You Know the Way to San Jose? Resolving the Problem of Illegal Mexican Migration to the United States*, 17 GEORGETOWN IMMIGRATION LAW JOURNAL 251, 291 (2003).

8. Christopher J. Cassise, *The European Union v. the United States under the NAFTA: A Comparative Analysis of the Free Movement of Persons within the Regions* 46 SYRACUSE LAW REVIEW 1343, 1349 (1996).

9. Id. at 1354.

10. Robert A. Pastor, *Toward a North American Community: Lessons from the*

Old World for the New, 29 (Washington, D.C.: Peterson Institute for International Economics, 2001).

11. Jeff Faux, *The Global Class War: How America's Bipartisan Elite Lost Our Future, and What It Will Take to Win It Back* 224 (Hoboken, N.J.: John Wiley and Sons, 2006).

12. Pastor, *Toward a North American Community* at 55, 81.

13. See Chapter 5 in this volume.

14. Faux, *The Global Class War* at 224.

15. Robert J. Flanagan, *Globalization and Labor Conditions* 98–99 (Oxford: Oxford University Press, 2006).

16. European Commission Delegation, *Enlargement,* available at http://www.delind.cec.eu.int/en/enlargement/enlargement.htm.

17. Focus Migration, *Country Profile: Poland,* July 2005, Migration Research Group, Netzwerk Migration in Europa at 5, available at: http://www.focus-migration.de/typo3_upload/groups/3/focus_Migration_Publikationen/Laenderprofile/CP03_-_Poland.pdf. The original fifteen members of the EU are Austria, Belgium, Denmark, Finland, France, Germany, Greece, Ireland, Italy, Luxembourg, the Netherlands, Portugal, Spain, Sweden, and the United Kingdom.

18. Andreas Schneider, *Analysis of EU–CEEC Migration with Special Reference to Agricultural Labour,* Hamburg Institute of International Economics, 2004 at 10.

19. Id. at 5.

20. Id. at 10

21. Id.

22. Timothy A. Canova, *Closing the Border and Opening the Door: Mobility, Adjustment, and the Sequencing of Reform.* 5 GEORGETOWN JOURNAL OF LAW AND PUBLIC POLICY 36, 41 (2007).

23. Trades Union Congress, *The Economics of Immigration,* June 19, 2007, available at http://www.tuc.org.uk/extras/migration.pdf.

24. Adam Roberts, *A World in Flux,* ECONOMIST, November 15, 2007, at 61.

25. Id.

26. EUROPA, glossary, available at http://europa.eu/scadplus/glossary/accession_criteria_copenhague_en.htm

27. European Commission, *Enlargement: Financial Assistance,* October 18, 2007.

28. Id.

29. Id.

30. European Commission, *PHARE,* December 2, 2007.

31. *The EU PHARE Program,* FORESTS AND EUROPEAN UNION RESOURCE NETWORK, available at http://www.fern.org/pubs/briefs/phare.htm; European Commission, *Supporting Enlargement: What Does Evaluation Show? Ex-Post Evaluation of PHARE,* July 2007 at 11.

32. *The EU PHARE Program.*

33. Id.

34. Id.

35. DG Regio-ISPA, *The Mini ISPA Report 2000–2004* at 3, available at http://ec.europa.eu/regional_policy/funds/ispa/pdf/stat20002004_en.pdf.

36. Id. at 7.

37. European Commission, *Regional Policy-Inforegio: ISPA, Sectors Receiving*

Assistance, June 20, 2008, available at http://ec.europa.eu/regional_policy/funds/ispa/ sectors_en.htm.

38. Id.

39. DG Regio-ISPA, *The Mini ISPA Report 2000–2004* at 5.

40. European Commission Directorate-General for Agriculture, European Commission, *Bulgaria Agriculture and Enlargement* (2002).

41. European Commission, *Enlargement: Financial Assistance, SAPARD,* October 3, 2008.

42. European Union, Europa, *Overviews of the Activities of the European Union, Agriculture: Meeting the Needs of Farmers and Consumers,* available at http://europa.eu/ pol/agr/index_en.htm.

43. Id.

44. Directorate-General for Agriculture, *Bulgaria Agriculture and Enlargement.*

45. Republic of Bulgaria. *Annual Report on SAPARD Implementation in the Republic of Bulgaria for the Period June 1, 2001–December 31, 2002,* June 2003 at 4.

46. European Commission, *CARDS,* October 25, 2007.

47. Id.

48. European Commission, *Enlargement: Financial Assistance, Economic and Social Cohesion,* available at http://ec.europa.eu/enlargement/how-does-it-work/finan- cial-assistance/phare/economic_and_social_cohesion_en.htm.

49. Id.

50. European Commission, *Regional Policy: The Cohesion Fund at a Glance,* June 20, 2008.

51. Id.

52. European Union, *The Common Agricultural Policy—a Policy Evolving with the Times: The CAP and Enlargement 10.*

53. Id.

54. *Charlemagne: Post Enlargement Stress,* ECONOMIST, November 10, 2007, at 68.

55. Roberts, *A World in Flux* at 76.

56. Pastor, *Toward a North American Community* at 59–62, 135–136.

57. Ireland is the example. EU funds for Ireland had a special impact because they arrived in 1989 when there was a substantial backlog of projects and infrastructure needs. That is exactly where Mexico is today: id. at 136.

58. Markus Euskirchen et al., *From Borderline to Borderland: The Changing of the European Border Regime,* MONTHLY REVIEW, November 2007.

59. Gregor Noll, *Africa Sells Out to Europe,* Paper presented at the Euro-African Migration Conference: Open Democracy, July 13, 2007.

60. Ajay Prakash and Antoine Lerougetel, *The EU Strengthens "Fortress Europe" against Migration due to Climate Change,* WORLD SOCIALIST, May 7, 2008.

61. Euskirchen et al., *From Borderline to Borderland.*

62. Id.

63. Id.

64. Id.

65. Noll, *Africa Sells Out to Europe.*

66. Id.

67. Id.

68. Id.

69. Euskirchen et al., *From Borderline to Borderland*. Also, note that six thousand deaths were counted off the Canary Islands in 2007: see Sharon LaFraniere, *Europe Takes Africa's Fish, and Boatloads of Migrants Follow*, NEW YORK TIMES, January 14, 2008.

70. Euskirchen et al., *From Borderline to Borderland*.

71. Id. See also Prakash and Lerougetel, *The EU Strengthens "Fortress Europe" against Migration due to Climate Change*.

72. Euskirchen et al., *From Borderline to Borderland*.

73. Tongkeh Fowale, *The African Thorn in European Flesh*, AMERICAN CHRONICLE, February 27, 2008.

74. Id.

75. Canova, *Closing the Border and Opening the Door*.

76. For example, in 2000, the World Bank convinced the countries of the West African Economic and Monetary Union to reduce their import duties for poultry parts from 55 percent to 20 percent. Overnight, this region became a dumping ground for chicken wings. This put an end to Senegal's poultry production, ten thousand people lost their jobs, and $3.8 billion in annual sales disappeared.

77. Noll, *Africa Sells Out to Europe*.

78. Fowale, *The African Thorn in European Flesh*.

CHAPTER 5

1. *Will Going to Third Level Still Be Worth Financial Pain?* IRISH TIMES, April 7, 2009.

2. *Ireland Gets an "F" for Spending on Education in World Report*, INDEPENDENT, September 19, 2007.

3. European Commission, *Eurobaromater 67: Public Opinion in the European Union—National Report Ireland*, Spring 2007, available at http://ec.europa.eu/public_opinion/archives/eb/eb67/eb67_ie_exec.pdf.

4. Eric Pfanner and Sarah Lyall, *Irish Vote for Treaty Centralizing Power in the European Union*, NEW YORK TIMES, October 4, 2009.

5. *The Tiger Tamed*, ECONOMIST, November 20, 2008.

6. Id.

7. Thomas Landon Jr., *The Irish Economy's Rise Was Steep, and the Fall Was Fast*, NEW YORK TIMES, January 3, 2009.

8. Id.

9. Id.

10. Liam Halligan, *Will the Credit Crisis Leave the Irish Economy All Washed Up?* TELEGRAPH, February 28, 2009.

11. Id.; see also *The Irish Economy: Reykjavik-on-Liffey*, ECONOMIST, February 5, 2009.

12. Henry McDonald, *Irish Economy Will Lead Europe within a Decade*, OBSERVER, January 11, 2009.

13. *Irish Economy to Grow in 2010*, IRISH TIMES, September 29, 2009.

CHAPTER 6

1. The subtitle of this chapter is from Russ Bynum, *Immigration Raid Cripples Georgia Town*, ASSOCIATED PRESS, September 15, 2006 (quoting David Robinson, a resident of Stillmore, Ga., following an ICE raid in the town).

2. Some states such as Arizona and Mississippi have passed legislation requiring all employers to use the system to determine the employment eligibility of newly hired employees.

3. Tom Barry, *Are Americans Willing to Pay for the Intensifying Crackdown on Immigrants?* AMERICAS PROGRAM COMMENTARY, May 16, 2008.

4. *Swift Raids Impact Families, Economy, and ID Theft Victims*, DENVER CHANNEL, December 13, 2006.

5. *Wal-Mart Settles Illegal Immigrant Case for $11M*, FOX NEWS, March 19, 2005.

6. Quoted in Ginger Thompson, *Mexican Leader Visits U.S. with a Vision to Sell*, NEW YORK TIMES, August 24, 2000, at A3.

7. Laura C. Oliveira, *A License to Exploit: The Need to Reform the H-2A Temporary Agricultural Guest Worker Program*, 5 SCHOLAR: ST. MARY'S LAW REVIEW ON MINORITY ISSUES 153, 170 (2002).

8. Nicolaus Mills, ed., *Arguing Immigration: Arguing Immigration: The Debate over the Changing Face of America* 48 (New York: Simon and Schuster, 1994).

9. Wayne A. Cornelius, *Death at the Border: The Efficacy and "Unintended" Consequences of U.S. Immigration Control Policy, 1993–2000*, Working Paper no. 27, Center for Comparative Immigration Studies, University of California, San Diego, 2001 at 3.

10. See Frank Trejo, *Putting Up Barriers: Proposed Border Wall near El Paso Divides Community*, DALLAS MORNING NEWS, July 30, 1995, at 43A.

11. U.S. Border Patrol, *Border Patrol Strategic Plan: 1994 and Beyond—National Strategy*, July 1994.

12. Id. at 6.

13. U.S. Border Patrol, *Border Patrol Strategic Plan* at 6–9.

14. Id. at 7; U.S. General Accounting Office, *Illegal Immigration: Status of Southwest Border Strategy Implementation*, Report to Congressional Committees, May 1999 at 3.

15. Id. at 3.

16. Id. at 1, 4, 8.

17. Id.

18. Id. at 8.

19. U.S. Border Patrol, *Border Patrol Strategic Plan* at 4.

20. Letter to Mary Robinson, September 30, 2000, on file with the author.

21. U.S. Border Patrol, *Border Patrol Strategic Plan* at 10.

22. Memorandum from Claudia Smith, March 18, 2000, at 21–22 (citing Cornelius, *Death at the Border*).

23. Binational Study on Migration (1997), cited in id. at 7.

24. Kevin R. Johnson, *Race Matters: Immigration Law and Policy Scholarship, Law in the Ivory Tower, and the Legal Indifference of the Race Critique*, 2000 UNIVERSITY OF ILLINOIS LAW REVIEW 525.

25. Memorandum from Claudia Smith at 11.

26. *Frustrating Illegal Crossers at Imperial Beach and Moving the Traffic Eastward*, INS fact sheet, October 17, 1997, in Memorandum from Claudia Smith at 20.

27. Id.

28. Cornelius, *Death at the Border* at 29.

29. Rosenberg Foundation, *Changing Environment*, November 22, 2000, at 2.

30. See the Web site of the California Rural Legal Assistance Foundation Border Project at http://www.StopGatekeeper.org.

31. *US-Mexico Border Deaths on the Increase*, AL JAZEERA, September 30, 2009.

32. Letter to Mary Robinson, November 19, 1999, on file with the author.

33. U.S. Border Patrol, *Operation Gatekeeper: Three Years of Results*, cited in Memorandum from Claudia Smith at 23.

34. Id.

35. Id.

36. Memorandum from Claudia Smith at 23–24.

37. Id. at 25. One migrant had to have his foot amputated because an injury became infected while he was crossing the river.

38. Letter to Jorge Taiana, July 22, 1999, on file with the author.

39. Douglas S. Massey, *An Exercise in Self-Deception*, NEWSWEEK, January 19, 2004, at 41.

40. Russ Bynum, *Immigration Raids Leave Georgia Town Bereft, Stunned*, SEATTLE TIMES, September 16, 2006.

41. Rick Lyman, *In Georgia Law, a Wide-Angle View of Immigration*, NEW YORK TIMES, May 12, 2006.

42. Patrick Jonsson, *Crackdown on Immigrants Empties a Town and Hardens Views*, CHRISTIAN SCIENCE MONITOR, October 3, 2006.

43. *SPLC Files Federal Lawsuit Challenging Constitutionality of Immigration Raids that terrorized Latino residents of Southeast Georgia Towns* P.R. NEWSWIRE, PUBLIC INTEREST SERVICES, November 1, 2006.

44. Bynum, *Immigration Raids Leave Georgia Town Bereft, Stunned*.

45. Id.

46. Mark Prado, *Thirty Illegal Immigrants Targeted in Canal Neighborhood Raid*, MARIN INDEPENDENT JOURNAL, March 7, 2007.

47. Id.

48. *ICE Workplace Raids: Their Impact on U.S. Children, Families and Communities*, Workforce Protections Subcommittee Hearing, 110th Cong., 2d sess., v. 154 CONGRESSIONAL RECORD D., no 83, May 20, 2008 (statement of Kathryn Gibney, principal, San Pedro Elementary School).

49. American Civil Liberties Union, *Civil Rights Groups Sue Immigration Officials for Unlawfully Detaining Six-Year-Old U.S. Citizen*, press release, April 26, 2007, on file with the author.

50. Jesse McKinley, *San Francisco Bay Area Reacts Angrily to Series of Immigration Raids*, NEW YORK TIMES, April 27, 2008.

51. Ken Maguire, *Factory Struggles after Immigration Raid*, WASHINGTON POST, March 28 2007.

52. Ray Henry, *Children Stranded after Immigration Raid*, BOSTON GLOBE, March 7, 2007.

53. Alexandra Marks, *After New Bedford Immigration Raid, Voices Call for Mercy and Justice*, CHRISTIAN SCIENCE MONITOR, March 16, 2007.

54. National Council of La Raza, *Paying the Price: The Impact of Immigration Raids on America's Children* 28–29 (Washington, D.C.: National Council of La Raza, 2007).

55. Anahad O'Connor, *Immigration Agency Learns from '07 Raid*, NEW YORK TIMES, March 6, 2006.

56. National Council of La Raza, *Paying the Price* at 36–37.

57. Id. at 50–51.

58. Antonio Olivio, *Immigration Raid Eoils Iowa Melting Pot*, CHICAGO TRIBUNE, May 18, 2008.

59. Id.

60. *Raids Could Make Postville a Ghost Town*, KAALTV, May 14, 2008.

61. Id.

62. Jonah Newman (Minneapolis), letter to the editor, NEW YORK TIMES, June 3, 2008.

63. Mary Ann Zehr, *Iowa School District Left Coping with Immigration Raid's Impact*, EDUCATION WEEK, May 20, 2008.

64. Jayne Norman, *Immigrants Feel Distress, Shock, Nun Says*, DES MOINES REGISTER, May 21, 2008.

65. Michelle Boorstein, *Raid on Slaughterhouse May Mean Shortage of Kosher Meat*, WASHINGTON POST, May 22, 2008, at A02.

66. Spencer S. Hsu, *Immigration Raid Jars a Small Town*, WASHINGTON POST, May 18, 2008, at A01.

67. Steven Greenhouse, *Shuttered Meat Plant Edges Back into Business, but Its Town Is Still Struggling*, NEW YORK TIMES, December 4, 2008.

68. Barry, *Are Americans Willing to Pay for the Intensifying Crackdown on Immigrants?*

69. *The Great Immigration Panic*, NEW YORK TIMES, June 3, 2008.

CHAPTER 7

1. Kevin Johnson, *Free Trade and Closed Borders: NAFTA and Mexican Immigration to the United States*, 27 U.C. DAVIS LAW REVIEW 937, 960 (1994) (citing Congressman Robert Matsui).

2. Embassy of Mexico, *Mexico and the Migration Phenomenon*, paper distributed at the Immigration Task Force meeting, Migration Policy Institute, Washington, D.C., February 28, 2006, at 2, 6.

3. Louis Uchitelle, *NAFTA Should Have Stopped Illegal Immigration, Right?* NEW YORK TIMES, February 18, 2007.

4. Id. (citing Dani Rodrik, a Harvard economist and trade specialist).

5. Jennifer E. Harman, *Mexican President Vicente Fox's Proposal for Expanding NAFTA into a European Union–Style Common Market—Obstacles and Outlook*. 7 LAW AND BUSINESS REVIEW OF THE AMERICAS 207, 220 (2001).

6. Pastor, *North America's Second Decade*, FOREIGN AFFAIRS, January–February 2004 at 9.

7. Directorate-General for Agriculture, European Commission, *Agricultural Situation in Candidate Countries: Country Report on Romania*, July 2002 at 7; Andreas

Schneider, *Analysis of EU–CEEC Migration with Special Reference to Agricultural Labour*, Hamburg Institute of International Economics, 2004 at 16–17.

8. European Commission, *SAPARD Rural Development Plan for Romania*, November 22, 2000.

9. Id at 352.

10. Id.

11. Id. at 484.

12. Id.

13. Id.

14. Robert A. Pastor, *Toward a North American Community: Lessons from the Old World for the New* 76 (Washington, D.C.: Peterson Institute for International Economics, 2001).

15. Id. at 77.

16. Id. at 93.

17. Id. at 137.

18. Id.

19. Id at 93.

20. Pastor, *Toward a North American Community* at 136.

21. Thomas L. Friedman, *Out of the Box*, NEW YORK TIMES, April 4, 2004.

22. Pastor, *Toward a North American Community* at 145.

23. Id. at 191.

24. Id. at 139.

25. Bradly J. Condon and J. Brad McBride. *Do You Know the Way to San Jose? Resolving the Problem of Illegal Mexican Migration to the United States.* 17 GEORGETOWN IMMIGRATION LAW JOURNAL 251, 255 (2003).

26. Id.

27. Id. at 267.

28. Id. at 267–268.

29. Id.

30. Id. at 256.

31. Id.

32. Portugal and Spain, with EU help, established small colleges in rural provinces. These colleges served as magnets that attracted professionals from more advanced regions, and they also radiated their influence into the wider rural community, helping to upgrade their education: Pastor, *Toward a North American Community* at 141.

33. Sandra Polaski, *Twelve Years of the North American Free Trade Agreement: Hearing before the Subcommittee on International Trade of the S. Comm. on Finance*, CQ Congressional Testimony, 109th Cong., September 11, 2006.

34. Penélope Pacheco-López, *Mexico's Country Report*, EIU VIEWSWIRE, July 2005 at 20.

35. Polaski, *Twelve Years of the North American Free Trade Agreement*.

36. Monica L. Heppel and Luis R. Torres. *Mexican Immigration to the United States after NAFTA*, 20 FLETCHER FORUM OF WORLD AFFAIRS 51, 63 (Fall 1996).

37. Id.

38. Eliza Barclay, *An Unraveling Industry: Apparel Manufacturing Jobs Are in a Steep Decline*, HOUSTON CHRONICLE, April 23, 2006.

39. Pastor, *Toward a North American Community* at 138.

40. Wayne M. Morrison, Marc Labonte, and Jonathan E. Sanford, *China's Currency Peg: A Summary of the Economic Issues* (New York: Nova Science Publishers, 2006).

41. Id.

42. Id.

43. Jim Davenport, *Biden: Blame Immigration Woes on Mexico*, Associated Press, November 28, 2006.

44. Interview with Professor Joe Hyman, Anthropology Department, University of Texas, El Paso, February 21, 2006; see also *America's Border Troubles, North and South*, Economist.com Web Site, September 6, 2005.

45. Jason Ackleson, *Achieving "Security and Prosperity": Migration and North American Economic Integration*, 5 Immigration Policy in Focus (February 2006).

46. *Special Report: Romanian Workers in Spain*, French EuroNews, January 3, 2008.

47. Id.

48. Id.

49. Id.

50. Sebastian Hess, *The Demand for Seasonal Farm Labor from Central and Eastern European Countries in German Agriculture*, Agricultural Engineering International: CIGR Ejournal, May 2006 at 8.

51. Id.

52. Harman, *Mexican President Vicente Fox's Proposal for Expanding NAFTA into a European Union–Style Common Market* at 216.

53. Christopher J. Cassise, *The European Union v. the United States under the NAFTA: A Comparative Analysis of the Free Movement of Persons within the Regions*. 46 Syracuse Law Review 1343, 1349 (1996).

54. Id. at 1354.

55. Jeff Faux, *The Global Class War: How America's Bipartisan Elite Lost Our Future, and What It Will Take to Win It Back* (Hoboken, N.J.: John Wiley and Sons, 2006).

56. Kevin R. Johnson, *Opening the Floodgates: Why America Needs to Rethink Its Borders and Immigration Laws* (New York: New York University Press, 2008); Kevin R. Johnson, *Open Borders?* 51 UCLA Law Review 193 (2003).

57. Gerald P. López, *Undocumented Mexican Migration: in Search of a Just Immigration Law and Policy*, 28 UCLA Law Review 615 (1981).

58. Ginger Thompson, *Mexican Leader Visits U.S. with a Vision to Sell*, New York Times, August 24, 2000, at A3.

59. Id.

60. Johnson, *Open Borders?* at 205, 208, 211.

61. Antoine Pécoud and Paul F. A. Guchteneire, *Introduction: The Migration without Borders Scenario*, in *Migration without Borders: Essays on the Free Movement of People*, ed. Antoine Pécoud and Paul de Guchteneire, 1 (New York: United Nations Educational, Scientific and Cultural Organization Publishing, 2007).

62. Id. at 9.

63. Id. at 1, 4.

64. Id. at 13.

65. Id.

66. Id.

67. Id. at 6.

68. Id. at 14. In fact, in the United States, stricter border enforcement after 9/11 has reduced circularity, and many undocumented who would regularly return home, no longer feel that can do so. In many respects, this has increased the undocumented population.

69. Id. at 6.

70. Id. at 7.

71. Id. at 10.

72. Id.

73. Id. at 15.

74. Id. at 17.

75. Id. at 11.

76. Id.

77. Id. at 18.

78. Id. at 20.

79. Id. at 22.

80. Robert J. Flanagan, *Globalization and Labor Conditions* 88, 93 (Oxford: Oxford University Press, 2006). Flanagan complains that restrictions on immigration have damaged the ability of migration to help equalize labor conditions across the globe today: id. at 112.

81. Id. at 108.

82. Id. at 89.

83. Id. at 103–104.

84. Id. at 115–116.

85. Id. at 104–106.

86. Id. at 107.

87. Johnson, *Open Borders?* Also, see generally Johnson, *Opening the Floodgates.*

88. Johnson, *Open Borders?* at 205 (citing Mark Tushnet).

89. Id. at 208 (citing Joseph Carens).

90. Id. at 205–206.

91. Id. at 230–232.

92. Id. at 244–252.

93. Id. at 221–222.

94. Id. at 216–217. Consider racist sentiment directed at Latinos in the United States and the increased discrimination and hate crimes directed at Arabs, Muslims, and South Asians after 9/11

95. Id. at 226–230.

96. Id. at 211 (citing R. George Wright).

97. Id. at 203–204.

98. Id. at 233–235.

99. Id. at 263–264.

100. López, *Undocumented Mexican Migration* at 640.

101. See, e.g., Bill Ong Hing, *Deporting Our Souls: Values, Morality and Immigration Policy* (Cambridge: Cambridge University Press, 2006).

102. Pastor, *Toward a North American Community* at 189.

103. Johnson, *Open Borders?* at 208 (citing Dowty).

104. Douglas S. Massey, *An Exercise in Self-Deception*, NEWSWEEK, January 19, 2004, at 41.

105. *Northward, Ho! Fox and Bush,* ECONOMIST, August 31, 2001.

106. Bill Ong Hing, *To Be an American: Cultural Pluralism and the Rhetoric of Assimilation* (New York: New York University Press, 1997).

107. Jeffrey S. Passel, *Unauthorized Migrants: Numbers and Characteristics* 26 (Washington, D.C.: Pew Hispanic Center, 2005).

108. Id.

109. Id.

110. Id.

111. Id. at 27.

112. Id.

113. Id. at 4.

114. Stephen Dinan, *Illegals Bill Drops Felony Provision,* WASHINGTON TIMES, December 15, 2005; Hubert G. Locke, *Strike Some Words from the National Lexicon,* SEATTLE POST-INTELLIGENCER, December 29, 2006; *The Fence Campaign,* NEW YORK TIMES, October 20, 2006, at A24.

115. *The Need for Comprehensive Immigration Reform: Serving Our National Economy: Hearing before the Subcommittee on Immigration, Border Security and Citizenship of the S. Comm. on the Judiciary,* 109th Cong., 2005 at 3–5 (statement of Thomas J. Donohue, president and chief executive, U.S. Chamber of Commerce).

116. *National Restaurant Association Annual Report, 2006–2007,* available at http://www.nationalrestaurantassociation.com/aboutus/annualreport.cfm.

117. Id.

118. Daniel T. Griswold, *Willing Workers: Fixing the Problem of Illegal Mexican Migration to the United States,* Center for Trade Policy Studies no. 9 (Washington, D.C.: Cato Institute, 2002).

119. Butch John, *Immigration's Local Impact: Hispanics, Asians Flowing In,* LOUISVILLE COURIER-JOURNAL, September 6, 2000, at 1A.

120. *Rustbelt 2.0: Immigration Initiative,* BURGH DISPORA BLOG, available at http://burghdiaspora.blogspot.com/2007/12/rust-belt-20-immigratin-initiative.html.

121. Faux, *The Global Class War* at 46.

122. Laura Carlsen, *NAFTA and Immigration: Toward a Workable and Humane Integration,* unpublished ms., March 2008 at 15–16.

123. Id. at 17.

EPILOGUE

1. Russ Bynum, *Immigration Raid Cripples Georgia Town,* ASSOCIATED PRESS, September 15, 2006.

2. David Bacon argues that passage of the Employee Free Choice Act (EFCA), pending in Congress, is needed for the protection of workers at companies such as Wal-Mart and Rite Aid. The EFCA would go a long way toward solving the problems workers have at three crucial stages in union organizing efforts—anti-union firings at the beginning, getting their union recognized, and negotiating a first agreement: see David Bacon, *Why Labor Law Doesn't Work for Workers,* NEW AMERICAN MEDIA , March 11, 2009.

3. Ricardo Alonso-Zaldivar, *Bush Would Open U.S. to Guest Workers,* LOS ANGELES TIMES, January 8, 2004.

4. Abraham Spencer and Lee H. Hamilton, *Immigration and America's Future: A New Chapter* 38–40 (Washington, D.C.: Migration Policy Institute, 2006).

5. George Lakoff and Sam Ferguson, *The Framing of Immigration*, HUFFINGTON POST, May 19, 2006.

6. Antoine Pécoud and Paul F. A. Guchteneire, *Introduction: The Migration without Borders Scenario*, in *Migration without Borders: Essays on the Free Movement of People*, ed. Antoine Pécoud and Paul de Guchteneire, 12 (New York: United Nations Educational, Scientific and Cultural Organization Publishing, 2007).

7. Michael Josephson, *Making Ethical Decisions* (Los Angeles: Josephson's Institute of Ethics, 2002).

8. Id.

9. Ken Georgetti and John Sweeney, *A New Prosperity Agenda for North America* (letter to President Barack Obama and Canadian Prime Minister Stephen Harper), February 18, 2009, available at http://www.boston.com/news/politics/politicalintelligence/jjs%20kg%201etter%20to%200bama%20and%20harper%20%20021809.pdf.

10. See Chapter 7.

11. Gordon H. Hanson, *The Economic Logic of Illegal Immigration*, Council on Foreign Relations, CSR no. 26, April 2007 at 14.

12. Faye Bowers, *Employers Risk Little in Hiring Illegal Labor*, CHRISTIAN SCIENCE MONITOR, April 18, 2006.

13. Immigration and Nationality Act (INA) § 101(a)(15)(H)(ii)(a).

14. Id. § 214(c), 8 U.S.C. §1184(c).

15. Id.

16. U.S. General Accounting Office, *H-2A Agricultural Guestworker Program: Changes Could Improve Services to Employers and Better Protect Workers* (Washington, D.C.: U.S. Government Printing Office, 1997).

17. Id. at 133.

18. Robert A. Pastor, *Toward a North American Community: Lessons from the Old World for the New*, 98 (Washington, D.C.: Peterson Institute for International Economics, 2001).

19. Id. at 111.

20. Heather Clark, *Ex-Mexican President Fox Says U.S. Should Spend to Narrow Wage Gap between Two Nations*, MINNEAPOLIS-ST. PAUL STAR TRIBUNE, September 21, 2009.

21. Oxfam America, *U.S. Farm Subsidies Fuel Mexican Corn Crisis*, press release, August 27, 2003.

22. Id.

23. U.S.–Mexico Border 2012 Program, *What Is Border 2012?* fact sheet, U.S. Environmental Protection Agency, June 23, 2009.

24. National Center for Environmental Health, *Border 2012 Program*, CENTERS FOR DISEASE CONTROL AND PREVENTION, Atlanta, n.d.

25. U.S.–Mexico Border 2012 Program, *What Is Border 2012?*

26. National Center for Environmental Health, *Border 2012 Program*.

27. Rogelio Sáenz and Karen Manges Douglas, *Environmental Issues on the U.S.–Mexico Border: An Introduction*, 24 SOUTHERN RURAL SOCIOLOGY 1 (2009).

28. Tim L. Merrill and Ramón Miró, eds., *Mexico: A Country Study* (Washington, D.C.: U.S. Government Printing Office, 1996).

29. Id.

30. See *Mexican Ministry: FDA Study Shows Mexican Tomatoes Not Salmonella-tainted Source*, XINHUA NEWS AGENCY, July 11, 2008.

31. In the summer of 2008, U.S. officials asked Mexican growers to stop importing tomatoes because of a salmonella scare. Mexico turned out not to be the source of these tainted tomatoes, and the investigation ended "in questions": see id.

32. See Randal C. Archibold, *Wave of Drug Violence Is Creeping into Arizona from Mexico.* NEW YORK TIMES, February 23, 2009; Alex Johnson, *In Mexico's Drug Wars, Fears of a U.S. Front,* MSNBC, March 9, 2009; Associated Press, *Mexican Military Losing Drug War Support,* SECURITY CORNER MEXICO, July 24, 2008.

33. See Emilio San Pedro, *U.S. Ready to Aid Mexico Drug Fight,* BBC NEWS, March 2, 2009.

34. That is, Mexican farmers' losing their ability to compete against subsidized products.

35. See *Latin American Drugs I: Losing the Fight,* Latin America Report no. 25, CRISIS GROUP, March 14, 2008.

36. See the discussions of the European Constitution and Lisbon Treaty in Chapters 6–7.

37. Pastor, *Toward a North American Community* at 125.

38. Id. As long as the ratio in incomes between the United States and Mexico ranges from 4 to 30, the incentives to migrate will be compelling. Until that differential can be reduced about half—and, under very optimistic projections, that could take thirty to forty years—a deliberate decision to relax U.S. immigration laws would have serious adverse consequences for Mexico's economy: id.

39. Bill Ong Hing, *Making and Remaking Asian America through Immigration Policy* (Stanford, Calif.: Stanford University Press, 1993).

40. Harry S. Truman, *Veto of Bill to Revise the Laws Relating to Immigration, Naturalization and Nationality* (June 25, 1952), AMERICAN PRESIDENCY PROJECT.

41. John F. Kennedy, *A Nation of Immigrants* (New York: HarperCollins, 1958).

42. *Reagan on Immigration* (editorial), WALL STREET JOURNAL, May 16, 2006.

43. *Obama Puts Immigration Back on the Agenda,* FAIRIMMIGRATION.ORG, March 19, 2009.

44. Barack Obama, *I Will Repair Our Relationship with Mexico,* DALLAS MORNING NEWS, February 20, 2008; emphasis added.

45. *The White House Agenda: Immigration,* WHITEHOUSE.GOV, n.d.; emphasis added.

46. America's Voice, *Our Plan for Comprehensive Reform,* AMERICA'S VOICE ONLINE, 2008; emphasis added.

47. See Chapter 7.

48. Laura Carlsen, *Obama Reaffirms Promise to Renegotiate NAFTA,* HUFFINGTON POST, February 11, 2009.

49. Tom Barry, *Napolitano's Hard Echo of Liberal Immigration Reform Strategy,* AMERICA'S PROGRAM COMMENTARY, February 19, 2009.

50. National Council of La Raza, *Comprehensive Immigration Reform,* NCLR.ORG, n.d.

51. See generally Timothy A. Canova, *Closing the Border and Opening the Door: Mobility, Adjustment, and the Sequencing of Reform,* 5 GEORGETOWN JOURNAL OF LAW AND PUBLIC POLICY 36 (2007).

52. Id. at 82–83. Canova continues, "Whatever future the polity can imagine and agree upon, the state can claim the resources to plan it; and with sufficient financial resources, the nation-state can mobilize armies, rebuild shattered societies, modernize public infrastructure, and train and educate millions of citizens. [Taking on debt may be necessary, but with] university students [who borrow for their education,] taking on debt is . . . a good investment in the future. . . . Such mobilization of financial resources would allow the federal government to influence and perhaps once again dominate events in the world by directing the pattern of production; spending on health and education, in foreign aid and public infrastructure. While enormous public spending will never guarantee success, without sufficient public spending, failure is only a matter of time. [Such an investment] would spur a generation of men and women to productive, creative, and meaningful work on both sides of the border": id. at 87–88, 104. He acknowledges that the United States is the largest deficit country in the world and that the dollar is exposed and vulnerable to foreign exchange and global capital markets. Yet, he believes that the United States is wealthy enough to support a massive foreign aid program for Mexico's regional development: id. at 98.

53. Gary Becker, *The Wise Way to Stem Illegal Immigration*, BUSINESSWEEK, April 26, 2004, at 28.

54. Juliana Barbassa, *Condi Rice: Immigration Reform Needed for People Who "Crawl across the Desert,"* SAN JOSE MERCURY NEWS, March 13, 2009.

55. In fairness to Secretary Rice, she went beyond the economic benefit of immigrants and stated, "If we . . . start to believe somehow that it is instead a threat to us to have [immigrants] come here, we are going to lose one of the strongest elements not only of our national wealth, but also of our national soul": id.

56. Jimmy Carter, *Our Endangered Values: America's Moral Crisis* 11 (New York: Simon and Schuster, 2005).

57. Pastor, *Toward a North American Community* at 2.

58. Marjane Satrapi, *Persepolis 2* 144, 148 (New York: Random House, 2004).

59. Douglas S. Massey, *Backfire at the Border: Why Enforcement without Legalization Cannot Stop Illegal Immigration*, Trade Policy Analysis no. 29, Center for Trade Policy Studies, Cato Institute, Washington, D.C., 2006 at 5.

60. As the *The Great Immigration Panic*, NEW YORK TIMES, June 3, 2008, reminds us, the rhetoric of the anti-immigrant contingent is grounded in a historical philosophy that is best cast aside:

The restrictionist message is brutally simple—that illegal immigrants deserve no rights, mercy or hope. It refuses to recognize that illegality is not an identity; it is a status that can be mended by making reparations and resuming a lawful life. Unless the nation contains its enforcement compulsion, illegal immigrants will remain forever Them and never Us, subject to whatever abusive regimes the powers of the moment may devise.

Every time this country has singled out a group of newly arrived immigrants for unjust punishment, the shame has echoed through history. Think of the Chinese and Irish, Catholics and Americans of Japanese ancestry. Children someday will study the Great Immigration Panic of the early 2000s, which harmed countless lives, wasted billions of dollars and mocked the nation's most deeply held values.

61. Financial institutions certainly recognize the strategic importance of Mexico to the stability of United States and the rest of the world. Consider 1982, when the fear that Mexico could default on $80 billion in foreign loans created a financial crisis. The central banks of the world and the International Monetary Fund were forced to broad bridge loans and loan forgiveness packages to avoid the collapse of the world system: see Steven Solomon, *The Confidence Game—How Unelected Central Bankers are Governing the Changed Global Economy* 199–210 (New York: Simon and Schuster, 1995).

Bibliography

Abraham, Spencer, and Lee H. Hamilton. *Immigration and America's Future: A New Chapter*. Washington, D.C.: Migration Policy Institute, 2006.

Ackleson, Jason. *Achieving "Security and Prosperity": Migration and North American Economic Integration*. 5 IMMIGRATION POLICY IN FOCUS (February 2006).

Allen, Mike. *Bush Proposes Legal Status for Immigrant Labor: Workers Could Stay Six Years or More*. WASHINGTON POST, January 8, 2004, at A01.

Alonso-Zaldivar, Ricardo. *Bush Would Open U.S. to Guest Workers*. LOS ANGELES TIMES, January 8, 2004.

Alvarez-Bejar, Alejandro. *Industrial Restructuring and the Role of Mexican Labor in NAFTA*. 27 UC DAVIS LAW REVIEW 897 (1994).

American Civil Liberties Union. *Civil Rights Groups Sue Immigration Officials for Unlawfully Detaining Six-Year-Old U.S. Citizen*. Press release, April 26, 2007. Available at http://www.aclu.org.

America's Border Troubles, North and South. ECONOMIST, September 6, 2005.

America's Voice. *Our Plan for Comprehensive Reform*. AMERICA'S VOICE ONLINE, 2008. Available at http://www.americasvoiceonline.org.

Andrews, William J. *An Environmental Perspective on the "Effective Enforcement" Provisions of the North American Agreement on Environmental Cooperation*. Winnipeg 95 National Legal Symposium, Canadian Bar Association, August 23, 1995. Available at http://www.wcel.org.

Annis, Roger. *Economic Crisis Slams Canada*. CENTER FOR RESEARCH ON GLOBALIZATION, March 29, 2009. Available at http://www.globalresearch.ca.

Arai, Adriana, and Patrick Harrington. *After Six Months, Mexican Leader Tries to Build Economic Momentum*. INTERNATIONAL HERALD TRIBUNE, June 25, 2007.

Archibold, Randal C. *Wave of Drug Violence Is Creeping into Arizona from Mexico, Officials Say*. NEW YORK TIMES, February 23, 2009.

Associated Press. *Mexican Military Losing Drug War Support*. SECURITY CORNER MEXICO, July 24, 2008. Available at http://www.securitycornermexico.com.

———. *Mexico: New Legal System Set*. NEW YORK TIMES, June 18, 2008.

Bacon, David. *Why Labor Law Doesn't Work for Workers*. NEW AMERICAN MEDIA. March 11, 2009. Available at http://news.newamericamedia.org.

Barbassa, Juliana. *Condi Rice: Immigration Reform Needed for People Who "Crawl across the Desert."* SAN JOSE MERCURY NEWS, March 13, 2009. Available at http://www.mercurynews.com.

Barclay, Eliza. *An Unraveling Industry: Apparel Manufacturing Jobs Are in a Steep Decline*. HOUSTON CHRONICLE, April 23, 2006.

Barry, Tom. *Are Americans Willing to Pay for the Intensifying Crackdown on Immigrants?* AMERICAS PROGRAM COMMENTARY, May 18, 2008. Available at http://americas.irc-online.org.

———. *Napolitano's Hard Echo of Liberal Immigration Reform Strategy*. AMERICA'S PROGRAM COMMENTARY, February 19, 2009. Available at http://americas.irc-online.org.

Basas, Richard. *Mexico 2009: Stimulus, Security and Neighbourly Assistance*. FOREIGN POLICY ASSOCIATION, January 8, 2009. Available at http://latinamerica.foreignpolicyblogs.com.

BBC News. *Slowdown Hits Mexico Remittances*. January 27, 2009. Available at http://news.bbc.co.uk.

Becker, Gary. *The Wise Way to Stem Illegal Immigration*. BUSINESS WEEK, April 26, 2004, at 28.

Bernstein, Nina. *Most Mexican Immigrants in New Study Gave Up Jobs to Take Their Chances in U.S.* NEW YORK TIMES, December 7, 2005, at A30.

Boorstein, Michelle. *Raid on Slaughterhouse May Mean Shortage of Kosher Meat*. WASHINGTON POST, May 22, 2008, at A02.

Bowers, Faye. *Employers Risk Little in Hiring Illegal Labor*. CHRISTIAN SCIENCE MONITOR, April 18, 2006.

Bynum, Russ. *Immigration Raid Cripples Georgia Town*. ASSOCIATED PRESS, September 15, 2006. Available at http://www.sfgate.com.

———. *Immigration Raids Leave Georgia Town Bereft, Stunned*. SEATTLE TIMES, September 16, 2006.

Calderón, Felipe. *Dropping NAFTA Would Damage the Economy*. WORLDNET DAILY, April 22, 2008. Available at http://www.wnd.com.

Calderón Vows to Look U.S. in the Eye. SAN ANTONIO EXPRESS-NEWS, April 1, 2008, available at http://www.mysanantonio.com.

Canada Attracting More Mexican Immigrants. WORKPERMIT.COM, May 5, 2005. Available at http://www.workpermit.com/news/2005_05_04/canada/canada_attracts_mexican_immigrants.htm.

Canada Becoming the More Attractive North American Immigration Destination. CANADIAN IMMIGRATION NEWSLETTER, August 2007.

Canadian Services Coalition and Canadian Chamber of Commerce. *Canadian Services Sector: A New Success Story* 3 (2006).

Canadian Wheat Board. *CWB Wins NAFTA Appeal on Tariff*, June 2005. Available at http://www.cwb.ca/public/en/hot/trade/brief.

Canova, Timothy A. *Closing the Border and Opening the Door: Mobility, Adjustment, and the Sequencing of Reform.* 5 GEORGETOWN JOURNAL OF LAW AND PUBLIC POLICY 36 (2007).

Carlsen, Laura. *NAFTA and Immigration: Toward a Workable and Humane Integration.* Unpublished ms., March 2008, on file with the author.

———. *Obama Reaffirms Promise to Renegotiate NAFTA.* HUFFINGTON POST, February 11, 2009. Available at http://www.huffingtonpost.com.

Carter, Jimmy. *Our Endangered Values: America's Moral Crisis.* New York: Simon and Schuster, 2005.

Cassise, Christopher J. *The European Union v. the United States under the NAFTA: A Comparative Analysis of the Free Movement of Persons within the Regions.* 46 SYRACUSE LAW REVIEW 1343 (1996).

Central Intelligence Agency. *The World Factbook—Canada.* Available at http://www.cia.gov.

———. *The World Factbook—Mexico.* Available at https://www.cia.gov.

Chacón, Jennifer. *Unsecured Borders: Immigration Restrictions, Crime Control and National Security.* 39 CONNECTICUT LAW REVIEW 1827–1891 (2007).

Condon, Bradly J., and J. Brad McBride. *Do You Know the Way to San Jose? Resolving the Problem of Illegal Mexican Migration to the United States.* 17 GEORGETOWN IMMIGRATION LAW JOURNAL 251 (2003).

Constable, Pamela. *"No Amnesty" Is Cry at D.C. Immigration Protest.* WASHINGTON POST, April 23, 2007.

Cornelius, Wayne A. *Death at the Border: The Efficacy and "Unintended" Consequences of U.S. Immigration Control Policy, 1993–2000.* Working Paper no. 27. Center for Comparative Immigration Studies, University of California, San Diego, 2001.

Cotis, Jean-Philippe. *Benchmarking Canada's Economic Performance.* 13 INTERNATIONAL PRODUCTIVITY MONITOR 5 (2006).

Davenport, Jim. *Biden: Blame Immigration Woes on Mexico.* ASSOCIATED PRESS, November 28, 2006.

Department of Finance, Government of Canada. *Advantage Canada: Building a Strong Economy for Canadians.* Ottawa, November 23, 2006. Available at http://www.fin.gc.ca.

———. *Canada's New Government Announces Tax Fairness Plan.* Press release, October 31, 2006. Available at http://www.fin.gc.ca/news06/06–061e.html.

———. *Canada's New Government Cuts Wasteful Programs, Refocuses Spending on Priorities, Achieves Major Debt Reduction as Promised.* Press release, September 25, 2006.

———. *The Canadian Financial Services Sector.* Ottawa, June 2005. Available at http://www.fin.gc.ca.

Dickerson, Marla. *Economic Data Show Mexico Still Struggling for Growth.* LOS ANGELES TIMES, February 16, 2006.

Dinan, Stephen. *Illegals Bill Drops Felony Provision.* WASHINGTON TIMES, December 15, 2005.

Directorate-General for Agriculture, European Commission. *Agricultural Situation in Candidate Countries: Country Report on Romania.* July 2002.

Dugger, Celia W. *Report Finds Few Benefits for Mexico in NAFTA.* NEW YORK TIMES, November 19, 2003.

Economist Intelligence Unit, *Canada: Country Fact Sheet.* EIU Viewswire Canada 54, March 13, 2007.
———. *Canada Economy: "Advantage Canada" Strategy Launched.* EIU Viewswire Canada 3, February 12, 2007.
———. *Country Profile Canada* 14 (2006).
Ehrenreich, Barbara. *What America Owes Its "Illegals."* Nation, June 13, 2007.
Embassy of Mexico. *Mexico and the Migration Phenomenon.* Paper distributed at the Immigration Task Force meeting, Migration Policy Institute, Washington, D.C., February 28, 2006.
Embassy of the United States, Ottawa. *Canada–United States Relations.* January 2007. Available at http://ottawa.usembassy.gov.
Emmott, Robin. *More Migrants Die as U.S. Tightens Border Security.* Reuters, July 12, 2007.
Europa. *Overviews of the Activities of the European Union, Agriculture: Meeting the Needs of Farmers and Consumers,* n.d. Available at http://europa.eu.
European Commission. *CARDS,* October 25, 2007. Available at http://ec.europa.eu.
———. *Enlargement: Financial Assistance,* October 18, 2007. Available at http://ec.europa.eu.
———. *Enlargement: Financial Assistance, Economic and Social Cohesion,* n.d. Available at http://ec.europa.eu.
———. *Enlargement: Financial Assistance, SAPARD,* October 3, 2008. Available at http://ec.europa.eu.
———. *PHARE,* n.d. Available at http://ec.europa.eu.
———. *Regional Policy, Regional Policy-Inforegio,* June 20, 2008. Available at http://ec.europa.eu.
———. *Regional Policy: The Cohesion Fund at a Glance,* June 20, 2008. Available at http://ec.europa.eu.
———. *Supporting Enlargement: What Does Evaluation Show? Ex-Post Evaluation of PHARE,* July 2007. Available at http://ec.europa.eu.
European Union. *The Common Agricultural Policy—a Policy Evolving with the Times: The CAP and Enlargement 10.* Available at http://ec.europa.eu.
Euskirchen, Markus, et al. *From Borderline to Borderland: The Changing of the European Border Regime.* Monthly Review, November 2007. Available at http://www.monthlyreview.org.
Exige Calderón a EU frenar ley migratoria. El Universal, March 25, 2006. Available at http://www.eluniversal.com.mx.
Extending NAFTA's Reach. Worldpress.org, August 26, 2007. Available at http://www.worldpress.org/Americas/2910.cfm.
Faux, Jeff. *The Global Class War: How America's Bipartisan Elite Lost Our Future, and What It Will Take to Win It Back.* Hoboken, N.J.: John Wiley and Sons, 2006.
The Fence Campaign. New York Times, October 20, 2006, at A24.
Fergusson, Ian. *United States–Canada Trade and Economic Relationship: Prospects and Challenges.* Congressional Research Service report no. RL33087, U.S. Library of Congress, October 13, 2006.
Ferris, Susan. *Twenty Years Later, 50 Percent Still Poor: NAFTA, Global Competition Have Left Millions Behind.* Austin American-Statesman, August 10, 2003.
Fidier, Stephen. *Going South.* Financial Times, January 8, 2009.

Flanagan, Robert J. *Globalization and Labor Conditions.* Oxford: Oxford University Press, 2006.

Foreign Affairs and International Trade, Government of Canada. *Canada's New Government Cuts Wasteful Programs, Refocuses Spending on Priorities, Achieves Major Debt Reduction as Promised.* Press release, September 25, 2006. Available at http://www.fin.gc.ca/news06/06–047e.html.

———. *Canada to Hold Public Consultations on Proposed Free Trade Agreements with Andean Countries and Dominican Republic.* Press release no. 139, November 4, 2002.

———. *The Economic and Fiscal Update.* Ottawa, November 23, 2006.

———. *Opening Doors to the World, Canada's International Market Access Priorities 2006,* June 5, 2006. Available at http://www.international.gc.ca/tna-nac/2006/7_06-en.asp.

———. *Regional and Bilateral Initiatives: Canada–Central America Four (CA4),* November 7, 2006. Available at http://www.international.gc.ca/tna-nac/ca4-en.asp.

———. *Regional and Bilateral Initiatives: Canada–Dominican Republic Free Trade Discussions,* February 6, 2007. Available at http://www.dfait-maeci.gc.ca/tna-nac/dr-en.asp.

———. *Regional and Bilateral Initiatives: Canada–European Free Trade Association (EFTA) Free Trade Agreement Negotiations,* January 11, 2007. Available at http://www.international.gc.ca/tna-nac/efta-en.asp

———. *Regional and Bilateral Initiatives: Canada–Korea Free Trade Agreement Negotiations,* February 27, 2007, available at http://www.dfait-maeci.gc.ca/tna-nac/RB/korea-en.asp.

———. *Regional and Bilateral Initiatives: Introduction to the Canada–Japan Economic Framework and Joint Study,* 2008. Available at http://www.dfait-maeci.gc.ca/tna-nac/RB/japan-intro-en.asp.

———. *Seventh Annual Report on Canada's State of Trade* 25 (2006). Available at http://www.international.gc.ca/eet/trade/state-of-trade-en.asp

———. *Trade and Investment Reports Pocket Facts Canada (Annual),* February 13, 2007. Available at http://www.international.gc.ca/eet/pocket-facts-en.asp.

Fowale, Tongkeh. *The African Thorn in European Flesh.* AMERICAN CHRONICLE, February 27, 2008. Available at http://www.americanchronicle.com.

Fox, Vicente. *Mexican Foreign Policy in the 21st Century.* Speech delivered in Madrid, Spain, May 16, 2002.

Free Trade Deals: What You Don't See May Be What You Get. GLOBAL ECONOMIC JUSTICE REPORT 5 (February 2003).

Friedman, Thomas L. *Out of the Box.* NEW YORK TIMES, April 4, 2004.

Gillman, Todd. *Obama Tells Calderón He Wants to "Upgrade" NAFTA.* DALLAS MORNING NEWS, January 12, 2009.

Glanton, Dahleen, and Tribune National Correspondent. *For Immigrants, Raid Dims Hope for a Better Life.* CHICAGO TRIBUNE, December 11, 2006.

The Great Immigration Panic. NEW YORK TIMES, June 3, 2008.

Greenhouse, Steven. *Shuttered Meat Plant Edges Back into Business, but Its Town Is Still Struggling.* NEW YORK TIMES, December 4, 2008.

Griswold, Daniel T. *Willing Workers: Fixing the Problem of Illegal Mexican Migration to the United States.* Center for Trade Policy Studies no. 19. Washington, D.C.: Cato Institute, 2002. Available at http://www.freetrade.org.

Halligan, Liam. *Will the Credit Crisis Leave the Irish Economy All Washed Up?* TELEGRAPH, February 28, 2009.

Hanson, Gordon H. *The Economic Logic of Illegal Immigration.* Council on Foreign Relations, CSR no. 26, April 2007.

Harman, Danna. *Mexicans Head North for a Better Life—Way North.* CHRISTIAN SCIENCE MONITOR, October 28, 2005.

Harman, Jennifer E. *Mexican President Vicente Fox's Proposal for Expanding NAFTA into a European Union–Style Common Market—Obstacles and Outlook.* 7 LAW AND BUSINESS REVIEW OF THE AMERICAS 207 (2001).

Head, Keith, and John Ries. *Regionalism within Multilateralism: The WTO Trade Policy Review of Canada.* 27 WORLD ECONOMY 1377 (2004).

Henry, Ray. *Children Stranded after Immigration Raid.* BOSTON GLOBE, March 7, 2007.

Heppel, Monica L., and Luis R. Torres. *Mexican Immigration to the United States after NAFTA.* 20 FLETCHER FORUM OF WORLD AFFAIRS 51 (Fall 1996).

Hess, Sebastian. *The Demand for Seasonal Farm Labor from Central and Eastern European Countries in German Agriculture.* AGRICULTURAL ENGINEERING INTERNATIONAL: CIGR EJOURNAL, May 2006. Available at http://journals.sfu.ca/cigr/index.php/Ejounral/article/view/647.

Hing, Bill Ong. *To Be an American: Cultural Pluralism and the Rhetoric of Assimilation.* New York: New York University Press, 1997.

———. *Defining America through Immigration Policy.* Philadelphia: Temple University Press, 2004.

———. *Deporting Our Souls: Values, Morality and Immigration Policy.* Cambridge: Cambridge University Press, 2006.

———. *Making and Remaking Asian America through Immigration Policy.* Stanford, Calif.: Stanford University Press, 1993.

Hsu, Spencer S. *Immigration Raid Jars a Small Town.* WASHINGTON POST, May 18, 2008.

Immigration Raid Still Hurting Pork Producer. ASSOCIATED PRESS, December 28, 2006. Available at http://wcco.com.

The Impact of the Financial Crisis in Canada, Economic Viewpoint. DESJARDINS ECONOMIC STUDIES, October 14, 2008. Available at http://www.desjardins.com.

Industry Canada. *Overview: Competitiveness Factors for Attracting and Maintaining Automotive Investment: Comparison between Canada and Mexico,* November 21, 2003. Available at http://strategis.ic.gc.ca.

———. *Report on Canada's Industrial Performance* 18 (first half of 2006).

Ireland Gets an "F" for Spending on Education in World Report. INDEPENDENT, September 19, 2007.

The Irish Economy: Reykjavik-on-Liffey. ECONOMIST, February 5, 2009.

Jacinto, Martin. *Calderón, NAFTA and Mexico's Campesinos in 2008.* COUNCIL ON HEMISPHERIC AFFAIRS, April 1, 2008. Available at http://www.coha.org.

Jiménez, Sergio Javier. *Obama planea reunir a familias de migrantes.* EL UNIVERSAL, January 14, 2009. Available at http://www.eluniversal.com.mx.

————. *Ofrece Calderón pagar pension a mexicanos en EU.* EL UNIVERSAL, March 30, 2006. Available at http://www.eluniversal.com.mx.

Johnson, Alex. *In Mexico's Drug Wars, Fears of a U.S. Front.* MSNBC, March 9, 2009. Available at http://www.msnbc.msn.com.

Johnson, Kevin R. *Free Trade and Closed Borders: NAFTA and Mexican Immigration to the United States.* 27 UC DAVIS LAW REVIEW 937 (1994).

————. *Open Borders?* 51 UCLA LAW REV. 193 (2003).

————. *Opening the Floodgates: Why America Needs to Rethink Its Borders and Immigration Laws.* New York: New York University Press, 2008.

————. *Race Matters: Immigration Law and Policy Scholarship, Law in the Ivory Tower, and the Legal Indifference of the Race Critique.* 2000 UNIVERSITY OF ILLINOIS LAW REVIEW 525.

Jonsson, Patrick. *Crackdown on Immigrants Empties a Town and Hardens Views.* CHRISTIAN SCIENCE MONITOR, October 3, 2006.

Josephson, Michael. *Making Ethical Decisions.* Los Angeles: Josephson Institute of Ethics, 2002. Available at http://josephsoninstitute.org.

Kennedy, John F. *A Nation of Immigrants.* New York: HarperCollins, 1958.

Kochhar, Rakesh. *Survey of Mexican Migrants, Part Three: The Economic Transition to America.* Pew Hispanic Center, Washington, D.C., December 6, 2005.

Lacey, Marc. *Mexico Accepts Anti-narcotics Aid from U.S.* NEW YORK TIMES, June 28, 2008.

LaFraniere, Sharon. *Europe Takes Africa's Fish, and Boatloads of Migrants Follow.* NEW YORK TIMES, January 14, 2008.

Lakoff, George, and Sam Ferguson. *The Framing of Immigration,* HUFFINGTON POST, May 19, 2006.

Landon, Thomas, Jr. *The Irish Economy's Rise Was Steep, and the Fall Was Fast.* NEW YORK TIMES, January 3, 2009.

Latin American Drugs I: Losing the Fight. Latin America Report no. 25, CRISIS GROUP, March 14, 2008. Available at http://www.crisisgroup.org.

Locke, Hubert G. *Strike Some Words from the National Lexicon.* SEATTLE POST-INTELLIGENCER, December 29, 2006.

López, Gerald P. *Undocumented Mexican Migration: In Search of a Just Immigration Law and Policy.* 28 UCLA LAW REVIEW 615 (1981).

Lyman, Rick. *In Georgia Law, a Wide-Angle View of Immigration.* NEW YORK TIMES, May 12, 2006.

Maguire, Ken. *Factory Struggles after Immigration Raid,* WASHINGTON POST, March 28, 2007.

Malkin, Elizabeth. *Mexico Enacts Tax Overhaul Bill.* NEW YORK TIMES, September 15, 2007.

————. *Mexico's Fiscal Prudence Fails to Avert a Slowdown.* NEW YORK TIMES, December 29, 2008.

Malkin, Elizabeth, and Marc Lacey. *Mexican President Proposes Decriminalizing Some Drugs.* NEW YORK TIMES, October 2, 2008.

Marks, Alexandra. *After New Bedford Immigration Raid, Voices Call for Mercy and Justice.* CHRISTIAN SCIENCE MONITOR, March 16, 2007.

Marosi, Richard. *Less Cocaine on U.S. Streets, Report Says.* LOS ANGELES TIMES, December 16, 2008.

Massey, Douglas S. *Backfire at the Border: Why Enforcement without Legalization Cannot Stop Illegal Immigration.* Trade Policy Analysis no. 29. Center for Trade Policy Studies, Cato Institute, Washington, D.C., 2006.

———. *An Exercise in Self-Deception.* NEWSWEEK, January 19, 2004.

McKinley, James. *Mexican President Assails U.S. Measures on Migrants.* NEW YORK TIMES, September 3, 2007.

McKinley, Jesse. *San Francisco Bay Area Reacts Angrily to Series of Immigration Raids.* NEW YORK TIMES, April 27, 2008.

Merrill, Tim L., and Ramón Miró, eds. *Mexico: A Country Study.* Washington, D.C.: U.S. Government Printing Office, 1996.

Mexican Ministry: FDA Study Shows Mexican Tomatoes Not Salmonella-tainted Source. XINHUA NEWS AGENCY, July 11, 2008. Available at http://news.xinhuanet.com.

Mexican Telecom Magnate Slim May Be World's Richest. SAN FRANCISCO CHRONICLE, July 4, 2007.

Mexican Workers in Canada on the Increase. CAMPBELL COHEN IMMIGRATION LAWYERS WEB SITE, August 19, 2007. Available at http://www.canadavisa.com/mexican-workers-in-canada-on-the-increase-070820.html.

Mexico: Taxes, Pemex, and Calderón's Reforms. STRATFOR GLOBAL INTELLIGENCE, July 5, 2007. Available at http://www.stratfor.com.

Mexico's Calderón Talked Energy Reform with Oil Co[mpanie]s at Davos. MORNINGSTAR, January 29, 2008. Available at http://news.morningstar.com.

Mexico's Peso Gains on U.S. Aid Hopes, Stocks Edge Up. REUTERS, January 16, 2009. Available at http://www.reuters.com.

Meyer, Josh. *White House Unveils Plan to Fight Drug Cartels at Border.* LOS ANGELES TIMES, March 25, 2009.

Meyer, Michael C., William L. Sherman, Susan M. Deeds. *The Course of Mexican History,* 7th ed. Oxford: Oxford University Press, 2003.

Mills, Nicolaus, ed. *Arguing Immigration: The Debate over the Changing Face of America.* New York: Touchstone, 1994.

Morrison, Wayne M., Marc Labonte, and Jonathan E. Sanford. *China's Currency Peg: A Summary of the Economic Issues.* New York: Nova Science Publishers, 2006.

National Center for Environmental Health. *Border 2012 Program.* CENTERS FOR DISEASE CONTROL AND PREVENTION, Atlanta, n.d. Available at http://www.cdc.gov.

National Council of La Raza. *Comprehensive Immigration Reform.* NCLR.ORG, n.d. Available at http://www.nclr.org.

———. *Paying the Price: The Impact of Immigration Raids on America's Children.* Washington, D.C.: National Council of La Raza, 2007.

Natural Resources, Government of Canada. *Statistics and Facts on Energy,* Ottawa, June 7, 2006. Available at http://www.nrcan.gc.ca.

Neipert, David M. *NAFTA Section 303, a Difficult Choice for Mexico NAFTA.* 10 CURRENTS: INTERNATIONAL TRADE LAW JOURNAL 25 (2001).

Noll, Gregor. *Africa Sells Out to Europe.* Paper presented at the Euro-African Migration Conference: Open Democracy, July 13, 2007. Available at http://www.opendemocracy.net.

Norman, Jayne. *Immigrants Feel Distress, Shock, Nun Says.* DES MOINES REGISTER, May 21, 2008.

Northward, Ho! Fox and Bush. ECONOMIST, August 31, 2001.

Obama, Barack. *I Will Repair Our Relationship with Mexico.* DALLAS MORNING NEWS, February 20, 2008.

Obama Puts Immigration Back on the Agenda. FAIRIMMIGRATION.ORG, March 19, 2009. Available at http://fairimmigration.wordpress.com.

O'Connor, Anahad. *Immigration Agency Learns from '07 Raid.* NEW YORK TIMES, March 6, 2006.

Olin, Cliff. *Masses of Immigrants Demand Amnesty.* LOS ANGELES INDEPENDENT MEDIA CENTER, April 9, 2007. Available at http://la.indymedia.org.

Oliveira, Laura C. *A License to Exploit: The Need to Reform the H-2A Temporary Agricultural Guest Worker Program.* 5 SCHOLAR: ST. MARY'S LAW REVIEW ON MINORITY ISSUES 153 (2002).

Olivio, Antonio. *Immigration Raid Roils Iowa Melting Pot.* CHICAGO TRIBUNE, May 18, 2008.

Oxfam America. *U.S. Farm Subsidies Fuel Mexican Corn Crisis.* Press release, .August 27, 2003. Available at http://www.charitywire.com/charity123/04224.html.

Pacheco-López, Penélope. *Mexico's Country Report.* EIU VIEWSWIRE, July 2005.

Passel, Jeffrey S. *Unauthorized Migrants: Numbers and Characteristics.* Washington, D.C.: Pew Hispanic Center, 2005. Available at http://pewhispanic.org.

Passel, Jeffrey, and D'Vera Cohn. *Trends in Unauthorized Immigration: Undocumented Inflow Now Trails Legal Inflow.* Washington, D.C.: Pew Hispanic Center, 2008. Available at http://pewhispanic.org.

Pastor, Manuel, and Carol Wise. *The Origins and Sustainability of Mexico's Free Trade Policy.* 48 INTERNATIONAL ORGANIZATION 459 (1994). Available at http://econpapers.repec.org.

Pastor, Robert A. *Toward a North American Community: Lessons from the Old World for the New.* Washington, D.C.: Peterson Institute for International Economics, 2001.

―――. *North America's Second Decade.* FOREIGN AFFAIRS, January–February 2004. Available at http://www.foreignaffairs.com.

Pécoud, Antoine, and Paul F. A. Guchteneire. *Introduction: The Migration without Borders Scenario.* In *Migration without Borders: Essays on the Free Movement of People.* Ed. Antoine Pécoud and Paul de Guchteneire. New York: United Nations Educational, Scientific and Cultural Organization Publishing, 2007.

Polaski, Sandra. *Twelve Years of the North American Free Trade Agreement: Hearing before the Subcommittee on International Trade of the S. Comm. on Finance.* CQ Congressional Testimony, 109th Cong., September 11, 2006.

Pollan, Michael. *The Omnivore's Dilemma—a Natural History of Four Meals.* New York: Penguin, 2007.

Poloz, Stephen S. *Exports More Diversified in 2006.* EXPORT DEVELOPMENT CANADA, March 7, 2007. Available at http://www.edc.ca.

Poulin, Denis, and Attah K. Boame. *Mad Cow Disease and Beef Trade.* Statistics Canada no. 11–621-MIE2003005, May 20, 2003.

Prado, Mark. *Thirty Illegal Immigrants Targeted in Canal Neighborhood Raid.* MARIN INDEPENDENT JOURNAL, March 7, 2007.

Prakash, Ajay, and Antoine Lerougetel. *The EU Strengthens "Fortress Europe" against Migration due to Climate Change.* WORLD SOCIALIST, May 7, 2008. Available at http://www.wsws.org.

Privy Counsel Office, Government of Canada. *Canada and South Korea Explore Possible Free Trade Agreement.* Press release, November 19, 2004. Available at http://www.pco-bcp.gc.ca.

Raids Could Make Postville a Ghost Town. KAALTV, May 14, 2008. Available at http://www.crownheights.info/index.php?itemid=11931.

Reagan on Immigration (editorial). WALL STREET JOURNAL, May 16, 2006.

Richburg, Keith B. *Worldwide Financial Crisis Largely Bypasses Canada.* WASHINGTON POST, October 16, 2008.

Roberts, Adam. *A World in Flux.* ECONOMIST, November 15, 2007.

Roett, Riordan. *Mexico: Political Update.* Memorandum, Emerging Markets Group, Chase Manhattan, January 13, 1995. Available at http://www.hartford-hwp.com.

Roig-Franzia, Manuel. *Mexico Revises Its Justice System.* WASHINGTON POST, June 18, 2008. Saad, Lydia. *Most Americans Favor Giving Illegal Immigrants a Chance.* GALLUP NEWS SERVICE, 2007. Available at http://www.gallup.com.

Sáenz, Rogelio, and Karen Manges Douglas. *Environmental Issues on the U.S.–Mexico Border: An Introduction.* 24 SOUTHERN RURAL SOCIOLOGY 1 (2009). Available at http://www.ag.auburn.edu.

San Pedro, Emilio. *U.S. Ready to Aid Mexico Drug Fight.* BBC NEWS, March 2, 2009. Available at http://news.bbc.co.uk.

Satrapi, Marjane. *Persepolis 2.* New York: Random House, 2004.

Schneider, Andreas. *Analysis of EU–CEEC Migration with Special Reference to Agricultural Labour.* Hamburg Institute of International Economics, 2004. Available at http://doku.iab.de.

Schott, Jeffrey J. *The Free Trade Area of the Americas: Current Status and Prospects.* 5 JEAN MONNET/ROBERT SCHUMAN PAPER SERIES, July 2005. Available at http://www6.miami.edu.

Schwartz, Jeremy. *Looming Economic Disaster in Mexico.* AUSTIN AMERICAN-STATESMAN, September 30, 2008.

Seth, David. *Responding to Striking Farmers, Mexico's Calderón Pimps NAFTA.* DOCUDHARMA BLOG, January 8, 2008. Available at http://www.docudharma.com.

Slowdown Hits Mexico Remittances. BBC NEWS, January 27, 2009. Available at http://news.bbc.co.uk.

Solomon, Steven. *The Confidence Game: How Unelected Central Bankers Are Governing the Changed Global Economy.* New York: Simon and Schuster, 1995.

SPLC Files Federal Lawsuit Challenging Constitutionality of Immigration Raids That Terrorized Latino Residents of Southeast Georgia Towns. P.R. NEWSWIRE, PUBLIC INTEREST SERVICES, November 1, 2006. Available at http://w3.1exis.com.

Swift Raids Impact Families, Economy, and ID Theft Victims. DENVER CHANNEL, December 13, 2006. Available at http://www.thedenverchannel.com.

Testing Teachers. ECONOMIST, May 22, 2008. Available at http://www.economist.com.

That "Buy American" Provision (editorial). NEW YORK TIMES, February 11, 2009. Available at http://roomfordebate.blogs.nytimes.com.

Thompson, Ginger. *Mexican Leader Visits U.S. with a Vision to Sell.* NEW YORK TIMES, August 24, 2000.

Thomson, Adam. *Calderón Pleads for Energy Reform.* FINANCIAL TIMES, May 27, 2008.

Thornburgh, Nathan. *The Case for Amnesty.* TIME, June 18, 2007, at 38.

The Tiger Tamed. Economist, November 20, 2008.

Trejo, Frank. *Putting Up Barriers: Proposed Border Wall near El Paso Divides Community.* Dallas Morning News, July 30, 1995.

Truman, Harry S. *Veto of Bill to Revise the Laws Relating to Immigration, Naturalization and Nationality* (June 25, 1952). American Presidency Project. Available at http://www.presidency.ucsb.edu.

Uchitelle, Louis. *NAFTA Should Have Stopped Illegal Immigration, Right?* New York Times, February 18, 2007.

Uddin, Sadam. *Impact of Higher Commodity Prices on Canada's Trade Balance.* Foreign Affairs and International Trade no. 3, Government of Canada, 2006. Available at http://www.dfait-maeci.gc.ca.

U.S. Border Patrol. *Border Patrol Strategic Plan: 1994 and Beyond—National Strategy.* July 1994.

U.S. Department of Agriculture (USDA) Foreign Agricultural Service. *Canada Agricultural Situation.* This Week in Canadian Agriculture, GAIN Report no. CA3049, August 12, 2003. Available at http://canada.usembassy.gov/content/emb-consul/fas_twica30_2003.pdf.

U.S. General Accounting Office. *H-2A Agricultural Guestworker Program: Changes Could Improve Services to Employers and Better Protect Workers.* Washington, D.C.: U.S. Government Printing Office, 1997.

———. *Illegal Immigration: Status of Southwest Border Strategy Implementation.* Report to Congressional Committees, May 1999.

U.S.–Mexico Border 2012 Program. *What Is Border 2012?* Fact sheet, U.S. Environmental Protection Agency, June 23, 2009. Available at http://www.epa.gov.

Vogel, Richard D. *Calderón's Nightmare: Renegotiating NAFTA.* Monthly Review, November 28, 2008.

Walker, Carson. *U.S. Ban on Canadian Beef Putting Farmers out of Business.* High Plains/Midwest Agricultural Journal, July 29, 2004. Available at http://www.hpj.com.

Wal-Mart Settles Illegal Immigrant Case for $11 Million. Fox News, March 19, 2005. Available at http://www.foxnews.com.

The White House Agenda: Immigration. White House.gov, n.d. Available at http://www.whitehouse.gov.

Whittington, Les, and Robert Benzie. *Harper, Calderón Agree to Oppose U.S. Trade Threat.* Toronto Star, February 6, 2009.

Wilson, T. A. *Lessons of the Recession.* 18 Canadian Journal of Economics 693 (1985).

Wilson, Thomas, et al. *The Sources of the Recession in Canada: 1989–1992.* Canadian Business Economics 3 (Winter 1994).

Yet Another Huge Bank Failure in the USA. Virtual Nonsense, January 13, 2009. Available at http://renaud.ca/wordpress/?tag=canadian-economy.

Zehr, Mary Ann. *Iowa School District Left Coping with Immigration Raid's Impact.* Education Week, May 20, 2008.

Index

welfare benefits: EU migrants and, 81, 109;
  Georgia and, 127
Whitaker, T. K. (Irish economist, secretary of
  finance of Ireland), 98
Windsor-Detroit corridor, 75
Wise, Carol, 48, 49
World Bank, 43, 94; and loans to Mexico, 139
World Trade Organization (WTO), 19, 23, 25,
  43, 55, 66, 72, 77, 94
World War I: economic slump and, 31;
  recruitment of cheap labor and, 31, 149

World War II: agriculture and, 65; Bracero
  Program and, 35; economic growth and,
  35; EU formation and, 79; GI bill and, 135;
  Marshall Plan and, 135; trade expansion
  and, 25
Wright, R. George, 143
WTO, 19, 23, 25, 43, 55, 66, 72, 77, 94

xenophobic ideology, 31

Zedillo, Ernesto, 24, 43, 44, 45, 46

Bill Ong Hing is a Professor of Law at the University of San Francisco and Professor Emeritus at the University of California, Davis. He teaches Immigration Law and Policy, Rebellious Lawyering, Negotiations, and Asian American History. Throughout his career, he has pursued social justice by combining community work, litigation, and scholarship. His books include *Defining America through Immigration Policy* (Temple) and *Deporting Our Souls: Values, Morality, and Immigration Policy*. Professor Hing was co-counsel in the Supreme Court asylum case *INS v. Cardoza-Fonseca* (1987). He is the founder of the Immigrant Legal Resource Center and serves on the National Advisory Council of the Asian American Justice Center.